East I
4700 L
Gram

D0348804

# Faith That Endures

*The Essential Guide to the Persecuted Church*

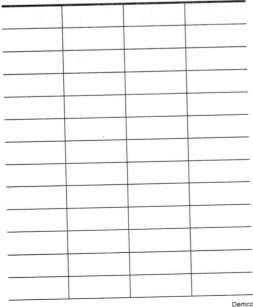

DATE DUE

Demco

ιcMillan

Andrew

© 2006 by Ronald Boyd-MacMillan

Published by Fleming H. Revell
a division of Baker Publishing Group
P.O. Box 6287, Grand Rapids, MI 49516-6287

Printed in the United States of America

All rights reserved. No part of this publication may be reproduced, stored in a retrieval system, or transmitted in any form or by any means—for example, electronic, photocopy, recording—without the prior written permission of the publisher. The only exception is brief quotations in printed reviews.

Library of Congress Cataloging-in-Publication Data
Boyd-MacMillan, Ronald.
    Faith that endures : the essential guide to the persecuted church / Ronald
    Boyd-MacMillan ; foreword by Brother Andrew.
        p.   cm.
    Includes bibliographical references.
    ISBN 10: 0-8007-3119-0 (pbk.)
    ISBN 978-0-8007-3119-9 (pbk.)
    1. Persecution. I. Title.
BR1601.3.B69 2006
272′.9—dc22                                                    2006009123

Unless otherwise indicated, Scripture is taken from the New Revised Standard Version of the Bible, copyright 1989, Division of Christian Education of the National Council of the Churches of Christ in the United States of America. Used by permission. All rights reserved.

Scripture marked KJV is taken from the King James Version of the Bible.

Scripture marked Message is taken from *The Message* by Eugene H. Peterson, copyright © 1993, 1994, 1995, 2000, 2001, 2002. Used by permission of NavPress Publishing Group. All rights reserved.

Scripture marked NASB is taken from the New American Standard Bible®, Copyright © 1960, 1962, 1963, 1968, 1971, 1972, 1973, 1975, 1977, 1995 by The Lockman Foundation. Used by permission.

Scripture marked NIV is taken from the HOLY BIBLE, NEW INTERNATIONAL VERSION®. NIV®. Copyright © 1973, 1978, 1984 by International Bible Society. Used by permission of Zondervan. All rights reserved.

Scripture marked NLT is taken from the *Holy Bible*, New Living Translation, copyright © 1996. Used by permission of Tyndale House Publishers, Inc., Wheaton, Illinois 60189. All rights reserved.

# Contents

# Foreword

If you want to change the world, you need at least three things.

First, you need to know the facts. It is shattering to me to know that over the fifty years I have been in ministry, the basic facts of the persecuted church have remained a mystery to the majority of the world's Christians. We *all* ought to know: Who are the persecuted? Where are they? How are they suffering? What are the causes? In an age where information is power, you will receive in this book the best global overview of the persecuted church with all its stresses, strains, and needs. Ron has always been part researcher and part journalist, so the facts are not boring in his hands, but dramatic and challenging.

Second, you need to have the right strategies. Once you know the facts, I know your heart will be moved. You will want to get involved. But first you need to know the dangers and mistakes that could be made. Serving the persecuted should not be a trial-and-error business. Like me, Ron has witnessed many good-hearted but emotional interventions on behalf of the persecuted. There are ways to help and ways to hinder. I made far too many mistakes in my early years as a Bible smuggler behind the Iron Curtain, mainly because I had no one to assist me in the tricky art of strategic intervention. Ron guides us through this minefield with expert precision.

Third, you need to feel the power of the persecuted church, because they are God's means to show us the way of Christ. Following Christ always involves suffering, as we have to cast self aside and embrace His cross. It is a way of joy and pain, and Ron gets this paradox across with great skill, in a way that attracts us to the message of the persecuted. Far too many books about persecution focus on the gory sufferings of the persecuted but never mention what they have learned. Ron brings their spiritual challenges home to us in a way that even the persecuted cannot do. It takes someone to stand in the gap between their experience and ours, someone who has the experience of both and can connect the two worlds. The great secret Ron exposes is simple—we all should learn the way of the persecuted, because the way of Christ is a way of trouble, and it is the trouble that brings the delight.

So allow this book to make you angry as you see so much ignorance in our churches about persecution today. The message of the persecuted church is needed in the West as never before. The British preacher Campbell Morgan once said that persecution was the devil's second-best tactic. His best tactic is materialism, and we in the West have been sleepwalkers in our faith for too long, forgetting in the midst of a life of material ease and manic busyness that we are even in a spiritual battle. Let this book recall you to the battle the church is always in. Who knows, you may find that persecution is already on its way to you. That should not make you despair but rejoice.

Brother Andrew

# Introduction

## *"You Need Our Faith to Find Your Own!"*

Beijing was still sullen from the events of the Tiananmen massacre eight months before as I crunched through snowy streets to meet my contact in the winter of 1990. I looked around to make sure no one was following. It was dark, but a sleek Mercedes of a high Communist Party functionary turned abruptly left, nudging an old man off his bicycle into the dirt. The car stopped, the rear window opened, and a face appeared, presumably to make an apology. He never got the chance. The old man picked himself up and, with all the disgust he could muster, spat a whirling comet of phlegm through the window. The car screeched off.

I shuddered against the biting cold. In years of visiting Beijing, I had never witnessed such impudent dissent, excluding of course the thousands of protesting students who flocked to the square months before to face a frightening fate—the bullets of the People's Liberation Army on June 4, 1989. There was something in the air besides the snowflakes. That trivial incident hinted at a greater shift. A change in the attitude of people toward government had occurred, even if it was still mainly subconscious. History was being given a shove, but in which direction?

The massacre story had been well covered in the press and was not my concern on this visit. I was making my way to the house of Mr. Bao, an elderly professor who also moonlighted as a Bible teacher to underground rural churches. I spied his dingy apartment building, picked my way around smoking piles of garbage, walked up three flights of dark stairs—which were lethal with ice—and knocked quietly on the door. No one came, but I could hear shouting from within. For a moment I stood irresolute, heart pounding, wondering if the police had got there before me. I listened more closely and realized the shouts were full of laughter. I knocked louder, and the door opened to reveal three elderly men dressed in dark suits and ties, all standing with wineglasses in their hands. The surreal interaction with them that followed forms the core convictions about the contemporary persecuted church that drive the writing of this book nearly fifteen years later.

"Come in; come in," said Bao. "Let me introduce you to my friends." One was Mr. Cheng, a smiley gray-headed science teacher. A mathematics genius, he returned from postgraduate study in the 1950s to help build the new Chinese society. Mao showed his appreciation by having him shovel sand in a work gang for twenty years. Bao introduced the other, with a wink, as "Nicodemus." The mystery man smiled, revealing yellow smoker's teeth, and said obliquely, "I only come to Jesus *at night* you see." I knew exactly what he meant. I recognized his face from a recent photo of higher-ranking Communist Party officials. If this man was a Christian, he had made a brilliant job of keeping it secret.

"Am I interrupting a party?" I asked, depositing some cashew nuts on the table.

"Oh, please join us," said Bao, and poured me a glass of radioactive-looking liquid. "This is a special occasion."

"What occasion?"

Cheng answered, "We are drinking a toast in memory of the man who did more than any other to bring to our beloved China the largest scale revival in the history of Christianity!"

Intrigued, I said, "I'll drink to that guy!" We raised our glasses.

"To Mao Zedong!" they chorused.

I coughed a cashew nut into the wineglass. "I'm sorry," I gasped. "I must have misheard. I thought for a second you all said Mao Zedong!"

"We did!" said Bao.

"I don't get it!" I said. "Surely Mao was a monster?"

"God has a use for monsters too!" answered Bao elliptically. "Ah, you need some more refreshment!" The liquid tasted like paraffin with an ammonia chaser. Two slurps and my head was pounding.

"You're all joking, right?" I said. "I thought you would say John Sung or Watchman Nee or Wang Mingdao." An idea dawned on me. "Is Mao Zedong code for one of those three or another?"

"No!" said Nicodemus. "Our Mao is *the* Mao."

"I don't get it!" I said again.

"Neither did we . . . for a very long time!" Mr. Cheng said softly.

"And many still don't!" added Nicodemus.

Bao settled back onto the one piece of quality furniture in his apartment—a lacquered rosewood sofa. "Chinese people," he began, "never were particularly religious, not religious in the sense that Indonesians or Indians are. We are a pragmatic people. Our culture is Confucian, and Confucius taught people not to waste their time asking unanswerable questions like, Does God exist? He counseled us to concentrate on truths to live by, simple ethics if you like. No, we are not a religious people! We don't let the gods interfere with making money."

I broke in, "What about all the temples? All the gods?"

Cheng replied, "Sure, we have folk religion, but it's superficial. If anyone wants some good fortune, they ram joss sticks into an orange, maybe spread a few nuts around, and offer it to the gods in the hope of getting some good luck." He smiled, "That's all it really amounts to. It's like reading your horoscope. There is no transcendent God that makes demands on us. No savior figure. No real notion of faith at all. We have an idea of a supreme being, but as our Confucian culture said, he was unknowable, we didn't seek him."

"That may be why Christianity never really spread in China," said Nicodemus. "For all the efforts of the foreign missionaries—Nestorian, Catholic, Protestant—we were too pragmatic, too materialistic a people to really become impressed with such an *otherworldly* gospel."

"And then along came Mao Zedong," said Professor Bao, "who changed all that. Do you know what he told us? He said we were going to build *heaven* on earth. He said we would build it through *truth*. He said we could only do it by *faith*—in each other. He said we would be part of an *eternal* China."

Nicodemus burst in. "Then he organized us. He gave us hymns to sing. He instituted rituals of confession and repentance, called 'struggle meetings.' He even forced us all to get together into small groups and expound a 'sacred' text together . . ."

"The Little Red Book!" I cried.

Cheng stood up. "At the height of it all, he would gather us together at Tiananmen Square. Millions would crowd in, especially the youth. Mao would walk out onto the balcony and spread his arms like this." Mr. Cheng raised his arms sideways, palms upraised, almost in the crucifixion position. "The crowd would thunder back their adulation, slapping their Little Red Books to their breasts. He wouldn't need to say a thing."

Bao asked, "Do you know what he was doing?"

"Playing God," I answered

"Exactly! Or more precisely, teaching the Chinese people how to worship!"

We all paused. I looked at the three of them. Their faces were etched with the worry lines of years of suffering. I wondered what tortures they must have endured, and for a moment I pictured Bao's face struggling to stay silent and faithful in the face of beatings and goading in the desperate years. "But you had to worship only him, right?" I asked. "That's what made it so tough!"

Bao replied more slowly, "Yes, he became god, and a jealous god at that. No other gods were allowed. He closed the churches, jailed the pastors, burned the Bibles—annihilated the visible church. Many dear Christians died. It was a horrible time."

Nicodemus said sorrowfully, "I was a persecutor then. I hated Christians with all my heart. I have bad things on my conscience. I threw a pastor from a second-floor window once. He broke his spine. He was still sent to the countryside for hard labor."

After a long silence I asked, "So how does this get us to the world's largest revival?"

"Well," said Bao, "Mao died in 1976. Now, gods aren't supposed to die. Then in 1978 Deng Xiaoping gets power again . . ."

"That's why he was always nicknamed 'Lazarus,'" said Nicodemus, "always rising from the political dead."

Bao continued, "Deng allowed the population to travel again from province to province without needing extensive paperwork and permissions. So the few evangelists that were left, like myself, began to go and preach the gospel in the countryside, and what happened next gave us the shock of our lives . . ."

"We would start telling them about Jesus Christ," broke in Mr. Cheng, "and the people would shout, 'Stop, we want to believe!'"

"And I would tell them, 'Wait a minute. You haven't heard the whole story yet,'" said Bao, laughing. "And they would say, 'No, this is the God whom Mao taught us to look for. We thought it was Mao who would save us, but it cannot be because he died. We see now that it must be Jesus.'"

Excitedly Bao and Cheng recounted their experiences of moving from village to village and seeing the gospel welcomed with a hunger they could scarcely believe. Other evangelists reported the same, and so by the 1980s a revival of gigantic proportions began to sweep the vast peasantry of rural China.

By the mid-1980s, China watchers such as Dr. Jonathan Chao were putting the size of the rural revival at fifty million and rising. No one knows the true extent of this revival, since large swaths of the Christians prefer to worship in house churches, independent of the state-controlled churches. The 2001 edition of the *World Christian Encyclopedia* stuck its neck out and estimated the size of the Christian community in present-day China at just under eighty-nine million.[1] All statistical totals are controversial in China. Suffice it to say that the number of Christians in China is millions more than officials admit to, and whatever figure you use, it still constitutes the largest numerical revival in the history of Christianity. In less than one generation, a church burst into being that is bigger than the entire population of the United Kingdom.

"That's why we say Mao brought us this huge revival," said Bao. "He created a society full of worshipers, and when their object of worship died, they became a society of seekers intent on finding another god."

"When the idol is smashed, the gospel grows," said Nicodemus.

"So what you are celebrating, then, is this irony. When Mao thought he was the greatest annihilator of the church, in fact he was doing pre-evangelism on a scale unique in human history," I said.

"Exactly!" said Bao. "Mao meant it for evil, but God meant it for good. Mao was used to prepare this country for the greatest outpouring of the Spirit ever seen in his church. He's God's fool! He planted in the people's hearts the desire for true religion, then failed them so spectacularly that they kept seeking until they found the one true God."

We laughed. We almost felt sorry for Mao, doing his worst to finish the church off and all the while laying the foundation for the world's biggest revival.

"But it was hell to live through," said Bao soberly.

As we talked, I began to feel a prickle of annoyance. This perspective on the suffering of Chinese Christians was thrilling, but why had I never heard it before? Hundreds of Western Christians had visited China over the years, and many books had been written, yet the faith interpretation of these significant men had never made it into print. Had we missed a key ingredient in the story of God in this land? All I had read were harrowing individual testimonies. I asked them why this was, and Cheng's answer haunts me to this day: "You cannot understand the full story of the persecuted church if all you write about and listen to are the stories of a few individuals who were martyred or miraculously delivered. We praise God for them, but for every story of deliverance, there are a thousand stories of endurance. That's the real story. Miss that, and you miss the bigger picture of how God brings us through. Too many Westerners just want a diet of deliverance when they really need to hear about endurance."

**First Conviction**

Without wagging the finger like teacher Cheng, this book is one attempt to tell that fuller story. The simple fact is that most books about the persecuted church feature either deliverance feats of a few remarkable Christians or the torture details of a few prominent Christians, but the larger picture of God's action among the many who merely endure—some quietly and some doubtfully—is left out. While one loves to hear the remarkable stories, they are only a slice of the story, the tip of the iceberg, and not to be mistaken for the fuller, more dramatic version.

Out of this came the first conviction that drives this book: *That the fuller story of the contemporary persecuted church remains a tragically untold story. We hear too much of the deliverance stories of the few and not enough about the endurance stories of the many. There is a grander, greater narrative of God's action underneath the stories of individual pain, suffering, deliverance, and endurance.*

Professor Bao gestured that night to a large bookcase full of brown-paper books. "These are the elephants," he said. This was his word for outsized translations of the Bible in Chinese, which very few Christians actually wanted. "I didn't refuse them because, of course, we will take Bibles any way we can get them, but most Christians would prefer the traditional Union Version, and some of the peasants won't even accept them."

"How did you end up with them then?" I asked.

"They dumped them on me!" he said. "I found them outside my front door. They were from some Western contacts I had never heard of. I never asked for them. And if they are found in this apartment, there will be problems for me." He sighed, "I just wish they would do more research on who needed what, instead of coming over here with all these Bibles thinking we will fall on their necks and kiss them. I even wonder whether they are more interested in feeling good themselves than really serving us."

In many quarters, it is worse not better. Ten years later I was back in Beijing listening to a tirade from a house-church leader against so-called "Bible bombers"—Westerners who came to China to "bomb" a town with Scriptures during the night, stuffing tracts into bicycle baskets and mailboxes so that, in the words of one of the smugglers, "when all the people woke up the next morning, there was Jesus everywhere." So impressed were they with the tactic that they contacted *Time* magazine and were profiled in the September 11, 2000, issue.

The house-church leader was thirty-two, from Hanzhou, and loved Bible smugglers. But he was angry. I remember him shouting, "Jesus is not a book!" He went on to argue that Jesus didn't spread His gospel by asking His disciples to write scroll scraps and scatter them throughout the towns of Galilee and Judea. With his fist banging the table in front of him, he shouted, "The way the gospel spreads the best is when one saved person tells an unsaved person, in a winsome fashion, what they are missing. Tell those people that!" He also claimed that the tactic of Bible bombing was counterproductive, as the local Christians usually get blamed by the police, who need scapegoats, and church leaders face harassment and arrest. And all because some Western Christians wanted to play James Bond!

Let them ask first! Let them understand the dynamics. Let them take time to realize that the situation is a lot more complex than they think. Let them build a relationship with the persecuted before attempting to serve them. It sounds so obvious, but so much ministry misses the mark in precisely this area.

If there is a generalization that works here, it is that liberal Christians tend to ignore the needs of the underground churches. Often they are taken in by state-sponsored clerics who are no more than paid propagandists. Evangelicals, on the other hand, have a tendency to demonize those who worship in state churches and are often slow to take advantage of more official opportunities when they arise. At any rate, tactical naïveté is rife and is only counteracted with a fuller understanding of the persecuted church. Understanding brings an awareness of the complexity; complexity brings humility; humility brings discernment; discernment brings effectiveness.

## Second Conviction

The second conviction: *Those who seek to assist the persecuted all too often end up using them rather than serving them, because they fail to understand the complexity of persecution. We must understand the dynamics of contemporary persecution better to ensure more effective intervention and assistance.*

It was time to take my leave. It had been one of the most enlightening evenings of my life. I thanked my friends for their stories, adding, "I'm so thankful I'm not going back to a land where Mao reigns. I feel guilty about it, though, that I don't have to pay such a price to bring revival to my country. It's like you have been living through the pages of the book of Revelation!"

Teacher Cheng licked his lips, and I could see another lecture coming. "Take this back from us," he said carefully. "*Everyone* is living in the book of Revelation, because we all are part of the persecuted church."

"Well, I don't think we're suffering like you folks," I replied.

Cheng explained patiently, "Wherever you go in this earth, you will be seduced by a false prophet, or coerced by a beast, into worshiping some idol that is not God. That is apocalyptic reality. Your worship is what you put your energy into. The only difference between you and us is that here it happened so brutally, we saw it so clearly; where you live, it happens so subtly, you cannot see it at all." He punched a fist into the palm of his other hand, and his glasses slipped down to the end of his nose. "Don't miss this," he said. "Please don't miss this—*you need our faith to find your own!*"

As I went out the door, Bao whispered, "Remember, as the idols are smashed, the gospel grows."

## Third Conviction

Thus was born the third conviction: *Western Christians require an encounter with the persecuted church to recover essential insights into*

*their own faith, especially the biblical truth that there is no such thing as*
*a* nonpersecuted *believer.*

These men gave me insights I could bring back to my own country, to my own faith, and use to gain a deeper walk with God. Was
my worship being stolen by idols without my knowing it? Were
there beasts and false prophets around that I had failed to identify?
Was the cult of celebrity an idol? Was the American Dream an idol?
Was a foolish patriotism an idol? Was a selfish materialism an idol?
I heard a preacher say recently, "An idol is something that becomes
more important to you than God." If an idol is anything that takes
my energy away from God, then these things very probably are. The
insights of the persecuted church brought a literal unveiling (*apoca-
lypsis*) of the world that I was in. How could I have been so blind?
After all, just because I live in a free country does not make the devil
less interested in stealing my worship away from Jesus Christ.

Yet the insight came with hope. God allows idols to build up and
then smashes them to create a hunger for himself in societies and
in the human heart. I could see this pattern rerunning in my own
context. We need the insights of the persecuted to learn the basics
of our own faith. Freedom brings many benefits, but it also blinds
us to certain truths. The faith of the persecuted contains insights
we can apply, not just admire. That is why this book closes with
three chapters answering the question, What can we learn from
the persecuted church? In so much writing on the persecuted, this
is a question seldom asked.

All too often I had related to persecuted believers through two
emotions—awe and guilt. The awe came from what they had endured. They seemed like super-saints. The guilt came from knowing
I would never face the same physical suffering as they, and it seemed
so unfair. Their faith seemed so exotic, and mine so mundane. But
I have come to see that these emotions prevent me from having an
experience of the persecuted that is useful to my own life, to my
own church, to my own nation. The persecuted have insights that
go beyond the usual clichés—pray harder, welcome strife, memorize the Word. They have a message that critiques and reshapes
my faith. Once I asked a Sri Lankan church leader, "Why does God

allow so many of his people to be persecuted?" The leader smiled, touched my arm, and replied, "Maybe so that people like you can see what true Christianity looks like!"

Let's face it. Most of the Bible is written by persecuted believers to strengthen other persecuted believers. If you want to understand it, better to talk to the group closest to the original community that wrote and first read it—the contemporary persecuted! Freedom has brought us many illusions, and there is none more foolish than the idea that we will not suffer for Christ. The battle comes to us all. As a Chinese pastor once put it, "We may not all sit on the same thorn, but we all sit on the same branch." The persecuted have much to teach us about simplicity, suffering, the Bible, prayer, and citizenship. It would be a tragedy if the only relationship we had with them were one of sending resources. They are anxious to bless us the only way they know how. Can we let them?

So here is a modest guide to the persecuted church in the world today. The book is organized around five key questions:

What does contemporary persecution look like?

What is persecution?

Where is the persecuted church?

How do we help the persecuted?

What can we learn from the persecuted?

It is my hope that by the end of this book you will feel informed rather than confused about persecution in a world of anecdotes and claims and counterclaims, become better aware of how to help the persecuted in a way that protects them rather than endangers them, and finally, actually encounter the story of the persecuted church so that it becomes your story also, where their insights into God are enfolded into your walk with God.

It is my prayer that you will discover that teacher Cheng was right when he said, "You need our faith to find your own!"

*Part One*

# What Does Contemporary Persecution Look Like?

# 1    The Dying

## *Kurdistan—Martyrs and Survivors*

Please don't read any malice into this, but I used to feel quite annoyed at martyrs. I would take pains to brief legislators and missions leaders on the overall dynamics of a church in a particular country, and then suddenly a martyr story would rocket onto the scene, and in an instant all the nuance was forgotten, and I was being asked the same question: "How many more martyrs can we expect?" A government that may have tried hard to bring religious freedom was instantly relabeled as "Christian killers." Churches that had no martyrs were described as "dead." Even missions that had long-term strategies to help the church were judged only on how well they eased life for the widow or orphan. The capacity of a martyr to shrink the story of a church of millions to the mortal wounds of a single person is staggering, and disturbing, because often those wounds tell a tale that is far from typical.

Even within the persecuted church, the vast majority of Christians are not martyrs and never will be. In twenty-five years of reporting on the persecuted church in Eastern Europe and Asia, the number of martyr stories I personally covered came to no more than five. Each year the Vatican publishes a list of martyrs. Out of a Roman Catholic community of 1.1 billion, the list rarely exceeds forty in number. The *World Christian Encyclopedia* puts the number of martyrs in history at 0.8 percent of the total number of Christians who have ever lived, and their figures are controversially high. The fact is, the story of martyrdom is almost always the story of a few, untypical Christians rather than the experience of the normal Christian. And in a book such as this, which seeks to give an overview of the entire persecuted church, martyrdom cannot, by definition, be the major element. Indeed, it would be fair to say this: *If all you focus on is the story of the martyrs, you will never understand the story of the persecuted church! Martyrdom is the dazzling tip of the iceberg that hides the dark bulk of the body.*

Yet despite the tendency of a martyrdom to control the perception of a church, I have repented of my earlier attitude. The capacity of a martyr story to deliver a shock message far outweighs its tendency to distort the overall situation. Bluntly speaking, the story of a martyr delivers two shocks to the spiritual system with a voltage we cannot receive from any other group of Christians.

First, there is an *unveiling* effect. A martyr story unveils the stark and dangerous nature of the conflict all Christians become a part of when they turn to Christ. We suddenly realize the world is a battleground, not a playground, and the gospel is a dangerous thing, not just a comforting thing. Indeed, this gospel we profess could get us killed! We realize, with a shudder, that this could happen to us, because we belong to the same gospel, and the foes of that gospel are powerful and crazed with hate.

Second, there is an *inspiring* effect. A martyr is someone who loves the truth more than life itself, and we are forced to ask of ourselves: "Do I come up to that standard?" We reevaluate our priorities in the light of the actions of someone who clearly knew that the gospel was the most important truth in the entire universe, and we reconnect through that person's sacrifice with the vast cosmic dimensions of the gospel, rescuing us from more trivial appreciations of its power. A martyr requires us to recall why it is worth dying for the Christian gospel.

Yes, this is easy to state in theory but hard to absorb in practice. I first began to really "get it" on a trip to Iraq.

On April 9, 2003, two weeks after President Bush declared that Operation Iraqi Freedom had been won, and only Saddam Hussein's boots remained on his huge statue in the center of Baghdad, I found myself traveling in close convoy at 180 kilometers an hour on the road from Amman to Baghdad. We were a group of eight men intent on visiting the Iraqi Christians, anxious to assure them that their Christian brothers and sisters in the rest of the world had not forgotten them, and seeking to find ways to pray and to assist in the rebuilding.

The Iraqi church was a sad story. Barely five hundred thousand Christians remained in this overwhelmingly Muslim state of twenty-four million, a country that contains so much of the biblical landscape, including Babylon, Nineveh, and Ur. Christians continued to leave at the rate of thousands per year, finding the mixture of Islamic culture and Saddam's harsh rule a throttling combination. We reached Baghdad to find a kind of controlled chaos. The traffic lights did not work, so everyone was inching their cars forward, refusing to give way and shouting at the other drivers to give way. Huge buildings lay in heaps from the bombing, girders exposed and hanging, glinting in the fierce dry heat. The portraits of Saddam were all defaced, the statues ritually toppled, and when we stepped out onto the street, we were plied with the looted passports of Iraqi personalities who had long fled their stylish villas for a life on the run. The glum face of Saddam's long-term foreign minister, Tariq Aziz, gazed up from his UN passport. "Your memento of the war for just five hundred U.S. dollars," said the enterprising robber.

We crept from house to house, visiting Christians to the sound of gunfire. Gangs of organized looters were cruising the streets with Kalashnikovs. Old family scores were being settled also, with the threat of punishment effectively removed. The Christians were happy to see the back of Saddam but apprehensive about the future, fearing Shia reprisals and a more Islamic state. Once again it was remarkable to discover the good news under the bad, as many Christians agreed with Bishop Salieba of Mosul: "The war was good for us—it made us desperate for God, and so we turned to him like

Old Testament psalmists and found him satisfying." So often, from a religious perspective, something that is bad for the country can be good for the kingdom. The Christian views news through a much more wide-angled lens than the materialist.

But one visit sticks in my mind more than any other. We were sharing fellowship with a group of nine nuns, sitting huddled around a few candles in a home. They were the traumatized remains of the Sisters of the Sacred Heart of the Chaldeans. The mother superior of their order, Sister Cecilia, had been martyred nine months before, in August of 2002. Killed at seventy-one years of age, she had been taken to the nunnery when orphaned as a five-year-old and took her vows at fourteen. On the night of August 15 she happened to be in the nunnery by herself, as the rest of the sisters were in the north of the country. Her devoted friend Sister Albertine told us through muffled sobs what she found in the morning. "I saw Sister Cecilia's body, naked. She had her wrists tied to her ankles, her legs were broken, a rag was stuffed in her mouth, and her throat was slit. She had seven stab wounds in her torso."

This was no robbery gone wrong. Sister Albertine continued, "The body was turned to face the mosque, and the stab wounds were in a crescent pattern." A single dried tear on the cheek of Sister Cecilia was all there was to show for her excruciating night of suffering.

Worse was to follow for the sisters. Sister Cecilia's killers were caught and tried. The three men were extremist Muslims, two of them neighbors living on the same street, recipients of the kindness of the nuns on numerous occasions. Duly jailed, they could not believe their luck when a month later Saddam Hussein, in a desperate attempt to stiffen resistance to the impending occupation, opened all the prisons and let the criminals flood back into society—more than fifty thousand of them. Sister Cecilia's killers, after four weeks of prison for murder, were at large again.

One murderer returned to his house across the street from the nunnery and held a raucous party. The sisters fled with the noise of celebration in their ears. Said Sister Albertine, with doubts wrinkling her forehead, "We tried to reach out to everyone on this street. We

East Parkway Church
Library
4700 East Roseville Parkway
Granite Bay, CA 95746

did nothing but good. How can we have hope for the future when this is our experience?"

The final straw was when the mother of the murderer came out and told them, "Even if my son was hanged, I would still celebrate, because he entered a Christian home and bought a place in heaven."

These were the most chilling words I heard in Iraq. How appalling, how dreadful, that a mother could take pride in her son's brutal and cowardly slaying of a defenseless seventy-one-year-old nun! What kind of warped thinking would ever convince her to assume that God would be pleased by such an act? It begs understanding. I shook my head in puzzlement for the next week, until a similar mystery assailed me in the north of the country, in Iraqi Kurdistan.

## No Friends but the Mountains

The northeast of Iraq is mountainous and green, in contrast to the desert, near-lunar landscape of southern Iraq. This area is home to 4.5 million Kurds—the Medes of biblical times. The Kurds form the majority in this region and heartily detest the Arabs, nursing memories of a long and painful series of humiliations from Arab leaders and countries, most recently in the 1980s when Saddam's armies launched chemical and gas attacks against them. More than 180,000 perished, whole villages were slaughtered, the hills were littered with mass graves, and more than two million Kurds fled the carnage. One Kurdish leader we met murmured sadly, "Only the mountains are our friends, and they only frown on our graves."

In 1991 the first Gulf War brought a measure of autonomy, however, as the Kurds were technically part of Saddam's Iraq but under UN administration, with the Americans enforcing a no-fly zone. Hundreds of thousands of refugees flooded back, and with them came Christian missionaries, anxious to plant churches among one of the Middle East's least evangelized peoples. Remarkably, an indigenous church of between one and two hundred Muslim converts was under way in the late nineties. The Kurds were open to the gospel, many Christians believed, because their suspicion of Arabs included a view that imposing sharia law was really an attempt to Arabize them, and so they remain one of the region's most unenthusiastic Sunni Muslim groups.

Despite increasing openness to the gospel, the Kurds still face persecution from their families and the state when they turn to Christ. The indigenous Kurdish Evangelical Church gained its first martyr in 1997. He was forty-three-year-old Mansour Hussein Sifer, who staffed a small Christian bookstore in Arbil, the largest town in Kurdistan. A convert for only a year and a half, he was a gentle giant of a man who wrote poetry and devoted himself to knowing his Bible.

On the morning of April 21, 1997, he told his wife, Ruth, and his young son that he was going into the bookshop for an "important appointment," even though, as the last day of a Muslim feast, the bookstore would normally be closed. At 10:00 a.m. he was seen cleaning the window of the store, and then at 10:40 his best friend, another Muslim convert, dropped in to make sure the shop had not been looted over the holidays. He found the door open, and his dear friend slumped on the floor. Thinking Mansour had fainted or collapsed, he ran to a neighbor for help to carry him into a taxi, but when they returned they both noticed a pool of fresh, bright blood near Hussein's head. He had been shot at close range with a pistol. The bullet hole was visible on the side of his head.

On the floor beside the body was one of the store's Arabic books for loan, titled *More Precious than Gold*. The chairs were stacked, and it was assumed that Mansour was still cleaning the floor when the assailant came in to return the loaned book and shoot him.

So often there is a grisly aftermath to these martyrdoms in Islamic countries. The government refused to fingerprint the book, claiming they did not have the technology. The name of the person who was loaned the book was found to be false, so that trail went cold. Instead, police picked up Mansour's best friend and tortured him terribly, trying to make him confess and pin the murder on a squabble between Christians. When the friend returned from jail, he was unable to sit down because of the pain.

The month of "investigation" was also hard on the widow, Ruth, who was being pressured by the authorities to accuse Mansour's friend. Police told her, "His friend has confessed to your husband's murder; now will you tell us what their real relationship was like?" Distraught with grief, she hardly knew what to believe and was preoccupied with the shattering discovery that she was pregnant with Mansour's second child. She eventually refused to cooperate, saying, "I cannot believe his best friend would kill him."

Instead of a community and government that should have been sympathetic in the light of the brutal slaying, the church experienced further harassment and persecution. As one member of the church in Arbil said afterward, "Now we know we are not in a football game."

And Mansour's killer has never been caught.

Yet, if one can say this respectfully, Mansour's mysterious martyrdom was old news in 2003. I was on my way to meet the widow of the second martyr of the Kurdistan church, thirty-eight-year-old Zewar Mohammed Ishmael. We wound our way over rough tracks under the snowcapped Zagros Mountains to the border town of Zahko in the company of Pastor Jousif Matty, one of the leading workers in the Kurdish church. He told us Zewar's story and confessed he was filled with some apprehension, as Zewar's widow, Layla, was still a Muslim. Would we get a welcome? Would she blame us for Zewar's conversion and his death?

Zewar had been a feisty man, a born fighter who came from a tribe known for taking the law into their own hands. Used to weapons and mountains, he served as a guerilla fighter in the Kurdish freedom army. But in 1999 he became a Christian and poured his bountiful energy into witness. He hosted the local church in his home, and when his fifth child was delivered, gave the boy a Christian name—Ephraim. Zewar lived only to see Ephraim enter his fifth month of life. A taxi driver, he used to keep Bibles in his car and give them out to interested passengers as he told them of Christ. Some were interested. Some were shocked. But he paid no heed when he was abused or warned. Once his father drove him out to the desert and threatened to leave him there if he did not return to Islam. "Drive away, Father," Zewar smiled. "My faith is more important to me than life itself."

The town of Zahko is close to the Iranian border, and many Islamic extremists sneaked over from there to radicalize the population. Also the Saudis built mosques and taught their own harsh version of the Islamic faith, Wahhabism. So Zewar's activities did not go unnoticed. He was denounced publicly from the mosques. At Friday prayers a mullah said that Zewar was responsible for five hundred Muslims leaving their faith. This was a lie, but it inflamed many extremists. Zewar began to be shadowed.

On the morning of February 17, 2003, Zewar came to the depot where the taxi drivers congregated. A man was seen walking up to him, and witnesses recalled the conversation. The man said, "Zewar, would you like to take some tea with me? I want to talk to you about coming back to Islam."

Zewar replied, "Brother, I am so happy in my new faith, but by all means, let us talk."

The two walked around the corner to a teahouse. Seconds later there was a loud shout, "*Allahu Akbar*,"[1] followed by rapid gunfire. The taxi drivers raced around to find Zewar lying dead in a pool of blood. In a split second, twenty-eight bullets had entered his body, eighteen in his face and ten in his chest.

His killer was chased and caught. This time there was no attempt to pin it on the local Christians, because the killer, a local extremist Muslim who had been inflamed against Zewar in the mosque, was proud to confess. He told police, "I dreamt that the Prophet Muhammad, peace be upon him, told me to kill Zewar, and then I would go to paradise." He waited four days before acting on his vision. It is a measure of how far the Kurdish government has come in their attitude toward Kurdish converts that Zewar's killer was given a ten-year prison sentence.

All these facts were relayed to me as the car bumped along the road toward Zewar's house. The facts were depressing, yet I was unprepared for the emotional experience ahead. We pulled onto a dirt road and drew up alongside a house with rusted iron gates. We rapped on the gates. They didn't open. Perhaps the family was not at home. Then there was a squeak, and a young girl peered out shyly. She led us to a carpeted room with cushions. This was where the church met. Soon the family filed in. A young man of eighteen came over to me and, quite unexpectedly, held me tight. This was Zewar's eldest son, Zerevan. His shoulders began to shake, and I felt his tears trickling down my neck. These tears seemed to scald my very soul. Holding him, I suddenly felt the utter senselessness of all that had happened. I remember repeating the questions to myself: *How could anyone take the life of this boy's father? How is it possible?*

Then in came Layla, Zewar's wife, smiling and holding back tears. In her late thirties, her face was full of worry lines. She was wearing a long green dress and a black Muslim headscarf, which she kept toying with self-consciously. Cradled against her hip was a smiling, spry little youngster dressed in red with a big yellow bib. This was Ephraim, Zewar's "Christian" child. He crawled toward us, drawn to the chocolate bar I was waving at him. Zerevan had let me go by then, and Layla and her five children sat against the wall opposite us.

We looked at each other. What could we say? I looked into the eyes of Layla and read such pain there. Her control slipped, and even though we were strangers, she wept. We all wept, and again a scalding wave of *Oh, God, why?* swept over me from head to toe. My mind just kept revisiting the questions: *How could anyone do this? How could anyone possibly do this—take a man's life and leave his family so desolate? How on earth could he think that would please God?* Martyrdom seemed an immense mystery. Layla's eyes and Zerevan's tears had connected me to the awful human tragedy of it and left me stunned. And almost for the first time I was asking God, "How can this happen?"

It was as if I suddenly realized my Christianity had been lived in a sealed container. No one was fanatical about anything in the United Kingdom, where I lived, least of all faith. The closest we got to fanatics were football hooligans, and they were regarded as idiotic. Where would I find the resources to try to understand how someone could feel so strongly as to kill another person in a desire to please God? And yet was this not what happened in the world of the New Testament?

The answers did not come as we continued to meet with Zewar's family. It was getting worse for them. Obviously the loss of the male breadwinner is a catastrophe in a Middle Eastern context, but it was even worse for Layla. Zewar's family was blaming her for not preventing his conversion. They told her, "We won't help you because you were a bad wife. You did not manage to convince him to remain a good Muslim. This would never have happened if you had been a good wife."

The only good news was that she had found a larger family. The church of Zahko had rallied around her. They would buy her a house and give Zerevan a job and visit her regularly with gifts and offer support. Her family would not have made it without the support of the Christian community. Yet Zewar's death shattered the local church. They dived underground, and today are a small, frightened community still. His martyrdom has not, so far, brought any apparent spiritual benefit for the Christian witness in the town of Zahko.

I was left with a burning problem. I was no longer a reporter. It was a matter of cardinal importance to find some kind of resolution to this question: how can people hate Christians so much that they want to kill them? It was *my* question now, not just Layla's. Not just Zerevan's. Through the eyes of Layla and the tears of Zerevan, it was as though I had stepped suddenly through the back of C. S. Lewis's wardrobe and found myself in another world—a violent, blood-and-guts world, where men had their faces shredded by machine guns and died in pools of blood on dusty streets because they had talked with delight about their faith in a taxi, and—horror of horrors—given a Bible away here or there. What kind of world was this? What kind of faith drew this reaction? What kind of God allowed it?

I stress this experience because I think it is one we all undergo as part of an encounter with martyrs. They wake us up to the way the world really is. We forget, but they remind us. They strip away the illusions that the world is a reasonable place, where conversions are the object of rational family or community discussions. The liberal ideal that a Westerner grows up with—that all ideas should be discussed and weighed objectively—gets cruelly shattered as surely as the bullets that hit the soft tissue of the martyr's body.

As we drove away, someone in the car said, "Well, life used to be a picnic, but not anymore. When I take the Eucharist this Sunday, I'll smell the blood this time!"

## Why Kill for God?

Though I had gained this new perspective, there was the incredulity of it to deal with. Why would someone want to kill another person over religion? I began to consider this question that evening, when it so happened that my Bible reading passage was the story of the first Christian martyr—Stephen.

There seemed to me two inadequate explanations as to why people kill in the name of religion. One focuses on the killer, the other on the victim.

The first view says, "The killer is crazy." It's a pathology issue, best left to the psychiatrist to explain. The killer is insane. This view is an old favorite of the secularist, who thinks that anyone who professes an absolute creed in a relativistic world is a potential danger to society. In Western Europe this view is hardly untenable given the past propensity for religious people to slaughter each other. Even religious figures give credence to the view. I heard Dr. Zaki Badawi, former principal of the Muslim College of Britain, tell a group of Cambridge University students when asked about the 9/11 bombers, "Well, religion is like medicine. You must be careful only to take a little of it. Take a lot and the cure will be worse than the illness." This is nonsense. The idea that the more enthusiastically you embrace a religious belief, the more unstable you become clearly owes its origin to the assumption that religion is not something that deserves a serious commitment; rather, it is trivial, like supporting a football team. Jonathan Swift, the great clergyman-essayist of the eighteenth century, gave the lie to that when he wrote, "We have just enough religion to make us hate, but not enough to make us love one another." Yet the media is full of op-ed writers lining up ten deep to tell us that all religion is essentially bad religion, and even the self-respecting Christian who obeys the government, pays taxes, and upholds family values is really just an "inner voice" away from turning into a prowling, murdering maniac.

The problem with this view is that it fails completely to understand that there is a strange kind of rationality to religious violence. The killing of believers in the name of God usually comes packaged in a complicated series of justifications. For example, when the killing of Zewar was reported in *Compass Direct*, the journalist discovered that few in Zahko thought that his killer, named as Abd al-Karem Abd al-Salam, would be sentenced to jail for the crime, because "Islamic law requires the execution of apostates who forsake Islam."[2] No Muslim leader in the town condemned the action of the assassin. Zewar's killer may have been an extremist, but he was not a lunatic. In fact, he was acting firmly within the canons of centuries of Muslim law.

Similarly, if one examines the circumstances of Stephen's death, the notion that those who put him to death "are just crazy" does not wash either. Stephen is examined by a council of Jerusalem's leading scholars and priests. Prejudiced they may be. Crazy? No. These men ran the city. They were a clever, elite group, learned and respected.

And yet let's not get over rational here—something so riled this group of scholars and priests that they turned into a hate-crazed mob that stoned a man to death, believing it to be a righteous, God-pleasing act. What incensed them so that they lost control?

Some say we need look no further than to the words of Stephen himself, which leads us to the second inadequate view, focusing on the victim. This view says that there is usually some recklessness in the victim that draws down the wrath of the persecuting community. It's a sad fact that there is always a whispering campaign that seeks to find in some aspect of the victim's behavior an explanation for his death. Even in Zahko some of the Christians murmured, "Zewar was much too bold. He never should have given Bibles away so openly in his taxi."

Certainly Stephen never had the benefit of reading Dale Carnegie's *How to Win Friends and Influence People*. After a lengthy defense, saying he had not spoken against the temple, because the God of Israel, historically, was a pilgrim God whose presence was never limited to a physical temple, these are the words that made the Jewish leaders lose their tempers:

> And you continue, so bullheaded! Calluses on your hearts, flaps on your ears! Deliberately ignoring the Holy Spirit, you're just like your ancestors. Was there ever a prophet who didn't get the same treatment? Your ancestors killed anyone who dared talk about the coming of the Just One. And you've kept up the family tradition—traitors and murderers, all of you. You had God's law handed to you by angels—gift-wrapped!—and you squandered it!
>
> Acts 7:51–53 Message

One could well imagine, after incendiary words like these, some of the Christians saying to each other, "How could Stephen have put his head into the noose like that?" And indeed, since the incident triggered a huge persecution, they might also have said, "Why did he put our heads in the noose as well?" One can well imagine the whispers as the persecution raged: "Because Stephen spoke so harshly, more Christian leaders have lost their heads, entire groups have had to leave their livelihoods and become refugees, and whole families have been broken up. It's awful on the children—how could Stephen be so insensitive?"

Yet not a single negative word is said against Stephen. He is described as a man who was "full of grace and power, did great wonders and signs among the people" (Acts 6:8). When his body is buried, there is no hint of censure: "Devout men buried Stephen and made loud lamentation over him" (8:2). Indeed, the way Luke constructs his narrative, it is clear that he believes that the persecution of Stephen benefited the church because it woke them up to serve the Great Commission. Stephen's death results in the scattering of the Christians away from Jerusalem. They are forced to spread the gospel as they were bidden by Christ in Acts 1:8: "You will be my witnesses both in Jerusalem, in all Judea and Samaria, and to the ends of the earth." How ironic that the world's most Spirit-filled church even failed to understand the Great Commission! Stephen's martyrdom changed that, and every Gentile today should breathe a prayer of thanks.

## People Kill to "Rescue" Their God

Often martyrdoms become markers or turning points in the history of a church. Sometimes the killing provokes a wave of outrage that topples even entrenched totalitarian systems. Kevin Ruane's book *To Kill a Priest* is subtitled *The Murder of Father Popieluszko and the Fall of Communism*. Father Jerzy Popieluszko, known as Solidarity's Priest, was a thirty-six-year-old Catholic priest who led inspiring Masses in Communist Poland during the dreary years of martial law in the early eighties. His abduction, torture, and murder at the hands of the secret police led to such revulsion toward the regime that it gave the people's union, Solidarity, a new impetus and enabled them to set in motion the events that led to the fall of the Berlin Wall. More than a million people attended his funeral on Saturday, November 3, 1984. No one claims his martyrdom brought down the USSR single-handedly, but his death definitely released forces of bravery and determination that marked a key turning point in the events that rewrote the balance of power in the world today.

Still, this does not get us any closer to *why* Stephen, or Zewar, was killed. Luke is disinterested in motive; he simply sets out the downward spiral of events that resulted in Stephen's death. It was a four-stage process. It began with a theological debate, but when Stephen's opponents felt bested in argument (Acts 6:10), they began a campaign of lies, bribing witnesses to say that Stephen had blasphemed (v. 11). Then a quasi-legal procedure was instituted to silence Stephen—the calling of the council—and finally when Stephen's defense proved too hot to handle, it ended in mob rage.

Clearly Stephen's words reached the very worst part of a human being and released forces that in normal civilization we all keep down. A great evil was unleashed. It begs the inevitable question—why, in the history of the world, are religious people so prone to violence?

Rowan Williams, the archbishop of Canterbury, argues that religious people are prone to violence because religion is so powerful an explorer of ourselves. He says:

> I think any kind of religious faith takes you much deeper into yourself and into reality than is comfortable, and going deeper into yourself of course makes contact with bits of yourself that don't normally appear. Therefore it can be heroic, it can be hugely generous, because those things are in us—as a religious person would say—in the image of God. It can also touch deep hurts, deeply buried angers and irrational passions and so it can also release a lot of violence.[3]

This is well put. Religion is such a central expression of one's individual and national identity that an attack on it seems like an attack on one's god. And so, in a bizarre way, *religious people kill to rescue their god*! That is their deepest motivation. The men that stoned Stephen were killing a heretic who had blasphemed against God. The man who shot Zewar was protecting Allah. Rage, of the deepest and darkest kind, is awakened here as by little else in the course of a life. Of course, joy is awakened also, and religion has enough ecstasy to go around for everyone. But the deepest places of a human being are opened up by religious faith, and this can have catastrophic as well as beneficial consequences, when the carnal comes up to the surface.

Of course motives are always mixed. Defending one's god is not the sole reason for violence. In one of the few places in Scripture where the authors show an interest in the motives of the persecutors, Matthew reports that Pontius Pilate saw that it was "out of envy" (Matt. 27:18) that the Jewish priests were handing Jesus over to him. They envied Jesus's power and influence with the masses. It was greed that made Judas hand Jesus over. It was out of political cowardice that Pilate did not put his neck on the line to save an innocent man. And it was also out of political necessity that Caiaphas, the high priest, made his fateful calculation that Jesus was too dangerous to let loose at Passover time with Rome itching to wipe out the Jews, and so "it is expedient for you that one man die for the people" (John 11:50 NASB). Caiaphas said far more than he knew, but he was trying to save his God, his people, his religion.

Applying all this to Zewar, we can see the same mixture of factors. He was killed for four main reasons:

Because an Islamic cleric, in a meeting of fanatics, lied and claimed that Zewar had led five hundred Muslims to Christ

Because an extremist had a vivid dream to rescue his god and kill Zewar

Because leaders got jealous of his influence

Because Zewar was bold and uncompromising in his witness

There is one aspect of this we have so far left out, without which the picture is not complete. It is the devil, the demonic hatred that lies behind all anti-Christian violence. Note that this hatred does not lie behind all religious violence. The devil's ire is directed at Christ, no one else. This adds an extra dimension of evil. Where did Mr. Abd al-Karem Abd al-Salam's dream come from to kill Zewar? Surely it came from the devil himself, waging his cosmic battle of spite against Jesus Christ. This is another source of rage.

Ultimately then the Zewars of this world are killed by other religious people who have convinced themselves, through lies, through demonic suggestion, and through their darkest fears being stirred up, that their god has to be rescued! And let it be admitted—Christianity has written a few dark chapters in this tale. I remember witnessing a terrible scene in Ambon, Indonesia, in the late 1990s. A priest was giving communion to a Christian militia and finished with the words, "Now go and anoint your machetes with Muslim blood." Beneath these chilling words was the same insecurity. The priest explained, "We're being overrun. If we don't strike now against the Muslims, the Christian God will be banished from these islands."

## Protecting the Racket

Still, the majority of Christians are martyred not because other religious people are trying to rescue their god but because nonreligious people are trying to *protect their racket*. For example, pastors in Colombia are executed by Marxist guerillas primarily because the pastors in the rebel-controlled areas refuse to participate in their drug-running rackets, which fuel the entire economy of these regions. In other situations, one has to peer more closely to discern the racket.

On the evening of October 9, 1998, forty-two-year-old Alexey Sitnikov was abducted from the premises of Grozny Baptist Church in Chechnya, where he was a pastor. Alexey was single, having devoted much of his life to nursing his elderly invalid mother. Muslim Chechens were becoming increasingly violent in their attempts to form a breakaway republic, and ethnic Russians fled in large numbers as the Russian army moved in to subdue the militants. But Alexey stayed to pastor the 170 members of the Baptist church, and miraculously through all the heavy bombing, the church building was unscathed.

Initially it was assumed that Alexey's disappearance was the work of Muslim extremists. They were in the pay of corrupt local officials who had been pocketing relief supplies intended for Alexey's church members. He had protested about this and had even been asked if he wanted to receive a big payoff himself to keep his nose out of it.

"I'd rather starve," he told a friend at the time when he had literally nothing to feed his own mother.

Subsequently Alexey was warned by being taken hostage twice for short periods. The second time he was beaten unconscious and left for dead outside a hospital. The third swoop on him was the last. It was only in August of 1999 that his severed head was seen on national television. Local police bulletins frequently included such footage in an attempt to identify the growing number of kidnapping victims. It was presumed that he had been killed soon after his abduction.

Alexey Sitnikov was a mild-mannered, gracious young man who, because of his Christian honesty, refused to participate in a lucrative racket ripping off foreign aid donations. Violent men, who set a low value on human life, killed him. Such men are responsible for the majority of Christian martyrs today.

Yet martyrs are not numerous in the church. Recently a mantra has been widely repeated: "More Christians have died for their faith in the twentieth century than in the previous nineteen centuries combined." The implication is clear: today we are at an all-time peak for the killing of Christians. The problem with this claim is that it is primarily a testimony not so much to an increase in persecution as to an increase in population. The fact is, you can say that more people have died of malnutrition, war, famine, whatever in the twentieth century than in the previous nineteen, simply because *more people have lived in the twentieth century than in the previous nineteen*. To imply that this is the most dangerous time to be a Christian in the history of the last two thousand years is possibly an exaggeration.

Ministries to the persecuted churches tend to steer clear of estimates of numbers of martyrs, though the *World Christian Encyclopedia* has not been reticent, claming that between AD 33 and AD 2000, a total of 69,420,000 Christians have been martyred, or 0.8 percent. They put the annual rate of martyrs at a staggering 160,000 plus, but it is hard to see how they derive such a high figure from such a restrictive definition of a martyr: "Believers in Christ, who have lost their lives, prematurely, in situations of witness, as a result of human hostility."[4] Only by counting as martyrs, for example, the tens of thousands of nominal Christians killed in civil war conflicts that may not even be related to religion, can one get to such a figure. I have learned to leave the counting to God and not get into foolish arguments about who is a martyr and who is not. Over time the church will recognize a true martyr. One should respect that process.

## Rare but Important

For all their rarity, though, martyrs are exceedingly important. They are killed primarily because religious people, in a bizarre demonic twist, wish to rescue their god from humiliation, or because nonreligious people, who have lost all notion of the sacredness of humanity, want to protect their moneymaking racket. The importance of martyrs stems from their ability to unmask for the ordinary Christian the hostile nature of the world in which we live. We sense the reality of Christ's warning to all His disciples that the world will hate us because of Him (see John 15:18–19), and we see the injustice of it, as Jesus also said, "They hated me without a cause" (v. 25). A martyr makes us aware that this world can never be our home. Also martyrs inspire us to a closer walk with Christ. We are moved by their witness to death (the essential meaning of the word martyr), and they call us to follow their example. "Give up your small ambitions," they cry from the grave, and their last words tell of the grandeur of this gospel, this Christ, we profess to follow. When Dietrich Bonhoeffer says before being shot by the Nazis on April 9, 1945, "This is the end—for me, the beginning of life," we wonder how we ever shrank down Christian living to a small, boring way of life, and we resolve never to allow that to happen again.

Historically, martyrs often create watersheds in the history of the church, as we have seen in the case of Stephen. It was the Latin church father, Tertullian, who first came up with the phrase, "The blood of the martyrs is the seed of the church." Ironically, he was wrong about his own city, Carthage, and much of North Africa, which had martyrs aplenty, yet the church virtually disappeared with the arrival of Islam. A martyr brings no guarantee of revival.

In fact, Christian history reveals an ambiguous legacy in this respect. Christians have been far too prone to idolize martyrs and venerate their remains, often at the expense of remembering their own gospel responsibilities. As a Christian pastor in Kurdistan once confided about the historic churches in Iraq: "They won't stop talking about the martyrs they have had over a thousand years ago, but they never ask why they don't have any martyrs today—it is because they are afraid to take the gospel to a Muslim." This pastor had taken converted Muslims for baptism to his local Chaldean Catholic bishop, who said to him, "Are you mad? If I baptize these people, we will all be finished." The pastor replied, "Aren't you supposed to do it because God commands you, not whether it suits the political survival of the church?" He realized, like many a reformer, that to follow Christ more fully he needed to leave the church of his birth.

### Remember the Living

Sometimes we overvalue martyrs and undervalue the living. This came home to me after meeting Mr. Ha, a pastor in China. He and his brother both became Christians and went on to become fine preachers. But his brother was jailed in the early 1970s and died in prison. As Mr. Ha put it, "His testimony moved from words in the air to blood in the ground."

Mr. Ha also served some time in jail, but on his release he continued to preach and pastor many house churches. He began to be a little concerned as he was always introduced as "the brother of the one who was counted worthy to suffer a martyr's death." He recalled, "I was proud of the way my brother had died for Christ. But people would come up to me and say, 'Oh, it must be marvelous for you to have been so close to a great man of God.' It seemed like my brother's martyrdom put him in a completely different spiritual category from me in most Christians' eyes."

Matters came to a head when one day he was presented with a small book of sermons. The house church network that produced them regarded them as a great and inspiring text. "These are the sermons of your great brother," they said. "We hope they will be as formative for you as they were for us." Mr. Ha did not have the heart to tell them the truth. The sermons were not his brother's sermons; they were Mr. Ha's! It had been quite common for them to preach each other's sermons.

The incident caused him to express great irritation to God. "Lord, am I so unworthy that my brother is regarded as so special because he was martyred, and my words are not taken as seriously because I was not counted worthy of death? What did I do wrong that I was not martyred also?"

Mr. Ha continued for some years in this distress. Then one day he was reading through Jeremiah and came across a verse that, he says, "wrote itself on my heart with fingers of fire." Jeremiah had just been put on trial for preaching a particularly fearless sermon, and then Mr. Ha read: "Ahikam son of Shaphan supported Jeremiah, and so he was not handed over to the people to be put to death" (Jer. 26:24 NIV).

It hit Mr. Ha that he was just like Jeremiah—they had both been spared from becoming a martyr. Mr. Ha said, "If Ahikam had not intervened, Jeremiah would be only twenty-six chapters long instead of fifty-two chapters. It was not the will of God that Jeremiah become a martyr. God needed him to do more preaching, and that was not second best!"

There was another contemporary parallel with Jeremiah's story— a man just like Ahikam had saved Mr. Ha from death. Once a gang from the world of organized crime had captured Pastor Ha because he had been instrumental in the conversion of some prostitutes, who then refused to work at their old trade. He was taken to a factory and thrown into a large industrial refrigerator. "I knew I was going to die," he recalled, "and after a few hours my body began to stiffen." But then some thugs came in and carried him to a warm office, where he sat shivering uncontrollably. In came a fat man in a smart suit. He was the owner of the factory, and for all Mr. Ha knew, the godfather of the crime syndicate. He was holding the small book of sermons that had been found in Mr. Ha's jacket pocket.

"Yours?" the fat man asked.

"Yes, mine," said Mr. Ha, telling the truth about the book of sermons for the first time in years.

The fat man said soberly, "Seems to me you are telling people to be honest, to be good, and to love God. That's a good creed." Then he smiled, "Of course, it would put me out of business eventually but not in my lifetime I think." His face went serious again, "I own this factory, and I won't have the death of a good man on my conscience. China needs people like you to live."

Mr. Ha was released with the words ringing in his ears—*China needs people like you to live!* He said, "That man could have been a Herod or a Nero and put me to death, but he chose to be an Ahikam. He let me live, knowing that the Word of God, which he barely understood, still needed more proclaiming."

Years later, when I interviewed him, Mr. Ha was not so active. His ministry was largely over. Advanced arthritis had gripped his frame, forcing him into strange positions. But he reflected on that experience in these words: "Thus I missed becoming a martyr like my brother. But I had come to a full realization that it is as much an honor to be spared as to be martyred. In China, Watchman Nee is not greater than Wang Mingdao, just because Nee died in prison and Wang survived. I took in at last that I was not less worthy than my brother because I was spared. God had need of me and sent an Ahikam. Being delivered to preach again is as great an act of God as being strengthened to die in faith."

He stopped and cupped some water in his arthritic hands. He sipped it thoughtfully, then declared, "But we in the suffering church make too much of those who have been killed for their faith and too little of those who have been spared. Maybe that is inevitable, but I do say quietly in response to that attitude, 'Why do you want your Bible to shrink in half? God spared many prophets so that they would finish speaking his words, but you want to stop them half-way through their ministries.'"

Mr. Ha died soon after I met him. And his final words to me were these: "If it wasn't for people like Ahikam, our Bible would be very thin. Thank God for the preacher who is saved from a martyr's death. It is no sin to be spared that the Word of God may continue to be preached. Not all God's words must be written in blood!"

The story of the persecuted church is seen most dramatically in the blood of the martyrs, but the larger story is also written in the flesh of the living. Both stories need to be put together for a true understanding to emerge. After all, stars can only shine at night!

We see, then, that if we are to understand the persecuted, it is necessary to step back and get the larger picture. If persecution isn't just about martyrs, then what is this larger story? Perhaps we might begin this journey by asking what conditions result in the creation of martyrs. An Indian Christian put it more color-fully: "You've got to realize the lies come before the lashes." The violence that results in martyrs usually takes place long after the church has lost its battle for freedom. Sometimes the church does not even know it is in a battle until it is too late. Persecution creeps up on the church unawares. To appreciate this, we must travel to the India of the 1990s and meet the world's cleverest persecutors of that era—the Hindu extremists.

# 2   The Creeping

*India—Vacuums, Villains,
Lies, Mobs, and Megaphones*

While smuggling Bibles into Poland in the early 1980s, I took a
detour to spend a morning visiting Auschwitz-Birkenau concentration camp. It was a bitterly cold day. My feet crunched snow and
I had to flail my arms to keep warm—something the inmates had
been forbidden to do.

At that time, the Polish authorities had left the camp much as
they had found it. There was no slick presentation of the tragedy,
no shrill audiovisuals warning us of the dangers of Nazism. There
were just the huts, the ovens, and a room filled with steep piles of
boots and spectacles, which made the horror more vivid.

Only three visitors were at the site that day. We gazed at the
solemn piles, trying vainly to get our minds around the fact that
every boot, every pair of glasses represented a person who should
have enjoyed a happy life but were gone forever, their hopes dashed,
their voices silenced.

I mused, *How could anything so horrifying ever be allowed to happen?*
At my elbow appeared a wrinkled old man, a rabbi, who seemed to

read my mind. He pulled up his sleeve to reveal a number stamped in the blue ink that never fades. "Ravensbrück," he said. Then he put his face close to my ear and whispered urgently, "You must understand this; *you must understand this.*" He gestured to the ovens, "These crematoria were not built first with bricks but with words!" He explained, "It started with lies, quietly released into the culture as jokes, slogans, and arguments, and soon we Jews were depersonalized, dehumanized, seen as no better than animals, and you can do anything to animals!" As we parted, he said, "We never saw it coming . . . until it was too late!"

That dear old rabbi revealed a crucial lesson—persecution creeps! As many Jews of 1930s Germany never saw something as dreadful as the Holocaust coming, Christians rarely see persecution coming until it is too late. We think that persecution will be recognizable. We think we will see the signs, and these signs will be obvious. We will spot a Hitler figure; we will be alerted when millions are mobilized to marginalize us; we will unmask the ideology of hate that drives the persecution before it gets embedded into the culture. But in practice, persecution is hard to see coming.

For example, the Hitler figure may stay in the background. Or Hitler may not look like Hitler . . . at first. A German pastor I greatly respected once confided to me, "Until 1937 I kept a picture of Hitler on my study desk." Hitler made the trains run on time, made the parks safe to walk for women, gave a shattered Germany some pride again as a nation. At first—hard as it may be to understand with the apocalyptic hindsight we have today—many ordinary Germans did not see Hitler's diabolical side until he was well entrenched in power, and some not even then. To put it more biblically, *antichrists* are adept at masquerading as angels of light.

We think that we will spot a crude ideology of hate, but in practice the persecuting justification is often cloaked in a beguiling lie that is quite popular and appealing. In Nazi Germany one of these successful lies was, "Why can't Germany just be run by Germans, rather than Jews who do not like us?" In modern India the lie was, "We have to stop the Muslims taking over our Hindu country." Even under slogans as apparently innocuous as, "We have to make our country strong," or "We have to make the world safe for our way of life," persecuting ideologies can take shelter and then arise to make the world suddenly unsafe for religious minorities.

We may think we will be alerted by millions on the march shouting, "Death to Christians!" In reality it does not take millions to create a climate of persecution. Often it is a tiny elite who manipulate some handpicked mobs, and they manufacture a chaos that leverages them into power. At the risk of melodrama, I must say persecutors are clever, sinister figures, who shoot their arrows from the shadows (Ps. 11:2). Few vote for persecution—knowingly! Persecutors gain power by spinning an elaborate deception, and only when the prey is caught in their web do they reveal their venom.

The creeping nature of persecution results in three historical facts about Christians and persecution that are rarely acknowledged:

- Rarely does persecution come the way we expect it.
- We often don't see it coming at all.
- When it comes, we see that we are partially responsible for its appearance.

This third realization cuts the deepest. The fact is, extremists who fuel persecution exploit a vacuum created for them. Because "evil triumphs when good men do nothing," extremists end up center stage because of a failure of the forces of moderation. Hitler gained power because Germany was bankrupt, and the political moderates could not restore stability. And in the German church, the great hero of the Christian resistance Pastor Martin Niemoller stirred up a huge controversy when he insisted on the clause "through us" being inserted into the 1946 Stuttgart Declaration of the Evangelical Church of Germany. The declaration read: "With great anguish we state: *Through us*, inestimable suffering was inflicted on many peoples and lands" (author's italics).[1] Many German Christians felt Niemoller had betrayed the German people by taking some responsibility for the Nazi excesses. No doubt his sensitivity stemmed from his own experience, memorably expressed and oft quoted in this form:

First they came for the socialists, and I did not speak out because I was not a socialist. Then they came for the trade unionists, and I did not speak out because I was not a trade unionist. Then they came for the Jews, and I did not speak out because I was not a Jew. Then they came for me, and there was no one left to speak for me.

This chapter will show how contemporary persecution gets started, how it creeps into a culture before it bares its teeth. I will argue that there is a five-part recurring pattern to look for and will examine this pattern in the contemporary scene—India in the 1990s. I hope we can learn to recognize and oppose the forces that bring persecution before they become irreversible!

### Howls of Laughter

In 1996 I attended a conference of pastors in New Delhi. Evangelical church pastors had lined up to meet Western contributors, and the whole meeting became a rather undignified scramble for money. During the proceedings, a pastor stood up and said, "What are we going to do about the Hindu extremists?" There was complete silence. Someone eventually said, rather testily, "Well, what about them?" The pastor replied, "We Christians are going to be severely persecuted in this country if we don't act now to stop them!"

This statement was greeted with howls of laughter. The pastor sat down, shamefaced. "We are a secular country," he was lectured by one eminent pastor, "the only country in Asia that refused to have a state religion. Our history is against it."

But history was already being rewritten.

In the most astonishing rise to power of religious extremists in the twentieth century, a party of religious zealots with a harsh, divisive message of "India for Hindus only"—who were a laughingstock in 1990 with only two seats in Parliament—panicked a vast block of voters into thinking that India was being overrun by Muslims and Christians and took power in 1998. Waves of communal violence were unleashed throughout the country. From 1964 to 1996 there had been only thirty-eight registered cases of violence against Christians in the whole of India.[2] By the time 2001 rolled around, even the extremist government was admitting that in the two years since 1999, a total of 33 Christians had been killed and 283 injured, and more than 417 acts of violence had been recorded against Christians and their property, including rape, church burnings, and lootings by the score. This figure was a grudging one. The true extent of the anti-Christian violence was far greater. Evangelicals quickly formed the All India Christian Council in 1999 and its vice chairman, John Dayal, put the number of deaths at "over forty" and the number of violent incidents at "nearer nine hundred."

International concern mounted as the number of martyrs soared, especially after the gruesome killing of fifty-eight-year-old Australian missionary Graham Staines, burned alive in a jeep with his two young sons at 12:30 a.m. on January 23, 1999, in Manoharpur, Orissa. They had been sleeping when a crazed extremist mob hacked at them with axes and knives, pushed lighted straw under the car, and propped planks against the doors to keep them shut as the fire spread, ignoring the terrified cries of the two boys, Philip, age ten, and Timothy, age seven. The charred bodies of the three were discovered with their arms around one another.

The grizzly martyrdom woke the church up to the fact that when they protested the increasing violence against them, they found the police and many government institutions reluctant to help them, as the extremists had infiltrated their ranks. Instead of being protected, Christians were accused of conducting "forced conversions" or being a "CIA-backed Trojan horse." Slowly the Indian church began to appreciate that the violence was not sporadic but well organized. Joseph D'Souza, director of Operation Mobilization—India's largest Christian organization—declared in the summer of 2000, "There is now a carefully orchestrated pattern to the violence propagated against Christians in India today."

The party turning a blind eye to the violence was the governing Bharatiya Janata Party (BJP), a front for the Hindu extremist organization, the Rashtriya Swayamsevak Sangh (RSS). Their ideology was called *Hindutva*, a frighteningly fascist interpretation of Indian history that insisted only Hindus had a right to live on the great Indo-Gangetic Plain. While the "Christian West" fretted over how

to stop Islamic extremists taking power in the Middle East, they
forgot to notice the rise in India of what Dayal labeled "the Hindu
Taliban." And so in the 1990s the world's largest democracy suc-
cumbed to the charms of extreme religious nationalists, almost
unnoticed by the international community, and belatedly by many
Indian Christian leaders. The U.S. government caught up with the
new dynamics only in 2003, finally designating India a "country
of particular concern" for its deplorable record of protecting the
religious rights of minorities.

## The Five-Part Recurring Pattern

How did India's religious extremists manage to gain power so
quickly and create a climate of persecution for many of India's Christians in less than a decade? We can observe in India the five elements
in a recurring pattern of contemporary persecution seen around the
world: a vacuum, a villain, a lie, a mob, and a megaphone.

### A Vacuum

First, there needs to be a vacuum, a power vacuum that gives
extremists an opportunity to move to the power centers of society.
This vacuum is rarely created by the extremists; they merely exploit it. It's a strange truth, but extremists usually get into power
because they are invited. Extremists flourish only when moderates
fail. People do not turn to extremists until all other solutions appear
to have been unsuccessful. Extremism always needs a vacuum to
step into. The Communists of Eastern Europe gained a foothold
in Europe only because of the vacuum that followed the chaos
of the two world wars. In China Mao gained his chance because
people gave up on Chiang Kai-shek, who ran off with the country's
savings. When the forces of moderation fail, only then do the extremists prevail.

In India this vacuum opened up in the 1990s. It was caused
by two factors—the fragmentation of the ruling Congress Party,
which had held power since India began its democratic journey

in 1950, and the collapse of left-wing ideology after the fall of the Berlin Wall. India's politics always organized around two extreme poles—communalism and communism.

Traditionally the Congress Party of Gandhi and Nehru occupied power by promising to keep both extremes at bay. But in the 1990s the Congress Party was riddled with corruption, and many of its leading lights left in disgust to form regional political parties. The grand coalition was breaking up. Simultaneously, with the political vacuum, an ideological vacuum developed.

The left-wing perspective was in high retreat after the fall of Eastern Europe and the apparent triumph of Western capitalism. Congress preserved a nominal socialist ethos, though in practice they were the party of the wealthy elites, but the party found itself temporarily without a compelling message to justify its reelection. Intellectuals looked around to espouse a new ideology. A huge vacuum opened up at the center of Indian politics, and ordinary, peace-loving people looked in desperation to bring to the government some new faces untainted by the scandals of the Congress Party. Enter the BJP!

Note a vacuum doesn't automatically mean that extremists emerge. They must play their cards right and exploit the vacuum. To do this successfully, four more elements are needed: a villain, to organize the power grab; a mob, to create instability and intimidate voters; a lie, to motivate the mob to acts of violence; and a megaphone, to continually reinforce the lies, creating a new way of thinking and guaranteeing that this new ideology gradually changes the culture itself.

### A Villain

The villain is the architect who comes up with the strategy to get the extremists into power. In India a prime candidate for the villain role is Lal Krishnan Advani, the leader of the RSS. He is reported to have examined the Christians in the 1980s and asked, "Why do they have so much power where they live and we do not?" Christians were barely 2.3 percent of the Indian population. Hindus were 85 percent. Yet 50 percent of all the schools in India were Christian-run. The elites of the nation were trained there, including Advani. Forty percent of all the social work in the country came from Christian organizations. How did such a tiny minority gain such influence?

Advani is said to have concluded—rather surprisingly—that it was because the Christians were *one*. They had one book, the Bible. Hindus had literally thousands of sacred texts. Christians had one God; Hindus had thirty-three million and rising. Christians had one church (he obviously didn't look too closely). Hindus had a whole range of competing institutions. So the RSS leadership under Advani called for a new power strategy that would ape Christianity. There would be one book, the *Bhagavad Gita*; one deity, Ram; and one focus, the message of *hard Hindutva*. They united a whole slew of organizations, such as the World Hindu Council (VHP), the Bajrang Dal, the RSS youth wing, and many others into a more concerted movement, known as the Sangh Parivar. Now they were a focused, disciplined unit with a single simple message.[3]

But what was this message to be? Here Advani had a further problem. The message of *Hindutva* was old, fascist, and elitist. It was a nationalist ideology spawned at the founding of the RSS in 1924, one that held that India could be free and prosperous only when its entire culture reverted to the pre-Western, pre-Aryan glory days of original Hinduism. Back then in a wonderful golden age, went this dubious argument first coined by Vinayak Damodar Savarkar and Madhav Sadashiv Golwalkar, Hindus were united in race, culture, and geography. The RSS set out to restore this "unity." Taking a secular turn, especially with the founders refusing to make India a Hindu state in 1950, was a grave mistake in their eyes and should be reversed. All recruits to the RSS take an oath that says, "For the betterment of my sacred Hindu religion, Hindu culture, and Hindu community, I will dedicate myself to the prosperity of my Holy Motherland." Anyone who did not support this Hindu vision—particularly Muslims and Christians—would be forced to leave or at least removed from positions of power, lest they sabotage the purity of this perfect culture that would make India strong.

But the polarizing language and racist undertones of *Hindutva*, which betrayed its roots as a bastard child of 1920s and 1930s European fascism, was not likely to boost the BJP into power, given that the more numerous lower castes were alienated from a form of Hinduism dedicated to keeping them backward. All the Hindu extremist movements, like the RSS and BJP, were Brahmanical movements, or high caste, and embraced a Hinduism that taught one must stay in the caste to which one was born and accept one's karma, for only then would one gain a superior incarnation in the next life. But 70 percent of Indians were of low caste or outcaste status and were beginning to see caste as a social evil the state ought to confront. How could Advani garner enough votes from them while essentially asking them to assist him in their exploitation? The answer—hide the true agenda of *Hindutva* under some irresistible lies.

### A Lie

A lie, or a series of lies, is the third element in the pattern of contemporary persecution. People don't put extremists in power just because they feel like it, nor can they be roused to violence without believing they are justified. That's why lies are needed. Lies create the desperation that justifies the chaos created by a mob—the prelude to power. The main lie Advani came up with was that the 130 million Muslims of India were culturally trying to displace Hindus. He focused attention on this rather abstract idea by claiming that a four-hundred-year-old Muslim mosque in Ayodhya, Uttar Pradesh, was in fact built over the birthplace of the god Ram and should be torn down and a proper Hindu temple erected. He came up with other lies when the Hindu extremists turned from Muslims and went after Christians. The Christians, he alleged, are the agents of Western powers, often CIA backed, and are intent on converting Hindus by bribery and other coercive measures. When the pope came to visit India in 2000, he was greeted by the Congress Party leader, Sonia Gandhi, the Italian Catholic wife of former leader Rajiv Gandhi. Advani thundered, "We want Ram-Raj, not Rome Raj" (Ram rule, not Rome rule).

To get the intellectuals on their side, Advani and others began a movement that equated conversion with violence. An obliging cohort in this strategy was the "Hindu pope," Swami Dayandanda Saraswati. He said,

> What is violence? When you physically hurt me it is violence. When you do anything that can instigate physical violence, that is an act of violence, too. And if you can hurt me emotionally, it is also violence. If you can hurt me spiritually, that is the worst violence, rank violence. All those are there in evidence in conversion because it leads to physical violence. When you convert someone, you have to criticize the person's religion, his worship, his culture; all of these hurt. . . . He has to disown his parents, and their wisdom and their culture, his ancestors and entire community; you are isolating him, uprooting him, and all uprooted people are emotionally unsettled.[4]

When the same swami was arrested in the fall of 2004 for murder, the World Hindu Council blamed—amazing as it may seem—the Christians. Ashok Singal, the VHP leader, said, "This is a conspiracy of Christians and Sonia Gandhi."[5] He repeated allegations that there was a global Christian conspiracy to malign Hindu leaders and take over the country. Absurd, but these lies are carefully thought through to distract from the real issues, in this case, from the trial for murder of one of Hinduism's most sacred leaders.

There are bizarre rules for creating powerful lies. The more brazen they are, the more effective they are. The timing of the lie is critical. It has to distract at just the right moment. Most important, a "great" lie has to be couched in such a way that nothing can falsify it, so that anything that happens subsequently "proves" the truth of it—a classic conspiracy maneuver. Take this lie: "Western Christians have a secret agenda to convert India to Christianity." When Graham Staines and his two sons were killed by Hindu extremist youths, the initial public condemnation was very damaging to the Sangh Parivar. But the more international outrage that was expressed, the more Hindu extremists twisted it to prove the lie, saying, "See, look how upset these international forces are about the death of this missionary. It *proves* they want to take us over." And so, in the words of Richard Howell, the chairman of the Evangelical Fellowship of India (EFI): "These lies changed the climate in the 1990s. *Conversion* became a dirty word. *Proselytization* became a filthy term.

*Christian* even began to be equated with *foreigner*, and at every turn we had to defend ourselves from ludicrous ideas that we were all conducting 'forced conversions' among the poor, and our whole agenda in India was called into question as part of a CIA-backed conspiracy." Another pastor added, "All of a sudden it was like we had just arrived in the country and were interlopers, rather than a presence since the first century."

Yet why are these lies believed, given that they are so brazen and so intrinsically unbelievable? The answer lies in the final two elements of the contemporary persecution pattern: mobs and megaphones.

### A Mob

Mobs are needed to actually create the chaos that the extremists can exploit to cower the opposition. Here Advani played his masterstroke. In August 1990 he embarked on his *rath yatra*, a mass procession through ten Indian states, starting in Gujarat and intending to finish at the Babri Mosque. It was led by Advani riding in a Toyota jeep decorated as "Ram's chariot." En route he made speeches of great power, urging the young men to take the law into their own hands to save the future of Hinduism. Needless to say, communal violence ensued. And in December 1992 a mob demolished the Babri Mosque, convulsing the country. Even the police joined in. The Muslims were outraged. Communal harmony was ruptured. The BJP was properly launched. The government resigned, and in the elections the BJP gained 120 seats, forming the official opposition. The whole campaign was covered by a secular documentary maker, Anand Patwardhan. In a hard-hitting film, *In the Name of God*, he set out to expose what he called "Advani's frenzy-building mechanism" to take power.

Patwardhan's phrase is significant. Mobs are rarely spontaneous. They are carefully organized, and in India this organizing was carried out by the RSS, with a secret membership of between 2.5 and 6 million. Dispersed throughout the country, they instigate mobs to close down churches, beat up evangelists, and force converts to renounce their Christian faith.

It's easily done. In December 2004 a typical incident occurred just an hour from Bombay. On the fifth, in Kolhapur, a Christian fellowship was meeting in a school when a mob crashed the service. They were from Shiv Sena, a Hindu extremist organization based mainly in Maharashtra state. Terrifying the congregation, they smashed chairs and amplification equipment, roughed up the pastor, and then called the police, claiming the church was engaging in "forced conversions." The police arrived, stopped the service, and brought the Christians to jail to answer the charges.

Dr. Abraham Mattai, the Christian vice chairman of the State Minorities Commission, berated the police. "Why did you not uphold the law? You should be arresting the thugs not the Christians!" The incident was then written up in the local paper, slanted to imply that Hindus had caught Christians conducting underhanded forced conversions. The school at which the church met withdrew permission to hold services there. Mattai concludes, barely concealing his annoyance: "The Christians have been demonized in that town. They will never find premises now to worship in again. No one would dare." All because an organized mob disrupted a service and made carefully crafted accusations that frightened the police. A church that was alive and doing good work in the community has now been closed down. Such tactics have been used against literally thousands of churches outside the large cities in India.

The mobs do not have to be numerous, just ruthless. The key is to realize how well organized they are. In 2002 the persecution-watch news agency Compass Direct obtained a chilling secret RSS internal circular that instructed field operatives in thirty-four anti-Christian tactics.[6] The tactics included raping Christian women during riots, selling Christians into the flesh trade, recruiting doctors to dispense poisoned drugs, and assassinating anyone who opposed the caste system. Said a local pastor at the time: "The scales fell from my eyes when I saw the degree of organization that lay behind mob violence. I used to think it was just spontaneous, but that's a myth. It is superbly planned. They come in with sticks and violence; then they complain to the police that 'communal harmony' has been disrupted. The police, once they hear a term like that, immediately blame the Christians for inciting the mob. They stitch us up every time."

## A Megaphone

Of course these mobs are motivated by lies, but a megaphone is crucial also. Abraham Mattai reveals the essence of the megaphone strategy: "Loud repetition is the key to victory here. You can't just tell a lie once, you must tell it twenty, thirty times, as loudly as possible, and stop anyone hearing other points of view. Then the mob have no alternative than to believe you, because your propaganda is all they hear." This is just another way of putting Goebbels's principle into action. Joseph Goebbels, Hitler's master of propaganda, said, "If you repeat a lie often enough, people will believe it to be the truth." Mattai adds, "*Hindutva* is all lies, but the ideology became powerful because the lies kept coming at us all the time."

Communist regimes were masters at monopolizing the megaphones, insisting on taking over all the media and even education, banning the airing of different points of view. This was harder to achieve in India, however, where there was a relatively free press. But another Advani masterstroke started the ball rolling. He was instrumental in commissioning a television series that serialized two Hindu epic texts, the *Ramayana* and the *Mahabharata*. Beginning at nine o'clock on a Sunday morning, the series ran for two years, from 1990 to 1992, and much of India stopped to watch while the programs aired. Even crime dropped dramatically during the episodes. It all had the effect, in the estimation of evangelical strategist C. B. Samuel, of "re-Hinduizing the northern Indian culture." The south of India was not so affected, but the program gave a huge boost to the belief, "We are Hindus and proud of it." On his *rath yatra*, Advani took the film star who played the god Ram in his "chariot." The star was later elected to the national assembly.

Then the *Hindutva* message was spread out into the mass media, and the Sangh Parivar kept their own presses busy with their propaganda. The final stage was when Advani, as home minister in 1999, began to do what most of the opposition had feared . . .

rewrite the school textbooks. Warned Christian educator Dr. Gabriel Gonsalves at the time: "The cultural commanding heights of India are under attack, and the extremists are out to create a false version of history, which in time, will become truth." The BJP government printed seventeen thousand textbooks that taught that Jesus Christ lived in Kashmir and learned his principles from Hindu gurus. They also claimed the Taj Mahal was a Hindu monument (it is a Muslim mausoleum), that Homer derived his *Iliad* from Hindu sources, and that the cow was the mother of all, in whose body gods were believed to reside. Stressed Gonsalves, "These were not to be taught as interpretations, but as facts . . . in all government schools from primary to high school." The takeover scenario was under way with the RSS vowing to set up six hundred thousand single-teacher schools of fifty pupils throughout the Indian countryside, to raise up the next generation of *Hindutva* warriors. The strategy was long-term, and it was working!

So in 1998 the BJP gained power, and the anti-Christian momentum suddenly increased, especially as the mobs felt they could now act with impunity. Gujarat was the first state to bear the brunt when a VHP leader, Swami Ashimananda, called for low and outcaste groups who had converted to Christianity to be "reconverted." Over the Christmas of 1999, rampaging mobs burned thirty churches on the pretext they had conducted "forced conversions." If Christians thought the government would protect them, they were wrong. Prime Minister Atal Bihari Vajpayee visited the area, and with the world's press in tow, refused to condemn the arsonists, calling instead for a national debate on the issue of conversion. The implication was clear. The Christians were to blame for inciting the Hindu extremists.

The mobs took this as a signal that the government would turn a blind eye to their activities. One Christian leader took the gloves off. He was Alan De Lastic, the archbishop of Delhi, the highest-ranking Catholic in the country. "Your silence kills, Prime Minister!" he thundered. But the killing went on. So much so that Richard Howell, the Evangelical Fellowship of India chairman, reckoned that his organization was hearing of "around a hundred martyrdoms" each year, catapulting India into the category of desperate persecution states like Colombia, Sudan, and North Korea.

For all this worsening climate, the persecution was selectively applied. Much of the Indian church escaped it, sometimes for reasons that did them no credit. Howell asserts there are three sections of the thirty-million-strong Indian church.[7] First, those who were into social action—mostly Catholics (two-thirds of the Christian total), who generally soft-pedaled the whole issue of conversion. Second, mainstream Protestants, often with a pluralist theology that made the leaders actively hostile to the whole notion of evangelism, preferring a never-ending dialogue with Hindus and Buddhists. Indeed, as the persecution increased, their ecumenical organization—the National Council of Churches in India—refused to assist arrested evangelists, forcing evangelicals to form their own advocacy organization in 1999, the All India Christian Council.

The other third of the church is the evangelical Protestants, who, like the Catholics, worked primarily among the lower castes and outcaste groups, but who also stressed conversion. This latter group bore the brunt of the onslaught, though many Catholic activists who were empowering the poor came in for some stiff persecution too. The Catholic equivalent of Graham Staines was Sister Rania Maria, who was dragged from a public bus in February 1995 and stabbed more than forty times by three men in the street. Her eyes were gouged out while onlookers stared but did nothing. Mercifully, she died almost instantly. Her crime was to create a lending bank for the poor living in shantytowns, who were at the mercy of loan sharks until Sister Maria came along. It is believed that the moneylenders got together and paid the thugs to kill her.

## The Good News under the Bad

This may all seem like gloomy news, and for many Christians it is. But there is usually a good news angle with persecution. Indeed, one of the points of this book is that the story of God's working among the persecuted is, in the end, always a Good News story.

### Doing Something Right

First, *persecution usually occurs because the church is doing something right.* And what the church was doing right in India was evangelizing and empowering the most vulnerable groups in society—the lower castes and outcastes. Caste is central to the persecution story. According to Father Monodeep Daniel, an Anglican priest of the Delhi Brotherhood, "Persecution was always aimed at Christians in three groups—women, Dalits, and tribals—all are at the bottom of the caste system, and as a result of their Christianity are refusing to prop it up any longer." Hindu extremism is primarily born out of insecurity, that Christians (and other religions) might bring the Hindu house toppling down. This may seem preposterous at first, given that there are reckoned to be 850 million Hindus in India and only 30 million Christians. But to understand the fear that drew the persecution, we need to look more closely into caste and the nature of Hindu religion.

Hindus divide society into four classes—priests (Brahmans), rulers (Khastriya), workers (Vaishya), and servants (Sudras). Within each class, there are thousands of so-called castes. A caste is a group based on inherited professions and occupations. For example, one belongs to the pig-slaughterer caste or the leather-working caste. It is by accepting one's caste destiny, or *dharma*, that one gains salvation. In other words, to get a better incarnation, if you are born into the pig-slaughterers, you must stay a pig-slaughterer. It's important to remember that Hinduism is a purity religion, like the first-century Judaism of Christ's time, so human beings are graded on a scale of purity-impurity. The first three classes are regarded as pure, but the Sudra class is impure. A Brahman, for example, must not use the same utensils as a lower caste person, lest they be contaminated and drive God away.

The Brahmans are only 5 percent of the population, the other two top classes form another 10 percent. The servant castes, the Sudras, are a whopping 64 percent of the population. They are expected to serve the high castes. Then beneath the caste system, there is a huge population so impure they cannot be touched, nicknamed "untouchables." This is the bottom, 150 million so-called Scheduled castes, also known as Dalits (oppressed ones), and 80 million so-called Scheduled Tribes or tribal groups. Being at the bottom, these two groups prop up the entire system. They make society work. If they defect to another religion, Hinduism will literally topple over like a body with no legs.

And this is where the church comes in. The Indian church is 70 percent Dalit! Not surprisingly, the Christian faith comes as extraordinary news to someone who has been taught that if you are born into a pig-slaughtering caste, that is what you must do to please God and get a better reincarnation. Christianity sweeps that away and says, "You can be what you like. You are just as pure as anyone else, because all are equal in the sight of God." This cuts diametrically across the tenets of traditional Hindu extremist teaching that says one is born low caste as a punishment for sins in a previous life. Dalits are leaving the Hindu faith in significant numbers, panicking the Brahmans who see their entire edifice of salvation as under threat.

It has to be said, however, that the church has not always reached out to the Dalits. Christianity first came to India as early as AD 52—about the same time as it came to Europe—and yet Christians are barely 3 percent of the population two thousand years later. It is one of the greater missionary embarrassments in the world today. Part of the reason was that India's original Christians—the Mar Thomas Christians—came from a high caste and refused to evangelize the lower castes. Even today in many village churches throughout India, high caste members sit at the front, low caste at the back. Alan De Lastic, with customary bluntness, remarked, "The Indian church failed to believe in conversion; otherwise there would be five hundred million Christians here today." It's ironic then that Hindu extremists should accuse the church of producing conversions when, in fact, they are quite poor at it.

Many Dalits return to Hinduism, finding it hard when they lose their state privileges after converting to Christianity. John Dayal reckons the fallback rate to be 30 percent—a factor not considered by those who put the Christian population at over 4 percent today. That said, in the words of C. B. Samuel: "The evangelical Indian church has made a mighty impact, and in villages where there was just a fear of the spirits and lack of self-respect, the introduction of Christianity brings dignity, a desire for education, and a belief that they matter. This threatens the Brahmanical groups." A persecuted church is usually a threat to the powers-that-be. India's evangelicals were persecuted for all the "right" reasons!

### Serving the Cause of the Gospel

Another good news angle to look for in persecution is this: *the persecutors always end up serving the cause of the gospel of Christ.* In the providence of God, He ensures they end up building the kingdom. As the apostle Paul wrote, "We know that God causes all things to work together for good to those who love God" (Rom. 8:28 NASB). For one thing, the extremist persecution has turned off many from Hinduism, causing a greater turning toward Christ, especially among the poorer castes.

As a Dalit woman told me: "I would never have become a Christian had the leaders of Hinduism not urged us to hate and kill, because it made me realize anew that they just want to keep me in the trap of my caste. They want me to stay an untouchable so they can look down on me. When they started attacking the Christians, I said to myself, *I better find out what it is about Christianity that annoys them. If it annoys them, it may satisfy me.*"

Even more remarkable, however, is how the Hindu extremists have made it easier for Christians to get involved in public life. Richard Howell reveals: "A surprising benefit of the extremists taking power is that it is now acceptable to discuss religion in the public square again. Beforehand, it was very difficult, very secular." C. B. Samuel agrees, adding, "Because the BJP brought religion back into the public sphere, it makes the culture easier to evangelize. It is always the secular culture that is hardest to evangelize. The church used to see secularism as its protector, but we were warned by Christians like Lesslie Newbigin that secularism would ultimately freeze the church out of the life of the nation. Thanks to the Hindu extremists, we have that chance again to share our faith in the public realm, without ridicule, without embarrassment." Christians in the West, where faith is kept firmly in the private sphere by secular forces, surely envy Indian Christians this new opportunity.

A final (and extremely unexpected) piece of good news was the fall of the BJP government in March 2004. Christians were ecstatic. Not one of the poisonous textbooks was ever distributed to the schools. Beamed Gonsalves: "For the moment, the educational culture is safe from *hard Hindutva*." Yet as Dayal warns, "The BJP may have failed to bring *hard Hindutva* into the culture, but *soft Hindutva* is here to stay; it has gone mainstream, and even the Congress Party espouses it." Soft *Hindutva* preserves a total suspicion of conversions, a commitment to monitoring foreign funding for Christians while ignoring the same for Hindus, and privileging the Hindu religion as an act of nation-building, even though it stops short of wishing to make India a Hindu state.

Many fear the BJP will be back, and persecution rages where it always did—in the villages. The RSS is already two-thirds of the way toward their target of establishing six hundred thousand schools in the countryside. Already eleven and a half million children are spoon-fed an extremist version of history, viewing Christians as deceitful, foreign-backed usurpers of Hindu purity. "As long as the church succeeds in bringing Dalits to Christ, they will face persecution," warns Dayal, adding, "Nothing is more foolish than to think persecution is over just because a government changes."

### The Five Elements in the Red Light District

So we have seen how persecution seeps and creeps into the contemporary world, often catching the victim unaware. But if we take any lesson from this chapter, it must be this: extremists flourish only when a vacuum emerges. If Christians engage with the world, support the forces of moderation, and fight the voices of extremism, then that consigns extremists to the margins, denying them the opportunity to take power. We fight this battle all the time. Becoming alert to these five elements of how persecution starts—vacuum, villain, mobs, lies, and megaphones—may make the difference.

These five elements do not just apply in the macro-sphere, however. They enable us to understand persecution even on an individual level.

Kamatipura is a square mile of fourteen narrow lanes in downtown Bombay and contains more human misery than most societies. Seventy thousand prostitutes work there. About thirty thousand are minors. Kidnapped, drugged, and starved, they are raped by pimps, policemen, and clients. Although an illegal trade, brothel keepers bribe the police to turn a blind eye, and the police often take payment in the form of sex with the girls. However, one Christian man, Anson Thomas, felt the call of God to "make the red light district into a green light district."

In December 2004, I rode in a car through this area with Thomas. The car had tinted windows, so no one could look in and recognize him. If they did, a riot could ensue. Thomas was in fear for his life.

This thirty-eight-year-old civil servant began working in Kamatipura in 1991, organizing night shelters for the young children of prostitutes, who otherwise roamed the streets while their mothers worked. With the help of his church, these shelters became schools. Then he began to speak to the customers going into the brothels. "Two minutes of pleasure for a lifetime of fear," he would say. Then he appealed to the pimps. They just laughed. Finally, he began to get to know the girls, who were often forced out onto the streets to drum up business. Their stories horrified him. "I saw that they had given up hope. They were living fifteen to a room. They all hated their work but could not escape—the police were part of the racket. If they tried to flee, they were caught, starved, beaten, and gang-raped." So it occurred to Anson to organize raids on the brothels, asking the police to rescue the minors at least. After all, it was illegal; the law forbade it.

So Anson Thomas went into the rescue business. In the past few years he has rescued eight hundred girls. But getting the police to intervene when they are being bribed by the brothel owners is not easy. Thomas explains: "When I organize a raid, I don't tell the police where we are going. Otherwise, they will phone ahead, and when we arrive there will be no girls. I just say, 'I'll show you.' Then I have to convince them to park their van on an adjacent street, otherwise the street will empty out, and again, no girls. Then the officers walk very slowly to give the brothel keeper time. I have to hurry them. Finally, if the element of surprise is on our side, I go in and force them to take the girls out and arrest the brothel keeper. We all go down to the police station, and the police turn to me and say, 'Okay, Anson, your work is done now!' I reply, 'Oh, no, my work is just beginning.'"

He files a complaint. Then he insists the girls be taken to a hostel; otherwise they will be abused by the police. Then he has to keep visiting the girls in the hostel, arranging for them to receive vocational skills, such as candle making. Then he has to hurry to the court to prevent the brothel keepers from posting bail. He explains, "The lawyers for the brothel keepers give false names, and they are let out and start another brothel the next day. Also the court sets the girls free, saying, 'Go back to your home village,' but they have no money. What often happens is they file out of the court back into the clutches of the brothel keeper, who is waiting for them." To stop this from happening, Thomas has to be proactive, almost bullying the courts and police to do their duty.

Thomas did this for years, until the owners of the brothels got together. He began to be persecuted, and the five elements can be clearly seen. The vacuum is obvious. The flesh trade flourishes all because politicians and police are corrupt, preferring bribes to truth. The police even pay to be assigned to the area so they can receive greater kickbacks from the brothel owners. The churches are absent. Rescue ministries are too extreme for them. Says Thomas, "They are happy running schools for the prostitutes, but that way you are only helping the trade to continue. They only raise a hand if they know they won't burn a finger."

And there are villains. The brothel owners got together and wrote a letter in early 2003 to the police complaining that Thomas was conducting "forced conversions" of the girls, as he distributed Bibles to those who asked for them. Then they enlisted a local Congress politician, who tipped off the local extremist organization Shiv Sena.

They provided the mobs. Four hundred of them staged a raucous and semiviolent protest against Anson Thomas at the local police station. The police wrote Thomas a letter, holding him responsible for the disturbance.

Shiv Sena also provided the megaphone. An article in their magazine, *Samna*, on December 9, 2003, accused Thomas of "converting Hindu sex workers." They also create the lies, accusing Thomas of sleeping with the girls, forcing conversions, and kidnapping the girls and their children.

Now the police have banned Thomas from the area. The Shiv Sena mobs keep the brothels under observation, and if he attempts another rescue, they will kill him. This fear is not due to an overactive imagination either. Once they were under the impression he was leading a rescue, and three hundred turned up with huge sticks chanting, "Kill Thomas; kill Thomas." Then he learned that the brothel keepers had hired a hit man to murder him.

Thomas points out the irony of it all. "The Hindu extremists only got involved when they heard I was giving out Bibles to the girls. My question is, why don't they want to put a stop to the trading of underage girls, whom they called 'Hindu sex workers'? If they are Hindus, let them as good Hindus stop the trade! But they don't, because their actions have nothing to do with true Hinduism. Their agenda is all about power."

As Anson and I cruised the streets of Kamatipura in the tinted taxi, I saw the fear in his eyes—not for himself but for his wife and two young daughters. "My worst nightmare," he confided, "is that they will kidnap or kill my daughters."

Yet he is undaunted. He smiles, and the worry lines flee for a moment, as he says, "Well, they say children only throw stones at a ripe mango tree, so I must be doing something right to be in this much trouble for Christ!"

If this is how persecution starts, how do we help? How do we render assistance to churches like the Indian church, or to the likes of Anson Thomas? No Christian is ever supposed to stand alone. The beauty of the body of Christ is that each part supports the other. But given that persecution can be so subtle and the contexts so confusing, how can we ensure that when we try to get involved, we help rather than hinder?

To answer that, we must go to China.

# 3 The Squeezing

## China—"Persecution
## Is Like a Bamboo Brush!"

Contemporary persecution looks a bit like a Chinese brush. A number of bamboo leaf spines are gathered together at the top with twine, and the bottom fans out to form a brush. When dust and dirt is brushed up, several strands are in contact with the dirt. It is the same with persecution! Every single act of persecution has multiple causes. When a person is persecuted, it's usually for more than one reason. Three or four strands of the "persecution brush" will hit them at the same time.

Why is this important? Because if we are unaware of which type of persecution is occurring, our intervention to help the persecuted Christian may well end up doing more harm than good!

### Getting It Wrong!

When I was living in Hong Kong in the 1990s, four young Christian men came from the United States. They had a burden "to make the spirit of Mao bow to Christ in China," as they put it. Their reasoning was simple.

1. China is a Communist country run by the Communist Party.
2. Communists are ideologically opposed to Christians.
3. Therefore, if you are a Christian in China, you will be persecuted.

True? Up to a point, it is. But it is only a single strand of the brush. And because they didn't realize there were other strands to the brush, they ended up making trouble for local Christians in China when their intention was simply to help.

Arriving with fairly full saddlebags, they used their wealth to print a few thousand copies of John's Gospel in Chinese—in the same format as Mao's Little Red Book. This was a small pocket-sized book, with soft red covers, containing quotations from Mao's speeches and writings that every Chinese was forced to study during the Cultural Revolution (1966–76).

Smuggling the books into China in four large suitcases (dubbed "Operation Hernia"), they reached their destination city and went to see a local pastor. To their chagrin, the pastor looked less than delighted. He told them bluntly, "We don't want these books. They remind us of the Cultural Revolution. We just want to forget that period."

The four protested, "Ah, but you see, we are going to make Mao bow to Christ." The pastor shot back a bit harshly: "Mao died twenty years ago. He's been bowing to Christ ever since. Or hadn't you heard?"

The pastor refused to distribute the Gospels, and they had no other contacts in the whole of China, let alone in that particular city. The four got together for a prayer meeting and decided they would scatter the books throughout the city. One of them received a "word from God" that justified the action—"Cast thy bread upon the waters: for thou shalt find it after many days" (Eccles. 11:1 KJV). "The Bible is bread," said the prophet of the four. "If we leave God's bread around the town, God will feed the people in His time, His way." So the four split up. One rode the buses. One went to parks. One ventured into office lobbies. One went and ate in seventeen *dim sum* restaurants in a single day. And everywhere they went, they dumped piles of copies of John's Gospel. "We blanketed the city," said one of them. "The people woke up to manna from heaven the next morning."

The police were not amused, and it didn't take them long to find the gang of four, especially as they had been witnessed multiple times sitting on benches and seats, in huge, bulging coats, and then rising minutes later leaving a pile of books. The police spoke no English and bundled them off to see the mayor of the town.

Undaunted, they said to him, "You'll have to jail us now, won't you? After all, you're a Communist and we're Christians!" Perhaps this was what they wanted. At any rate, the mayor just sat looking at them from behind his desk, blowing smoke rings from a clove-scented cigarette.

"No, I'm a Christian actually," he said after a long pause. "I belong to the Party. That's true, but remember this—very few Party members in China today are Communists!"

They gaped at him. "So you're not going to arrest us?" they asked.

"Why on earth should I do that?" replied the mayor.

"Well, are you going to deport us?" they asked, with an air of desperation.

"No," he said, adding with a twitch of his lips, "I want you to travel around China spending lots of dollars to help our capitalist economy."

Much to their disappointment, they were released to continue a tour throughout China, minus any remaining Gospels of John in the form of Mao's Little Red Book.

I met up with them in Beijing and took them to Tiananmen Square. We went to one end of the square and gazed up at the huge portrait of Mao Zedong hung over the red arches to the Forbidden City. Serene, composed, blemishes airbrushed out, his face gazed out over the square like a benevolent deity. Mao was still a factor in China all right. But then I led them to the other side of the square and bade them look up at another huge face. This one was avuncular, grinning, with a white goatee lit up in garish neon. This was the face of Colonel Sanders perched atop the world's largest Kentucky Fried Chicken store.

Mao at one end of the square, Colonel Sanders at the other. "Who is having more influence on China today?" I asked the four American Christians. They shrugged. I answered, "It's probably the Colonel!"

China has been slowly selling off its state-owned enterprises to the private sector. Though ideologically still Communist, the nation's economy is rapidly becoming more capitalist. Those four Christians had misread the spirit of China. The spirit of Mao is still around for sure, but a more powerful spirit at the moment may well be that of the Colonel.

Back in the town the four had blanketed with unwanted Gospels, police arrested six house-church leaders. The police felt they had to do something to placate the intense annoyance of the people who had found the red books and remembered the past with such distaste. The Cultural Revolution really was a horrible period for everyone. The pastor who refused to distribute the books had been thrown from an upstairs window by teenage Red Guards in the sixties. He was denied hospital treatment. Instead, they came and jumped on his broken leg, chanting, "Imperialist capitalist roader." He passed out from the pain. Eventually he was smuggled into a hospital, but the surgeon was also a Red Guard, with no medical experience. He had been bidden to operate according to a Maoist directive: "Learn swimming by swimming!" Needless to say, the pastor still limps.

The police arrested these local believers mainly out of spite, holding them responsible for the actions of their foreign brothers. "Look what Christians do," they said. "They bring back all that's bad about the past."

If those four Christians had done their homework, studied a little of contemporary China, and consulted some local Christians, they would have realized there were types of persecution other than the ideological dimension they fixated on. *Their failure to appreciate the contemporary complexity of persecution resulted in the jailing of six believers whom they had never met.*

## The Seven Strands

There can be at least seven strands to contemporary persecution, and the chances are, when a single act of persecution occurs, two, three, and sometimes more of these strands all have a role. *Distinguishing between them is critical to effective assistance.* Let's stick with China to examine this, though the list applies to many other countries also.

### 1. Persecution from the Ideology

Slaving away in the British Museum library, Karl Marx famously wrote, "Religion is the sigh of the oppressed creature, the heart of a heartless world, and the soul of soulless conditions. It is the opium of the people." His thought launched an ideological war on Christians resulting in millions of deaths in the twentieth century when many of his followers took power.

Not that Marx meant to start a blood bath. All he said was, if you are unhappy and poor, you will create God as a form of escapism from your woe. Make the same people wealthy, and religion will wither away (which has been true in some societies, though ironically, always in non-Communist ones). But Lenin, Stalin, and Mao did not share Marx's naive belief that religion would quietly disappear if the social conditions that created it were removed. Perhaps they knew better. They decided to get rid of religion by force.

In China there were two periods after Mao's Communists took power in 1949 when a white-hot ideological campaign was waged against Christians. Simply to *be* a Christian in China during the early fifties and in the mid-sixties brought ridicule, rejection, and in many cases "reeducation through labor"—the official name for incarceration in a work camp. To refuse to be a Communist brought instant trouble. One cannot hide from ideological persecution.

This phrase "reeducation through labor" is interesting, and you still find it in China today. Communists were so sure their ideology was correct, they felt all they had to do was send the deviant to the fields for some good, honest toil, watered with some night classes from the writings of Chairman Mao, and they would soon espouse the correct ideology. They were simply "reeducated." Human beings were either enlightened by the truth or unenlightened. Reeducation was a coercive way of making them see the light.

So there was no room for pastors like Wang Mingdao and Watchman Nee, who refused to join the servile official church, called the Three Self Patriotic Movement (TSPM). They both went to jail for more than twenty years, resisting "reeducation" with heroic endurance. Nee died in a labor camp in 1972. Wang Mingdao emerged, feeble but unbowed, in 1979.

The essence of an ideology is that it lays claim to be the only truth. When an ideology is reinforced by the government, a totalitarian state is born. All must subscribe to the truth or face sanctions. In countries like North Korea today, the ideological warfare against Christians is still red hot. But in China, since the death of Mao in 1976, the ideological dimension has faded somewhat, as leading Communists realized their system was impractical. The failure to put rice on the table meant that the supreme leader, Deng Xiaoping, launched his "open door" policy in 1978, two years after Mao was safely dead, opening up sections of the Chinese economy to the influence of Western markets. He demoted ideology in favor of pragmatism. He died in his nineties and will probably be remembered for his maxim "It doesn't matter whether a cat is black or white, so long as it catches mice!"—a strange epitaph for a lifelong Communist.

But the transition to a free market economy is far from complete, and much of the rhetoric and the structure of government in China today are still Communist. The Chinese Communist Party still broaches no rivals, and genuine democracy is many years away. But it is fair to say that one is no longer in trouble in China merely because one is a Christian—a sure sign the ideological dimension has decreased in importance.

Yet the literature of some mission organizations gives the impression that all Christians in China are either in jail, just out of it, or just about to go into it again. That's the reason Western Christians who swallow this propaganda travel to China and are shocked to see churches open, Bibles legally printed, and many worshiping without fear—some even in unregistered churches in the bigger cities. So they come back disgusted, saying, "I'm not believing any more of this. I saw no persecution. That's all in the past." They are wrong, because there are other types of persecution that are still felt, but they are right to mistrust the presentation of the Chinese church as persecuted primarily by an oppressive ideology. That was true in 1955 and 1966 but not today!

## 2. Persecution from the Government

Any authoritarian government feels very insecure. They are paranoid that somewhere a group of people is plotting insurrection. The more power the government takes to itself, the more paranoid it becomes, regardless of whether it is left wing or right wing. Ideology is not paramount here.

This is why the earliest Christians were persecuted. For the first two and a half centuries, all underground groups were regarded with great suspicion by Roman emperors, who said, in effect, "If you want to get together in groups, it must be in my name and for my benefit." Christians could not swear the oath of allegiance to the emperor, because it required that they call him a god—an appellation they reserved solely for Jesus Christ. This forced them to worship in secret, and in the eyes of the emperor, anyone meeting in secret must be up to no good!

This is common in China also. On March 16, 1997, nine house-church leaders were arrested. One was a very famous evangelist called Xu Yongze, often labeled the Billy Graham of China. He led a large movement centered in Henan Province, central China. The leaders were arrested mainly because they were having talks about getting their movements together. The talks were not proposing any formal unions, but these leaders represented movements with memberships totaling millions.

These unity talks worried the Chinese government more than virtually anything else in the 1990s. If the leaders of millions of people were getting together without government permission, they became power rivals overnight.

I remember interviewing a high-ranking government official in 1987 and asking him, "Do you consider the house churches to be a threat?" He threw back his head and laughed, "I don't think so. They squabble, fight, and pick on each other. They are more interested in fighting each other than fighting us." But the moment the same house-church leaders tried to stop the infighting, the more the government feared the house churches might become an alternative political society. In Beijing the fear was that some messianic figure would emerge and unite the masses, and the government would be overthrown.

Far-fetched? Paranoid? Partly, but then there is a certain rationality in it. After all, the present leaders of China gained power exactly that way. A charismatic schoolteacher from nowhere called Mao Zedong rallied the peasantry in the thirties and forties, toppling the U.S.-backed Chiang Kai-shek, chasing him off the mainland to Taiwan with inspired guerilla warfare.

And just a century and a half ago, a religious figure called Hong Xiuquan came along, announced he was the younger brother of Jesus Christ, and before long gathered millions of peasants to his side, establishing a new power center in the south of the country. It was called the Taiping Rebellion, and it nearly toppled the Manchu Dynasty. Today's Chinese leaders remember it as if it were yesterday. Consequently, they are frightened of the sixty to ninety million house-church Christians, all the more so since 80 percent are peasants, susceptible (in government eyes) to following the mad visions of any charismatic leader. House churches are targets not primarily because they are full of Christians, but because they choose to organize outside of state control. An authoritarian government has to know everything that goes on in society. Every independent group is a potential enemy.

So the mark of a totalitarian government is that they refuse any group of people the right to gather without permission, whether they are a guild of firemen, a group of French chefs, or a small band of Christians seeking to mind their own business and worship God in peace. A paranoid state will *never* leave you in peace. If the group persists in meeting without permission, they become an object of suspicion, surveillance, and harassment.

A house-church Christian, then, may get arrested for the same reason that a secular Chinese might get arrested for reading Dostoyevsky in a study group—he or she never sought permission! Dr. Tan Che Bin, a Taiwanese Bible scholar and keen observer of the mainland, puts it this way:

> In China, every act is political. That is what is hardly understood abroad. But because a totalitarian government dominates all aspects of society, there can be no such thing as a non-political action. I see some American observers saying, "Why can't you just tell the Chinese government about the separation of church and state?" This reflects this misunderstanding. There is no sphere separate from the state in China. So when Christians meet in a home, or in a cave, without informing the government, it is—through no fault of their own—a political act! And it is a political act that says to the government, "You have no right to control us." That's when it gets dangerous, because that is precisely what the Chinese state claims . . . the right to control all aspects of society. This is the main reason house-church Christians are persecuted in China today. By meeting together outside state control, they become political subversives in the eyes of the government.[1]

### 3. Persecution from the Family

One of the most exciting developments following the Tiananmen Square massacre of June 4, 1989, is the number of students becoming Christians. Compass Direct estimated that some thirty to fifty thousand students became believers in the 1990s, and considering that intellectuals of China were rarely enamored of religious belief, this is a significant trend indeed. But these new believers face persecution from their parents on a scale we can only imagine in the West.

Mr. Li (not his real name) became a Christian in 1993. Despite graduating from one of the best universities in China, he was given a poor work assignment once his dean of studies found out he was a Christian. His parents were furious. They said to him, "We have sacrificed everything to give you an education. You are all we have. And you bring disgrace on us. You might at least have kept your beliefs quiet." So they said to him, "Unless you renounce your faith, you are no longer our son. You cannot continue to bring disgrace on our family."

This is common. While we might hear headlines about pastors in jail for their faith in China (and that's bad!), we will not hear tens of thousands of parents say to their children, "You are no longer part of our family." This is one of the worst things you can say to a Chinese person, where family honor is more important than life itself. Sadly, Li recanted. He now earns a high salary in an import-export bank. His parents are happy. The family honor is intact. But his soul is in ruins.

Or take another category of Christian in China: women. I heard a house-church leader estimate that in a single county of Henan Province, 40 percent of women Christian converts faced severe beatings from their husbands.

The same leader told me the story of "Sister Tang," a woman in her early forties who was a leader in his house church. When she told her husband she had become a believer in Christ, his response was to punch her in the face. He whipped her with a bamboo pole, tied her to a cart, and paraded her about the village. He felt humiliated. He screamed, "How dare you throw out the family gods without asking my permission? I decide who we worship, not you."

He left her out in a hailstorm still tied to the cart. Sympathetic neighbors untied her, but they never dared to take her in. When she crawled back to the house, her husband was ready for her. He beat her unconscious, and she awakened later in a hospital to find her mother sitting anxiously beside her. The mother's first words were, "Give up this Jesus. Your husband beats you because he loves you. Go back to the family gods."

So when we consider the scope of persecution in China, this is massive. Seventy percent of house-church members are women. That's anywhere from twenty to fifty million people. When they declare they have become Christians in a non-Christian household, literally millions can expect major opposition, often involving physical abuse. The culture permits it. When Sister Tang complained to the police, they laughed and said, "A man has a right to beat his wife."

### 4. Persecution from the Culture

Though the number is diving downward, still more than 60 percent of the Chinese population lives in rural villages. Many in these villages follow folk or traditional religions that have formed the culture over hundreds, even thousands of years. Becoming a Christian can draw the ire of this culture in many ways. When the culture persecutes you, it's as though every breath you take is polluted. It is the most all-pervasive form of persecution.

One couple in Gansu Province, China, became believers only to suffer a horrid accident six months later. Their two-year-old son was killed in a freak farming accident. The local folk religion taught that demons were the spirits of humans who had died prematurely and would come back as unhappy spirits seeking to do mischief. The spirit of their dead son was bound to bring trouble. The only way the villagers believed they could be protected from the attentions of these demons was to have guardian gods everywhere, so they would erect clay gods in the yard, in the kitchen, and in the living room.

But this couple had thrown their gods away when they became Christians. This was disastrous for the rest of the village, because the understanding was that if any god is removed from one house, then *the protection over the entire village is also removed*. The protecting canopy, according to Chinese folk religion, had been ruptured. In the village it was now "open season" for the demons. Even worse, with the angry spirit of the dead son on the loose, there was sure to be trouble.

So as a result of a centuries-old religious belief, this Christian couple found themselves isolated and persecuted. The villagers begged them to restore the gods to their house, pleading, "We don't say stop believing in Jesus. That's okay. Put up a god to him as well, but restore the old ones too—just for our peace of mind." When the Christian couple gently refused, explaining that with Jesus they had no fear of demons, the pressure increased.

Every night for three months, groups of villagers would gather outside their house and bang gongs, clash cymbals, and light firecrackers in the hope the noise would drive the demons away.

Every illness or problem in the village was blamed on the spirit of the dead son and on the refusal of the Christian couple to restore their gods. They said, "Look, these gods have protected us for thousands of years, and you've only known Jesus for two or three, so learn from history." A village elder suffered from a goiter; "It's those Christians!" said the people. A man was killed in a mine; "It's those Christians!" was the cry again. Even a poor harvest was blamed on the Christians.

Eventually, when no one would serve them in the market, the couple had to leave their village. They said, "Our ancestors have lived here for hundreds of years—it's our home—but since we trusted Jesus, it has become an alien place. We are homeless till we find our home in heaven."

Chinese folk religion is practiced in various forms by huge numbers of China's rural population of eight hundred million people, in the areas where 80 percent of China's Christians live. Even if the Communist government were to disappear tomorrow, persecution from this cultural source would continue for years to come.

### 5. Persecution from the Church

Yes, "persecution from the church" is not a misprint. In fact, from virtually the third to the nineteenth centuries, the biggest persecutor of the church was, well, the church! Calvinist slaughtered Anabaptist. Catholic slaughtered Protestant in the Inquisition. You could say in the twentieth century the Communists simply took over where the bishops left off. And in some countries like Russia, the bishops took over where the Communists left off, when the Russian Orthodox hierarchy in the 1990s returned to their old totalitarian ways and tried to expunge the evangelicals in the name of cultural purity. We can wish this were not so, but we have to reckon with it, and it can take many subtle forms. There are three different kinds in China alone.

Pei Jo was a youthful pastor in a town deep in the interior. The congregation belonged to the only official Protestant denomination allowed in China, the Three Self Patriotic Movement, which countrywide has about 18 million members. Though very compromised at the top level, where the leadership toadies up to government leaders, at the local level the situation is often not so grim. In fact, most congregational pastors are extremely evangelical and in many cities are often left alone to run the church as they see fit.

Pei was on fire for God, but his senior pastor, a man of seventy-seven, hated him. Perhaps he was jealous of Pei's gifts and the affection the small congregation showed him. He looked for an opportunity to get rid of the young man, and two years later, it came.

Pei had sent to Hong Kong for some theological literature he heard advertised on a radio broadcast. Naively, he asked that the material be mailed to the church address, but the day it arrived, only the old pastor was in the office. Even though it was not addressed to him, he opened it without a blush. Seeing it was from Hong Kong, he went straight to the head of the local police and said, "Pastor Pei has been receiving illegal material from abroad."

This was technically correct, but the policeman was loath to act. He said, "Can't you just confiscate it and give him a warning?"

"Certainly not," said the old pastor. "You have to make an issue out of it, or I'll make an issue out of you not doing anything."

So Pei was reported to headquarters and removed from the church. He was sent one thousand miles away and given a junior job in a shirt factory. He was heartbroken. So was the congregation.

Persecution—from the church. It was the elderly pastor who forced the police to act. This story does have a happy ending, however. The old pastor died shortly afterward, and the congregation sent a letter secretly to the young man, saying, "Come back to us and be our pastor. We are a long way from HQ, so we can do as we like."

He went back and actually took the name of the dead pastor, so that in Shanghai the administrators think the old pastor is still in charge of the church. They will not learn otherwise for years to come.

But happy endings are not the norm, as the following two stories will attest. In December 1994 the pastor of one of Beijing's largest churches was forcibly dragged from the pulpit on a Sunday morning and taken away under arrest. It looked like a shocking act of state censorship, which it partly was, but it never should have happened.

This church had been split for years into two rival factions. One favored the ousting of the pastor; the other his continuance. The issues were financial and spiritual. Church meetings were bitter but inconclusive. The pastor managed to stay. In despair, one influential member of the "let's oust him" camp decided to call on his friend at the Public Security Bureau. He managed to persuade him that forcibly removing the pastor would be a good thing for his career. And so it happened. A new pastor was installed.

If you were a visitor sitting in the pew that morning, you would think it was a terrible act of state persecution—which it was. But, more important, it was also an act of *church* persecution. If those two factions had managed to deal with each other as Christian brothers, this never would have happened.

Then there was the high profile case of Xu Yongze, the charismatic leader of the Henan-based house-church group called "The Born Again Movement," because of their emphasis on rebirth. Arrested in March of 1997, he received a four-year jail term in September (later commuted to three years in December after appeal) for leading a "criminal cult." Some of the case against him was supplied by other house-church leaders, angry at him for teaching a doctrine of assurance of salvation that was unorthodox. In writings attacking him, these other Christian leaders alleged he was not a Christian and was leading a cult. Once the government heard the word *cult*, they panicked. Cult leaders are potential messianic figures that could ignite the peasantry against the Communist Party. Perhaps if Xu had not been condemned so intemperately by his own fellow house-church leaders, he would not have merited such close government scrutiny.

Of course being thrown in jail is also still an act of state persecution. None of the house-church leaders asked the government to jail a heretic. But this is my point—each act of persecution is multicausal. In Xu's case, he was persecuted by both the church and the state.

### 6. Persecution from Corrupt Individuals

When the primary motive for persecution has to do with money, it is the work of corrupt individuals. This form of persecution takes two main forms: one is where the persecutor is out to make money from the act of persecution; the other is when he persecutes out of spite because he has lost money due to the actions of Christians.

I have noticed that arrests of Christians in China rise quite sharply in the period just preceding a public holiday and very dramatically before the big party—the lunar new year. This is mostly due to policemen jailing Christians and then saying, "You can get out of jail if you pay a fine." Most Christians do, and in recent years some fines have risen hugely to 20,000 RMB—about 2,400 U.S. dollars, many times the average yearly salary. These policemen pocket a part of the fine. Some very corrupt ones keep all of it. And they are quite unabashed. I once interviewed a policeman in Henan Province. He said, "We are paid so little, and I must have income to pay for presents especially at New Year." He shrugged, "Everyone has to manage somehow."

Christians can be seen as a soft target. They have resources for one thing. Many will pass around the hat and get enough money to pay the fine. Sometimes they have links to Western cash, which makes them a real target for extortion. In Nepal Christians are often viewed as people supported by Western aid money, and Maoist revolutionaries think all they have to do is kidnap a Protestant pastor and hold him for ransom to fill their coffers with arms money.

### 7. Persecution from "Over Boldness"

There is a school of thought that suggests that where Christians living in a hostile context act rashly or recklessly, they invite arrest or harassment unnecessarily.

An example of this is the tactic of so-called "tract bombing." One Western mission advertises in Europe for Christians to go and spread the gospel in China. Their method is to take thousands of Scripture tracts and blanket the landscape wherever they land.

Teams literally "bomb" areas with tracts, and no doubt some are converted through reading the literature.

But the question still remains: is this the *best* way to spread the gospel in China today? What normally happens is that local Christians get blamed for this act, which is quite illegal inside China. Some are even jailed. In one area where a "tract bomb" team went through, a Western Christian couple living in the area were held responsible and sent out of the country. This is surely a tragedy. After three years of language study, they had made friends with local Chinese and were truly living out the gospel in a way the tract bombers would never get to enjoy. They were discreet but firm in their witness, and over time they believed a proper incarnational witness for the gospel could be established. They never got the chance. And as they exited China in tears, they said, "It didn't have to happen like this."

All tentmakers face this dilemma. China offers thousands of foreigners the chance to teach English in universities and colleges each year, and many Christians take advantage of this invitation as a means to spread the gospel. But these teachers must be careful not to mimic Billy Graham each time they lecture the class. To do so would be in breach of their contract—to teach English first. But a discreet witness, especially outside and sometimes even inside the classroom, is often welcome. It is a tightrope most are able to walk successfully. Of course this is not to say that any Christian teacher deported from China has been overzealous. Paul was not ashamed to be kicked out of some cities, and there is a place for boldness.

The point of all this is to understand what persecution is like for *most* Christians in a particular country, in this case China. It is understandable that we hear most about those who have suffered martyrdom or are severely beaten in jail, but they are rarely the norm. In China most ministries can muster a list of one hundred-plus Christians actually serving jail terms for the cause of the gospel, but the church numbers well in excess of sixty million, all of whom are in some sense persecuted.

Always our task is to ask, How are *most* Christians persecuted and how can we assist? Only with an understanding of the difference between *extreme* persecution and *typical* persecution can effective intervention occur.

But even more important than knowing this difference is something far more basic—knowing what persecution actually is. Does persecution involve all forms of suffering for Christ? Does it occur everywhere, independent of political conditions? When Paul writes "all who want to live a godly life in Christ Jesus will be persecuted" (2 Tim. 3:12), does that mean that every Christian, whether in America or Africa, Paris or Pyongyang, should consider themselves part of the persecuted church? Before we work out any strategies of intervention, we need to have a clear idea of what persecution is. We are about to discover the most challenging truth of all: that persecution is an honor you have to deserve!

*Part Two*

---

# What Is Persecution?

# 4   Legal Definitions

*Why the United Nations*
*Can't Help Lucy!*

Everybody thinks they know what persecution is. But the moment someone says, "Oh, Sally is persecuted," or "Herbert is a martyr," howls of protest can be heard. It's just a fact of life that whenever you use the term *persecution*, it is usually followed by a storm of controversy over whether the use of the term was justified.

You'd think it would be simple. Persecution is Christians getting stuffed into black vans at midnight in cold war Berlin. It's Christians getting beaten up in the streets by hate-crazed Muslim mobs in Indonesia or Pakistan. It's Christians languishing in labor camps in North Korea, forbidden to raise their eyes to the sky. But is it also the young man in California who was cut out of his Jewish father's will because he became a Christian? Is it also the health worker in the United Kingdom sacked by the local authority because she prayed with a client?

It's not simple, as the following cases will illustrate.

## Cassie Bernall

Some said seventeen-year-old Cassie Bernall was "persecuted" for her faith. But others did not.

When two gun-toting killers rampaged through her school in Littleton, Colorado, on April 20, 1999, they singled her out. Putting a gun to her head, they asked, "Do you believe in God?" When she answered, "Yes," they pulled the trigger, killing her instantly. America had a martyr.

But was this an act of persecution? "No," said one of the world's most distinguished spokespersons for the persecuted church, Dutchman Brother Andrew. In widely publicized remarks, he said:

> This terrible tragedy was not persecution. We must keep our terminology clear. Persecution is not individual cases but when either a political or religious system takes away the liberties of Christian witness such as the Bible, outreach toward youth and children, missions, et cetera. Rather, I would call it "opposition," and opposition is there for every Christian. If we don't know anything about opposition in our Christian life, then we ought to worry about our effectiveness.

For Andrew, it is illegitimate to use the term *persecution* to describe an individual tragedy that occurs in a society that grants religious liberty. It is a term to be reserved for entire communities who face orchestrated campaigns of repression and discrimination.

But is this not rather a cold war definition, where it was always left to a super-powerful state to decide on the degree of freedom an individual was allowed? Why can't an individual perpetrate persecution against another individual? Must the source always be a system? It seems bizarre not to call losing one's life for Christ's sake an act of persecution. If that's not persecution, then what is? After all, Jesus did not say, "Blessed are you when *government officials waging anti-religious campaigns* revile you and persecute you . . . on my account." He said, "Blessed are you when *people* revile you and persecute you . . . on my account" (Matt. 5:11). If only a state or religious system can persecute, then much of what the

New Testament community called persecution has to be rejected, because the primary persecutors were not the Roman state, nor even the Jewish political leaders, but individual, jealous Jewish priests.

## Liu Xiaobo[1]

Some would say Liu Xiaobo was persecuted for his faith, but others say the term is too strong.

Mr. Liu is a genius in his forties. He graduated at the top of his class in mathematics from Beida University in Beijing. He was earmarked for a professorship while still very young, producing academic papers that astounded his more senior peers. But Liu never became a professor. In fact, he never even became an ordinary lecturer. He holds a job teaching algebra to nine-year-olds in a remote border town far from the capital.

The reason is his faith. Liu became a Christian in his final year of studies and took the public step of resigning his membership in the Communist Party. This immediately signaled to the dean of studies that he was no longer a trustworthy citizen. The offer of a lectureship was abruptly withdrawn. His new work placement was as a primary schoolteacher in Dandong, far away on the border with North Korea.

Now he sits in his tiny room, unable to emigrate to the United States, where a high-tech company has offered him a salary of two hundred thousand dollars. Liu has not been jailed, beaten, or hurt, but he has been denied the right to professional fulfillment because of his Christian commitment.

Is that persecution? "Certainly not," answered Allen Yuan, a famous house-church leader in Beijing until his death in 2005. He served more than twenty years in prison for refusing to join the officially approved church, and he argued, "No Christian can truly call themselves persecuted unless they have been in jail for their faith. *Persecution* is an extreme term. You have to be beaten, thrown in jail, or lose your life. That's persecution. Merely to have lost a career—that's unfortunate, but it's not persecution."[2]

Yet when Jesus talks of persecution, he is not speaking only of its extreme manifestations. He includes false accusation in his famous "persecution beatitude" in Matthew 5:11, and an expanded version of the forms of persecution is provided in Luke 6:22, which includes hatred, rejection, insults, and slander. So when the Pharisees come to Jesus and say, "We were right all along when we called you a Samaritan and said you were crazy—demon possessed!" (John 8:48 Message), that also would constitute persecution. Jesus is persecuted not only by being crucified. On this basis then, perhaps Mr. Liu is persecuted after all. And who is to say which is worse—to lose one's job for life but not be beaten, or to be beaten badly but to retain one's livelihood? One may be less extreme in form yet more extreme in result.

## Problems with Interpretation

So we have seen two different views of what has to be involved for persecution to occur:

- For some, persecution can take place only if waged as part of a government campaign.
- For some, it must involve physical suffering.

The trouble is, you can't spend all your time arguing about what constitutes an act of persecution, because you have to try to put a stop to it. But to do this, you need to have a clear idea of what persecution is.

I'm astonished at the number of books about persecution that never actually define it. Nina Shea's *In the Lion's Den*, the book that became the manifesto of Christian conservatives in the late 1990s, nowhere defines it. Nor does David Limbaugh's 416-page broadside, *Persecution: How Liberals Are Waging War against Christianity*. Only in Paul Marshall's *Their Blood Cries Out* are clear definitions given, and the two he gives are contradictory.[3]

At this point, we can offer three preliminary conclusions about the attempt to provide a definition of persecution.

## No Consensus

*No consensus exists about the correct use of the term* persecution, *and probably there will never be one.* Apart from the fact that the area is complex, as we have seen, two further reasons lead to this conclusion.

First, because *persecution* is a highly emotive, political term, nation-states tend to discourage its use because it requires the kind of urgent intervention states are loath to offer. The word *persecution* demands that states act—if you can make the charge stick! It is akin to the words *genocide* and *holocaust*. One cannot stand by and do nothing when the word *genocide* is used. Given, then, that the word has such power, huge deniability structures kick in to contest its usage. I have yet to meet any government that admits it persecutes anyone. Accuse the Chinese government of "persecuting Christians," and you will be told by their representatives, "Christians are in jail because they have broken criminal laws, not because they are Christians." That's clever, because it deflects human rights criticism. But in actuality all that has happened is that certain practices of Christianity—for example, organizing meetings outside church buildings—have been criminalized. No government on the planet will ever admit it persecutes. So when the word *persecution* is used, it acquires a political character, and as long as there are political consequences over its use, there will be furious debates over its meaning.

Second, the terminological disagreement stems from an inevitable legal distinction: the right to believe is an *absolute* right, but the right to exercise that belief is a *conditional* right. You may believe whatever you wish privately, but your right to express that belief in society is always subject to a series of qualifying clauses. In human rights documents these clauses are usually couched in this kind of language: "such limitations as are prescribed by law and are necessary to protect public safety, order, health, or morals or the fundamental rights and freedoms of others."[4] That's quite a lot of qualifiers, and many governments use them to curtail religious liberty unfairly.

Every believer has to accept some limitations on the expression of their liberties. Rights are always balanced with responsibilities, and living in societies always involves give-and-take. In every culture there is always debate as to how to balance the exercise of one's religious liberty with what is deemed to be the public good. The line of religious freedom always flutters as each society continually examines the questions of what to believe and how to express it. The debate is inevitable, healthy when civil, unhealthy when un-civil. And in societies that are more hostile to religion having any role in public life—such as in Western ones—the line is going to be drawn in a way that will increasingly disadvantage the believer—if the believer gives up on the fight!

### Two Distinct Uses

*The term* persecution *is used in two distinct senses: generally, to mean any violation of one's religious freedom, no matter how slight; or specifically, reserved for more extreme, gross violation of one's religious freedom, such as torture and imprisonment.*

In deference to a recent clash between two prominent activists and lawyers in the world of persecution, we could call this twin usage the Limbaugh line or the Horowitz line.

When David Limbaugh published his book *Persecution*, it became clear that he was using the term to refer to the discrimination against some Christians in America by a liberal elite, a group he said was particularly active in the judiciary. Much of his argument rests on the claim that the separation of church and state principle, a concept enshrined in the Constitution (though the language is not found in the documents), has been misapplied. Originally intended to ensure that the state did not privilege one denomination over another or one religion over another, it is now interpreted to mean that the state should keep religion out of public life entirely. Instead of preserving a helpful neutrality over religion *in* public life, the state is now trying to drive religion *from* public life. So *persecution*, for Limbaugh, includes Christians being unable to practice prayer on school premises, parents being obliged to remove Christian symbols from a municipal memorial wall for the Columbine High School massacre, and a Christian or other religious perspective in the education curriculum being driven out in favor of a purely secularist worldview.

Michael Horowitz would not dispute the argument that Christians have been sidelined in their own country by an aggressive and secularist elite, but he would strongly refute this marginalization being called "persecution." He has another word for it: "whining." The Jewish lawyer who lent his political skills to the Christian community and assisted the passage of the International Religious Freedom Act of 1998 took one look at Limbaugh's book and said to me, "Look, you can give as good as you get in this democratic society. You fight for your rights. You get pilloried for it, but that's democracy. You can't just cry foul when something goes against you. You fight on. It's the same for everybody. I know evangelicals are patronized, marginalized, and discriminated against, but you can change it. Persecution for me is where vulnerable people are murdered and tortured, starved, raped, and have absolutely no comeback." He added a warning: "To whine about persecution here [in the United States] only dilutes the desire to do something about it elsewhere. I mean, in North Korea if they find you with a Bible, you become a laboratory rat in a labor camp for germ warfare. That's what I call persecution. The idea of equating what we go through with what they go through in North Korea or China or Pakistan or Sudan or Cuba is wrong."[5]

So there are two schools of thought when it comes to defining persecution. One school, the Limbaugh line, includes all of the ways one's religious freedom is impugned, from discrimination and marginalization all the way to martyrdom. And to be fair, when one complains of a loss of income in Los Angeles because of one's faith, that does not mean to say the person is claiming the same *degree* of persecution as the Pakistani Christian on death row because he has been accused of blaspheming the prophet. Persecution, in this view, sets out to describe the entire *process* of victimization for one's faith.

The other school, the Horowitz line, wishes to retain the word *persecution* as a descriptor of extreme, usually physically violent incidents that have occurred as a result of faith. This school believes that to use the word too broadly devalues its impact and thus makes it ineffective in expressing the intensity of the suffering of many, even to the point of death. When the impact of the word is diluted, so is the will of the hearer to work for change.

### Inconsistent Use

*Confusion increases as the broad and specific implications of the term* persecution *are used inconsistently and even interchangeably.* Even those within the world of persecution will frequently use the word *persecution* to mean something like "torture" in one sentence, and then use it again in the next sentence to mean "discrimination." Take for example the World Evangelical Alliance's report to the UN Commission on Human Rights in 2004. They write, "Persecution usually passes through three phases," two of the phases are "disinformation" and "discrimination," but the third phase is also called "persecution."[6] How can persecution be both a phase of the phenomenon and the phenomenon itself?

Another example of this flip-flop usage occurs in the latest Lausanne paper on the persecuted church. On the one hand they argue, "Suffering and persecution are inevitable for those who follow the Lord Jesus,"[7] but on the other hand they can't bring themselves to stick to that usage when describing the discrimination in the West: "While the deteriorating situation in the West does not (yet) merit the term 'persecution,' it should be recognized that there is a reduction in religious freedom which is primarily affecting Christians."[8] That logic puts us in a strange position. If persecution is truly inevitable in the act of following Christ, yet no one in the West is persecuted, then clearly no one in the West follows the Lord Jesus—an untenable position.

Paul Marshall, always sensitive to nuance, is refreshingly honest in admitting that the definition shifts about in his book. On the one hand he says, "By religious persecution, I mean, in general, the denial of *any* of the rights of religious freedom,"[9] and he uses terms like *harassment* and *discrimination*. On the other hand, he admits that there are times when he uses the term "to refer to instances which *are severe* but are somewhat less than genocide."[10]

So with our heads buzzing, we must turn to the two essential sources that will assist us in defining persecution today—the United Nations Covenants, on which the human rights communities base their activities, and the Bible, since Christians must critique all documents and ideas in the light of Scripture. We'll look at the UN Covenants here and the Bible in the next chapter.

## Contemporary Definitions—from the Human Rights Community

The place to begin is Article 18 of the most august document that modern nation-states look to for guidance—the 1948 Universal Declaration of Human Rights, one of the founding documents of the United Nations. Coming in the shocked aftermath of the Second World War, this famous document attempted to set universally acceptable standards for governments on how to treat people justly. Article 18 was the paragraph dealing with religion, and below is the expanded version of the article in the 1966 (enacted 1976) International Covenant on Civil and Political Rights.

1. Everyone shall have the right to freedom of thought, conscience and religion. This right shall include freedom to have or to adopt a religion or belief of his choice, and freedom, either individually or in community with others and in public or private, to manifest his religion or belief in worship, observance, practice, and teaching.

2. No one shall be subject to coercion which would impair his freedom to have or to adopt a religion or belief of his choice.

3. Freedom to manifest one's religion or beliefs may be subject only to such limitations as are prescribed by law and are necessary to protect public safety, order, health, or morals or the fundamental rights and freedoms of others.

4. The States Parties to the present Covenant undertake to have respect for the liberty of parents and, when applicable, legal guardians to ensure the religious and moral education of their children in conformity with their own convictions.

In this document the word *persecution* is never mentioned. It does not occur in any of the UN Covenants, and, in general, representatives of the human rights community use the term reluctantly, preferring to talk instead of "violations of religious freedom." The emotive aspect of the term *persecution* often generates more heat than light, so the word is rarely used. Nevertheless, as an insight into the content of persecution, the discussion is clearly keyed to the notion of religious liberty; only the question of degree is left unresolved. In the broad sense then, a person may be said to be persecuted if he or she is deprived of *any* of the key elements of religious liberty. But some prefer to reserve "persecution" for severe deprivations of religious liberty. Article 18 sets out five essential rights that constitute religious liberty today in the Human Rights community:

1. You have the right to *believe* your religion.

   This aspect came in as a response to Communist societies that attempted to outlaw religious belief completely. No government is allowed to prevent its citizens professing a religion of their choice. This right also guarantees the freedom not to profess a religion. Say you are in an Islamic society and wish to be an atheist; this right guarantees that freedom. In practice, however, you would be well advised not to advertise it.

2. You have the right to *practice* your religion.

   States are forbidden to unduly interfere in the practice of one's religion. In China, for example, Christians are forbidden to worship in churches that are not state organized or state controlled. So if you get together in a home for a prayer meeting without obtaining official permission, it is an illegal gathering. This definition of religious freedom—where you can practice your faith only in a state-approved church—is universally regarded as an infringement of the freedom to practice religion. Only where the practice of the religion could be a matter of public order is the state justified in restricting it. For example, if a group of Christians had a church ritual that burned the flag of the country, the state might consider banning it on the grounds that they were fomenting rebellion.

3. You have the right to *spread* your religion.

   The right to practice religion presupposes the right to share it, though in reality there is a lot of controversy over what constitutes "forced conversion." Some argue that if Christians treat Hindus in hospitals and share their faith, and the Hindu patient becomes a Christian, that would constitute an "unethical conversion." Others say it is unethical solely if Christians agree to treat Hindu patients only if they convert. More secular societies are uncomfortable with the whole notion of conversion at all, believing that if all religions are equal, propagating one's religion should be discouraged completely. But so far, the UN Covenants affirm that if you have discovered the truth, it is only natural and right to share one's findings with a view to encouraging others to enjoy the same discovery.

4. You have the right to *change* your religion.

   Jo was an eighteen-year-old in Yemen who converted to Christianity soon after her birthday. She was killed by her family two days later, and the authorities refused to do anything about it. The family was only following what they held to be Islamic law, which mandates the stoning to death of those who "apostate"—change their religion. The Yemeni authorities failed miserably to uphold Jo's right to change her religion.

   The *World Report on Freedom of Religion and Belief*, published in 1997, revealed that the consensus in the international human rights community was that the individual has the right to replace his or her current religion with another, then added ruefully: "but there is no Islamic state that will formally accept that position."[11] The best the UN has been able to do is to ensure that the Special Rapporteur for Religious Toleration is a Muslim. He hasn't had much impact.

   This single feature probably explains why Muslim societies rank the highest in being hostile to Christians. In the Open Doors World Watch Lists of recent years, which rank countries according to how severely they persecute Christians, twenty of the top thirty are always Muslim countries, and two—Saudi Arabia and Iran—rank consistently in the top five.

5. You have the right to *transmit* your religion to your children
or dependents.

In many ways one of the most important rights is to be allowed to pass on one's faith to one's children, which guarantees the survival of the faith, as the torch of truth is handed
from one generation to the next. Communist nations in particular snatched this right away from parents, insisting that
all education be in the hands of the state, making atheism
the curriculum. Parents have the right within the family to
teach their faith to their children and to send their children,
if they wish, to religious schools.

So where does this leave us with the question of defining persecution? Again, it depends on whether you opt for a broad or a
narrow definition. If you take Marshall's broad definition of persecution as "the denial of any of the rights of religious freedom,"
then more than a third of the world's Christians are persecuted.
The *World Churches Handbook* reveals that 22 percent of Christians
live in Europe, and 27 percent in North America, leaving the rest
(51 percent) living in Asia, Africa, or South America, where more
likely than not Christians would be living in states that deprive
them of one or more of these five rights.[12]

That in a nutshell is the great contribution of Article 18. In
focusing on legal rights, it gives the broadest possible definition
of persecution, from martyrdom at one end of the spectrum to
discrimination and slander at the other. It attempts to provide a
universal standard that enables us to spot and eradicate persecution no matter what the country or culture. But if you wish to
reserve the word *persecution* for "gross violations" of one's religious
freedom, then you end up with a figure which Marshall puts at
200–250 million.[13]

## Limitations of the Legal Paradigm

The legal paradigm has its limitations. Christians harbor deep
doubts over whether Article 18 is adequate for understanding the

fuller dimensions of persecution. These doubts take two main forms.

### Inadequate Interpretation

*First, Christians fear that Article 18 could be reinterpreted to hamper evangelistic religions, especially as the main interpreting community—the Western human rights community—assumes an increasingly secular and pluralistic character.*

Christians and human rights campaigners should be bedfellows. Human rights discourse owes its origin to Christian concepts, and historically freedom of belief comes as a result of freedom of religion, not the other way around. But this has been forgotten in recent years in the human rights movement, where the concept of rights is underpinned with relativistic assumptions about equality that make Christians uneasy.

Christians argue that the proper basis for human rights is that everyone is sacred, but increasingly human rights campaigners are saying it is because everyone is equal. Yet equality carries no moral component. So a Christian teacher in a UK state school is required to teach that we should no longer frown on sex outside marriage. This "value-free" approach to sex education comes from this new notion of equality—all sexual behavior is equal. As the same teacher says, "If I fail to recommend a homosexual lifestyle alongside a heterosexual one, I'm labeled 'homophobic,' and the homosexual lobby will soon be after me claiming I have impugned their human rights." She is also required to say that pedophilia is wrong, yet she freely admits, "If society tells me that sex with young boys is okay tomorrow, then I'll have to teach that too."

The concern is that the human rights community is degenerating into a series of super-aggressive lobbies, with human rights being awarded in direct proportion to the marketing savvy of victim organizations. Can the world of human rights be trusted then to protect our religious freedoms? Indeed, can it be trusted not to change the definition? Rights are always evolving, and today's definition of religious freedom will not be tomorrow's. From which tradition or traditions will the new definitions come? The preamble of the European Convention on Human Rights is quite explicit. It promises to maintain human rights in accordance with "the protection and promotion of ideas and values that lie at the heart of a democratic society. These values are the concepts of 'pluralism, tolerance and broadmindedness.'"[14] These buzzwords set off alarm bells in the minds of Christians, since they can mask what Cardinal Ratzinger (before he became pope) called "Christophobia." He loudly protested the exclusion of all mention of Christian values from the preamble of the proposed and ill-fated European Constitution.

*Pluralism* can be a loaded term. If it simply means that each person should be free to choose the values he or she lives by, fine. But there is another version of it that carries the idea that religious differences are trivial. I remember attending a conference where a leader of a major human rights organization said to a Christian and a Muslim on the panel, "Come on. You are just worshiping the same God, so don't rock the boat by trying to evangelize each other." He was unaware of how extremely condescending his remark was.

It is not a trivial matter to a Christian whether Christ swooned (as Muslims teach) or died on the cross (as Christians teach). In fact, for a Christian, salvation for all humankind cannot take place unless Christ died on the cross. Could I trust a man like that human rights leader to uphold my right to share my faith and maintain that religions have important differences, even if that concept is offensive to some people? I suspect not. Yet many human rights advocates seem to have no notion that pluralism hides an antireligious agenda of its own. Even in the Freedom of Religion and Belief report, the editors, who should know better, state that human rights values are "essentially pluralist and neutral."[15] Pluralist is hardly neutral!

Of course this new understanding is an incentive for Christians to engage more significantly in the human rights realm, but it also begs the question whether Article 18 contains a paradigm that can properly protect the boundaries of religious freedom—which leads us on to the next doubt.

### Inadequate Model

*Second, Christians doubt whether Article 18 provides a good enough model to understand the spiritual dimensions of persecution.*

Lucy was raised in Singapore. Born into a wealthy Chinese family, she became a Christian at age fifteen. One evening she came down to the dinner table and asked timidly, "May I say grace for this meal?"

Her father stood up, crossed to where she was sitting, and slapped her hard across the face. "How dare you attempt to say grace to God for this meal. *I* put it on the table for you with my own sweat!"

Tears sprang into her eyes, and she answered, "But, Father, I was just wanting to thank God that he gave you the opportunity to put my food on the table." Her father was not mollified, however, and from that moment on she changed from being his favorite daughter to his least favored child. She used to massage his neck in the evenings, but now he shoved her brusquely aside and beat her at any opportunity. What a traumatic experience for a teenager who was used to her father's love, which was abruptly withheld because of her decision to give her heart to Christ!

It did not get better for Lucy. It got worse. Soon the family business began to falter, and Lucy got the blame because "you have upset the spirits of our ancestors by changing your religion."

This is a form of persecution that goes beyond Article 18. Lucy's father hates Christ and is responding to that hatred by abusing his daughter. Yet she lives in a state where—in a human rights sense—there is religious freedom. Clearly there's a lot more to persecution than defined by the law.

In sum, the problem with Article 18 is that it is a legal definition of religious freedom but not a spiritual one. It's hardly surprising that it is purely legal. The charter was drawn up primarily by lawyers, and the human rights community tends to be dominated by lawyers. But persecution is not just about the law. The danger with this definition is that it contains three assumptions that Christians know not to be true:

- The state is the primary perpetrator of persecution and thus the primary agent in reducing persecution.
- Changes in the law will reduce persecution.
- All forms of persecution *can* be eradicated.

The problem is that, in addition to the state, there are four other distinct sources of persecution. These are vividly portrayed in the New Testament—priests, families, merchants, and mobs— and are still active today. In many countries the biggest persecutors of Christians are their neighbors or religious leaders from other religions. The state may or may not be complicit, and the laws universally ignored. Indeed, most persecuted people do not have access to the legal system in their country to stand up for their rights. Even more critically, the Bible implies that some persecution will never be eradicated, since it is based on a spiritual enmity between Christ and the world. The danger of the Article 18 approach is that it overplays persecution as a legal phenomenon and excludes it as a spiritual phenomenon.

As a Chinese pastor once told me, "Some kinds of persecution you have to fight with all your might; and some kinds of persecution you have to embrace with all your heart."

We must turn to the Bible now to tell the difference.

# 5 Biblical Definitions

*Everyone Ought to Be
Persecuted!*

A man steps gingerly into a rickety four-foot-wide basket hanging in the dark, sixty feet above the ground. If the basket tips, he may fall to his death. The night should be dead still, but as he descends, lowered jerkily by his friends, the basket crashes into vines and bushes growing on the outside of the city wall. A vine seems to dart bony fingers out to snag the basket, stopping the furtive descent. While the basket rotates, the dizzy occupant hears fierce whispers from above. He feels sure, for a fleeting moment, that his pursuers are bound to hear. Or maybe they will notice the deafening creaking of the basket itself. Then with a loud snap the vine releases its grip, and the basket lurches downward. After what seems like an eternity, it hits the ground, and a balding man in his thirties leaps out and scampers away into the desert with all the alacrity of a mouse in the sights of an owl.

Never in his life did the apostle Paul expect to make an exit like this. But he did, from the city of Damascus, early in his service for God. The scion of a wealthy merchant, from an important city, brilliant at studies, and connected at the highest levels of Jewish society, he was a man of position and power. Not long before this, he had come to the city of Damascus with the status of an ambassador, a whole retinue of police and servants at his command, and in his bag letters of diplomatic immunity to conduct religious cleansing. The very mention of the name "Saul" would chill the heart of any Christian.

Yet in that basket he was as helpless as a kitten in a cage, knuckles white as he gripped the sides. Gone were his letters of immunity from Jerusalem's elite. He was no longer an ambassador. He was a fugitive. Gone were his staff and servants. He had no one now and would have to go back to manual labor to make a living. Gone were his status and power as a Jewish bright light. He wouldn't be staying at the presidential suite of the Hilton anymore. It was the YMCA from then on. He would hop from hostel to hostel for the rest of his life, and many times he languished in bare and stinking prison cells, enjoying the hospitality of the government. See him scampering away into the night, with nothing but his clothes.

Oh, and a gospel . . . recently discovered.

Look at him in that basket and remember that you are gazing at one of the most influential men in human history. The fact that it doesn't look like it is part of the wonderful drama of God's gospel, hidden so often to our eyes, where He clothes true power and influence in the drab and ragged garb of weakness and humiliation. That's how God builds His kingdom.

This is the reason it is probably very instructive to think about this question: *what went through the mind of Paul as he was lowered in this basket?* I've urged people to use their imagination and try to sit in this basket with Paul and ask, *What becomes clear about the Christian life from the inside of this basket?* Some of the answers Christians give as a result of this exercise have released great blessing into my life. They've had insights such as:

The Christian life involves utter dependence on others.

The Christian life involves feeling powerless.

The Christian life involves an uncertain but exciting future.

But as I led this exercise throughout the world, one aspect of the responses began to surprise me. Wherever I conducted the exercise in the "free" West, the list was similar to the ones above. But whenever I led it in the more "persecuted" East, like China or Indonesia, these groups always came up with a primary characteristic about the Christian life that Western Christians almost never mentioned. It was this:

The Christian life involves being pursued!

Why is Paul in the basket at all? Because he's fleeing! He is on the run. You can imagine him sitting in the basket musing, *This God is dangerous to know. One moment I was heading for a glittering career as a rabbi, but now after meeting him, I am on the run for my life.* The people who educated Paul and commissioned him to track down Christians have now turned on Paul because he has "changed sides."

There is a sense in which every Christian has changed sides. When we become a Christian, we put on a new identity; we become a "new creation" (2 Cor. 5:17). Suddenly a trio of forces that did not take much interest in us before begin to pursue us. This ungodly trinity is the flesh, the world, and the devil, and when these three react to the expression of our new identity, persecution is the result! Our world is no longer a playground but a battleground.

This is the spiritual meaning of the word *persecution*. The verb form literally means "to pursue." As soon as we align ourselves with Christ, we become the object of a pursuit, and this pursuit goes back to a divine-diabolical tension that Christ warned his disciples about as he was about to leave them on earth. He said, "I have chosen you out of the world—therefore the world hates you. . . . If they persecuted me, they will persecute you" (John 15:19–20).

This reveals the two central elements of persecution that take us way beyond Article 18. First, in the words of a Palestinian preacher, "It isn't about us." Persecution is about Christ, and the ungodly trinity is trying to get at Christ *through us*. We are not, strictly speaking, the object of the pursuit. We are the victims of it. Second, persecution is universal. This ungodly trinity is after Christ, our new Lord, whether we are languishing in a labor camp or lying on the deck of the love boat. Quite simply, if we take our new identity of Christ with us, we will be pursued.

But what does this pursuit look like in practice?

Let's start with Paul. Who is pursuing Paul?

In Acts 9:23–25 we read: "After some time had passed, the Jews plotted to kill him, but their plot became known to Saul. They were watching the gates day and night so that they might kill him; but his disciples took him by night and let him down through an opening in the wall, lowering him in a basket." This account says that the Jewish leaders of the city of Damascus were pursuing Paul. They were upset that they could not refute his preaching. Yet when Paul refers to this incident in 2 Corinthians 11:32, he writes, "The governor under King Aretas guarded the city of Damascus in order to seize me." Odd. He makes no mention of the Jewish leaders at all. King Aretas is a Gentile and happens to be the king of Arabia. So the plot thickens. Who is after Paul?

The mystery is resolved in Galatians 1, where Paul details the movements of his early apostolic career. After his conversion in Damascus, he spent time in Arabia. Three years later he returned to Damascus, the place of his spiritual rebirth, and preached in the synagogues, building up a following and incurring the wrath of the Jewish leadership. So he was sitting in the basket approximately three years after his conversion.

What he did in Arabia he never says. Some reckon he was on retreat. What is more probable is that he was preaching, and his preaching must have upset the king. We all know this much about Paul—everywhere he went, he preached, and everywhere he preached, he got into trouble! One would hesitate to call Paul to pastor one's church. Damascus would not be the only city from which he beat a hasty retreat. Aretas's writ ran right up to the wall of Damascus but possibly not inside the city. Hence, the guards were outside.

So he was getting it from both sides. Inside the city, the religious leaders were after his neck. Outside the city, the king's guards were waiting to arrest him. Yes, this man was pursued, and it's all because he had an incendiary gospel. That's persecution!

So much for Paul. What about the rest of the New Testament Christians?

## Five Sources of Persecution for the New Testament Christian

New Testament Christians faced persecution from at least five distinct sources: rulers, priests, merchants, mobs, and families, and of course these usually occur in combination. The followers of Jesus tend to unite the enemies of Jesus, and unlikely alliances can result. Jesus himself saw this when the Pharisees and the Herodians—two groups that hated each other—got together to plot his assassination after he healed a man with a withered hand on the Sabbath (Mark 3:6).

Let's look at each of the five.

### Rulers

It's surprising to some that rulers are not the biggest persecutors of Christians in the New Testament. That dubious honor falls to a section of the Jewish priestly caste. But there is no doubt that strong opposition came from the rulers. Pontius Pilate was complicit in the death of Jesus, Herod Agrippa killed the apostle James in Jerusalem (Acts 12:2), and of course Nero initiated a terrible persecution against the Christians of Rome in AD 64. Most scholars believe Mark wrote his Gospel to encourage this community.

The actions of governments are always going to be central to the persecution story, if only because they make laws and command armies, thus making them the most powerful group in any society. Even so, governments can be the pawns of other forces and elites, as we shall shortly see.

### Priests

It's not politically correct to say so, but it was Jewish leaders who were primarily responsible for putting Jesus on the cross (Matt.

26:3–4). Peter does not mince his words when he says to his first Jewish audience on the day of Pentecost: "Jesus whom *you* crucified" (Acts 2:36). Though it was Pilate's order, it was really the Jewish high priest who inveigled Pilate into giving the order for the persecution when he was inclined to let Jesus go (see John 18:31), trying to accomplish this by arranging a crowd clemency scene. All throughout his ministry, Jesus's bitterest enemies were religious leaders. This was also true for the early church. The first flogging of Christians was administered under the auspices of the Sanhedrin (Acts 5:40), and the first martyrdom of a Christian (Stephen) was carried out by enraged clerics (7:54–59).

It is a sad fact that the class that feels most threatened by radical Christian faith is the clerical class, whether of one's own religion or of a rival religion. As Dean Inge of St. Paul's Cathedral used to growl, "A priest loves nothing better than a prophet to stone." This is not to say all clerics are persecutors. Many Pharisees became followers of Jesus, and some, like Nicodemus and Simon, were the very model of courtesy and open-mindedness. Nevertheless, most violence to believers in the history of the church is done by other religious people. In Sri Lanka today Christians most often face persecution from mobs that have been whipped up by the local Buddhist priest, angry that Christians no longer pay a donation to him to run the village.

### Merchants

Merchants represent the economic establishment. Often they are the same as the priestly caste, as in New Testament times the political and economic elite were all Sadducees. But sometimes they are distinct and oppose Christians purely because they are a threat to their businesses. Christianity will undermine any person or structure that is seeking to be enriched through exploitation.

The two clearest examples of this are Paul's visits to Philippi and Ephesus (Acts 16 and 19). In Philippi, Paul and Silas end up in jail because of the actions of the owners of a demon-possessed psychic who was healed. Seeing their source of income disappearing because of her conversion, they pressed a false case against Paul and had him jailed for "disturbing the peace." But the Scripture makes clear their economic motive: "when her owners saw that their hope of making money was gone" (16:19).

Then when Paul gets to Ephesus, the impact of his preaching is so great that it causes the former members of the Artemis cult to hold a bonfire of their trinkets and shrines. A shop steward called Demetrius, on behalf of the silversmiths of the town, figures anything that reduces the appeal of the temple of Artemis is going to be bad for business. He stirs up a riot, and Paul has to hurry out of the city.

### Mobs

When persecution occurs, who is it that actually grabs the Christian by the scruff of the neck? Chances are it is rent-a-mob. Mobs play a major role in persecution, often when an elite group cannot induce the government to do their dirty work for them. Mobs are easily manipulated. They can be believers swayed by the heady rhetoric of clerics or ruffians ready to commit grievous bodily harm for the sake of a shekel.

The clearest example of this is in Acts 17: "The Jews became jealous, and with the help of some ruffians in the marketplaces they formed a mob and set the city in an uproar" (v. 5).

### Families

Last but not least in this list of sources of persecution is families. Anyone who has become a Christian in a family of unbelievers can testify to the hundreds of painful ways persecution can be experienced. Jesus warned about this in chilling language: "I have come to set a man against his father, and a daughter against her mother, and a daughter-in-law against her mother-in-law; and one's foes will be members of one's own household" (Matt. 10:35–36).

Jesus experienced this from his own family, being chided and misunderstood (see Luke 2:48; John 7:3–5), and "his own people did not accept him" (John 1:11). Bear in mind that most families in the world are not nuclear in nature but extended, so an entire web of kinship relations are fouled up when one member becomes a Christian, and this can make it very difficult to make one's way in the world. We could even say it is one's family culture that rejects the Christian witness. One reason for this is overfamiliarity. Jesus generalizes from his experience of rejection in Nazareth, saying, "Truly I tell you, no prophet is accepted in the prophet's hometown" (Luke 4:24).

This goes right back to the dawn of human history. The first recorded act of violence was due to family persecution—Cain murdering his brother Abel out of religious jealousy. It continues through the historical section of the Bible. King David bemoans the betrayal of a close friend in Psalm 41:9: "Even my bosom friend in whom I trusted, who ate of my bread, has lifted the heel against me." And among the prophets, Jeremiah experiences persecution when members of his own family are involved in an assassination plot against him: "Even your kinsfolk and your own family, even they have dealt treacherously with you; they are in full cry after you" (Jer. 12:6).

## The Inevitability of Persecution

New Testament Christians were persecuted for their faith in five ways. Over the course of a normal life, *at least one of the five always applies*, no matter when or where the Christian lives, or what he or she does. But seeing *how* this happens is not necessarily to understand *why*! Indeed, young Christians often have a very hard time understanding the inevitability of persecution. In a Bible study I was leading, a newly converted actress from Pasadena once confessed, "I don't get it. People should like me more after my conversion. I'm more honest, more loving, and more responsible. But for some reason, people like me less. Why do they take such a dislike to me?"

The whole matter goes back to the issue of one's new identity, which is in Christ. Whenever we identify with Christ, a change takes place, and this new allegiance means that we are no longer comfortable with the way things are. Suddenly there are a whole lot of tension points with our surroundings that were never there before.

I remember a policeman friend in Scotland getting into big trouble for Christian reasons. The law of the land required that two policemen witness a crime for charges to be brought. In practice, often one policeman would see a crime and would say to his partner, "This is what happened; back me up," and the partner would go into court pretending he or she had witnessed the crime also. After his conversion, my friend no longer felt comfortable lying in court to back up his partner. When he refused to do so, the whole police station shunned him, saying, "I'd never want you for a partner." But his new faith compelled him to put telling the truth above peer loyalty.

This conflict does not just happen to new Christians of course. Once I went up to Beijing with a group of journalists from the big international weeklies. We got on very well as a bunch until one night we all went out together, and I realized—a little late—that we were sitting in a brothel. I immediately left, and not a single journalist ever spoke to me again on that trip. They thought I considered myself "holier than thou," and it damaged my reporting, because a journalist needs camaraderie to check sources and discuss stories.

All of this delivers a new awareness that we are "aliens and strangers" (Heb. 11:13 NIV) in the world. Where we were once at home in our culture, we are now in conflict with it, or at least, with parts of it. As the Indian Christian philosopher Dr. Gabriel Gonsalves puts it, "Persecution is the default standard of the Christian life because the world hates Christ, and we bear in our own lives the marks of that enmity."

But why does identifying with Christ bring such conflict? What, or who, are the sources that orchestrate this conflict? The two primary ones are the world and the devil.

### The World

Persecution is the consequence of the world's hatred toward Christ. As Heinrich Ohler puts it, "The persecution of Christians arises out of the inner contradiction between the world's way of life and Christ's message and His church."[1] The "world" stands for everyone who chooses to live without Christ and resents anyone who tries to live with Christ, so this resentment is the wellspring of all persecution.

The essential characteristic of the world is not its atheism (for most of the world remains religious) but its refusal to center itself on Christ. As John writes: "He was in the world, and the world came into being through him; yet the world did not know him" (John 1:10). And later in the same Gospel, Jesus is even more specific, "If the world hates you, be aware that it hated me before it hated you" (15:18).

It's worth sticking with John's Gospel to get a deeper handle on this question of why the world persecutes Christ. In his prologue John writes: "The light shines in the darkness, and the darkness did not overcome it" (1:5). *Light* and *darkness* are key terms in John. When he says that Jesus is the light, he means that Jesus is the One who chases away the darkness of chaos at the creation. But Jesus is also light in the sense that He is a revealing light. He exposes this primal darkness in which we prefer to worship ourselves instead of Him—the sin in the Garden of Eden. As William Barclay writes: "The light which Jesus brings is something which shows things as they are. It strips away the disguises and concealments; it shows things in all their nakedness; it shows them in their true character and their true values."[2]

So the blood-red light of the cross reveals our deepest fears and shames, and unmasks our deepest identity as a creature that resents the creator. The natural reaction is to lash out to try to extinguish this glaring light. In our natural state we are in darkness, according to John. Those who love darkness therefore will hate the light. He puts it this way: "And this is the judgment, that the light has come into the world, and people loved darkness rather than light because their deeds were evil" (3:19). The darkness, then, stands for the natural sphere of all who hate the good. In other words, *people persecute Jesus because they fear His light.*

The message of John is also that the darkness can never win. It can never overcome. The light is too strong. Just as Christ's Word was sovereign over the dark chaos at the beginning of time, so His Word in His life and death is also sovereign over our darkness. The Christless life is a life in the dark, and John points this out symbolically most poignantly when Judas betrays Jesus and goes outside. He writes, "And it was night" (13:30)! Darkness comes when we turn our back on Christ. So the darkness will always try to extinguish the light, but it is never strong enough. That is the drama of this world. That is why persecution is its central motif—if you allow your eyes to be opened!

Essentially, the world is our culture. Every culture has a part of it that resents Christ and will find ways to hate him. Persecution occurs when the world finds out our new identity in Christ and reacts to it. This reaction comes usually as a result of our witness. In more religious societies, such as Hindu India or Muslim lands, a key moment in bringing persecution is when the new convert declares their new allegiance in becoming baptized. But as we have seen, our new identity means that we are no longer comfortable with the way our culture works. We are living in contradiction to it, and the culture does not like it. Luther described it: "When a man becomes a Christian and begins to confess his faith with his words and his life, the world becomes angry and begins to persecute, to torment."[3]

### The Devil and the Powers

The act of identifying with Christ not only sets us against our world but also against the powers that control our world. Throughout the Gospels Satan is referred to as "the ruler of this world" (see John 12:31), and Satan's hatred of Christ and his manipulation of the world make him the ultimate author of persecution. The battle is personal for Satan. When John wrote the book of Revelation to strengthen persecuted Christians, he portrayed Satan as a dragon who has been persecuting the church since the birth of Christ (Rev. 12:13).

Satan persecutes in two ways. Sometimes he tempts us directly, as he did Jesus in the wilderness (Matt. 4:1–11). And Paul talks of Satan "blocking" his way (1 Thess. 2:18) and preventing a visit to the believers at Thessalonica. There is the risk of direct demonic attack, something our ancestors in the faith were more attuned to than we tend to be today. I am always very interested to see how sensitive African Christians are to this. A Sudanese pastor told me, "When you become a Christian here, you sense a direct spiritual oppression. It's a heaviness. It's persecution of the spirit by an evil spirit."

But Satan also uses intermediaries through his power of suggesting temptation. He prefers to work in disguise and can even appear as an angel of light (2 Cor. 11:14), spawning teachings within the very church itself that lead the faithful away from a Christ-centered life. These teachings are spread by an intermediary, a person who may not even be aware he or she is serving Satan. Satan is behind all persecution, but rarely do people realize it. Nine times out of ten the agent of persecution that we recognize is a priest, a ruler, a family member, a thug, or a rich person.

So the conflict that results from identifying with Christ widens out from fighting one's own inner inclinations to struggling against the pressures of one's culture until one finally sets out to confront the forces that shape our culture. These forces are what the Bible calls "the powers," and although their meaning is in some dispute, most commentators believe they are distinct from Satan himself. The most well-known reference to them comes in the famous spiritual battle passage in Ephesians 6: "We wrestle not against flesh and blood, but against principalities, against powers" (v. 12 KJV). Powers are humanly created structures of earthly existence, such as tradition, government, and order, which are designed to help human society but in the end—thanks to demonic suggestion or the actions of fallen human beings—end up oppressing people rather than freeing them. We often talk about how "the system" is against us. We find ourselves stuck with a reality that prevents us doing what we want to do.

Take aid for example. We have more food in the world than the entire population can eat, we have sufficient money to get this food to the hungry, and yet never in the history of humankind have we been able to create a structure that gets food in sufficient quantity to the majority of the world's population. The system that we set up to deal with aid is the power—a whole host of institutions—yet despite our best efforts, while many at the bank get a bigger bonus, the poor of Africa can't find enough medicine or food. Often the biggest and subtlest battle the Christian faces is how to change these powers so that they do what they are supposed to do—serve Christ and not Satan.

## Definition Time

So where does all this leave us as we try to develop a more biblical definition of persecution? We have argued that Article 18 is inadequate because it cannot reflect the spiritual hatred that drives the persecution of those who identify with Christ. What definition must we now embrace?

Let's start with two definitions already written. The first one comes from Dr. Jim Cunningham and Paul Estabrooks in their introduction to *Standing Strong through the Storm*—a manual to help churches cope with persecution. They use Luke 6:22 (NIV) as a definition: "Blessed are you when men *hate* you, when they *exclude* you and *insult* you and *reject* your name as evil, because of the Son of Man" (author's italics).

Four verbs in this verse describe the process of persecution, forming the acronym HEIR: hate, exclude, insult, reject. Cunningham and Estabrooks link this to the use of the word *heir* in Romans 8:17, where Paul says we are heirs of God if we share in his sufferings. So they argue: "The interesting thing is that these four verbs can be experienced in varying degrees of intensity. We tend to think of persecution as only the very intense forms. But even when you experience hatred, exclusion, insult, and rejection in a lighter intensity, you are still being persecuted and therefore an heir."[4]

Perhaps the most comprehensive definition of *persecution*, though not the catchiest, is the one coined by Geoffrey Bromily in the authoritative *International Standard Bible Encyclopedia*: "Persecution is the suffering or pressure, mental, moral, or physical, which authorities, individuals, or crowds inflict on others, especially for opinions or beliefs, with a view to their subjection by recantation, silencing, or, as a last resort, execution."[5]

Both definitions are significant in that they opt for the broadest possible understanding of persecution—encompassing all types of hostility, not just extreme forms.

My own definition is a bit shorter: *Christian persecution is any hostility, experienced from the world, as a result of one's identification with Christ. This can include hostile feelings, attitudes, words, and actions.*

Why should we use a definition that is all-encompassing? Is it not an insult to the severely persecuted? There are six main reasons.

1. *The New Testament calls a very wide range of actions "persecution" and does not limit the word to extreme physical suffering.* Among the kinds of persecution mentioned are mockery (Heb. 11:36), slander (Matt. 5:11), disparagement (John 8:48), excommunication (Luke 6:22), and contemptuous treatment (Mark 15:16–20). Glenn M. Penner's book *In the Shadow of the Cross,*[6] is currently one of the most thorough biblical theologies of persecution. He points out that in John's Gospel alone, the "hatred" Jesus experiences takes six different forms: being rejected by His family (7:1–10), being threatened with arrest (7:30–52), being threatened with stoning (8:59; 10:31), having His reputation besmirched (9:24–29), being slandered (10:19–21), and being finally arrested and killed (18:1–19:37).[7] Also, to do justice to the verb form of *persecution,* "to pursue," as we have seen, it is clear that the verb does not refer to the effect of the pursuit so much as to the fact of it. Finally, it is very subjective to call one kind of suffering, for example, slander, not severe, and another kind, for example, a beating, severe. Who is to say that the slander may not be severer in kind and consequence?

2. *Justice must be done to the many New Testament affirmations that persecution ought to be a universal experience for every Christian.* The most oft-quoted verse in this connection is 2 Timothy 3:12: "All who want to live a godly life in Christ Jesus will be persecuted." There is no getting away from the universal range of this verse. And there are certainly many others. "It is through many persecutions that we must enter the kingdom

of God" (Acts 14:22). Jesus, in His eighth beatitude, seems to regard persecution as inevitable as He says "when"—not if—"people revile you and persecute you" (Matt. 5:11). John and Peter both warn Christians not to be surprised when persecution occurs, but to regard it as normal (1 Pet. 4:12–13; 1 John 3:13). This is because persecution is seen in spiritual terms. It is the consequence of the cosmic battle between Satan, the ruler of the world, and God. This leads us to the next point.

3. *Because persecution is seen as a consequence of a spiritual battle, it must extend to the experience of every Christian, regardless of location.* In other words, if it's spiritual, it's universal. Paul puts it bluntly: "He that was born after the flesh persecuted him that was born after the Spirit" (Gal. 4:29 KJV). Persecution is the pursuit of Christ through us, carried on by the flesh, the world, and the devil. This is why, when Saul is stopped from his murderous rampage, Jesus asks him on the Damascus road, "Why do you persecute me?" (Acts 9:4). Therefore this pursuit must occur through every nation; and let us say it plainly, even those who live in nations that uphold religious freedom will face persecution, because their Christ is just as hated by their world as elsewhere. The hatred that spiritual forces bear toward Christ does not diminish in democracies. We are all persecuted because we all live in the same world!

4. *The majority verdict in the history of the church has held persecution to be a universal phenomenon, embracing all types of hostility.* Even when Christianity became the official religion, its finest leaders still held that persecution should afflict the Christian. Space forbids a lengthy list. We've seen how Martin Luther defined it. Perhaps an even more significant church figure is Augustine of Hippo (AD 354–430), who regarded as one of the most convincing proofs of the efficacy of Christianity the fact that the whole known world had become Christian. But even in a Christian culture, he taught that "all times are open season for martyrs."[8] On Paul's 2 Timothy 3:12 admonition, he comments, "If you want to prove the truth of what he

said, start living loyally in Christ, and you'll soon see that
what he says is true."[9]

5. *The pastoral benefits of realizing we are all members of the persecuted church need not obscure the reality that the severely persecuted
require our urgent help.* Nothing is more damaging to the body
of Christ than the notion that some are spiritually different
from others. Saying that there is a persecuted church and a
free church represents an artificial divide that is simply not
there spiritually, as we have seen.

Often this divide results in idolatry. So-called persecuted
Christians who languish in jail or are beaten are viewed as
heroes, and a mentality develops among freer Christians that
says, "I could never do that" or "Their faith is just so much
greater than mine." But it isn't, as the severely persecuted
will attest. A young Muslim convert tortured for his faith in
Egypt told me, "We are in the same fight, you and I; that's
why we are one. The only difference is that your fight takes
a subtler form; mine is brutal, but it is the same fight." The
terrible danger is that Western Christians, who do not regard
themselves as part of the persecuted church, often fail to see
themselves in a spiritual battle at all. And those who are not
aware of the fight are losing it.

6. *Limiting the persecution definition to extreme manifestations of
physical suffering for one's faith runs the risk of failing to address
some of the causes of persecution.* One member of a religious
liberty mission told me: "If we talk about persecution in
the broadest sense, then we will find it much harder to
mobilize faithful Christians to help torture victims and
martyrs." But the objection to that is, if you pour all your
effort into building the house for the martyr's widow or
springing the tortured Christian out of jail, then you have
not addressed the reasons why the martyr was killed in
the first place or why the Christian was tortured. The fact
is, we can more effectively prevent certain types of persecution where it starts—when lies begin to spread, when
the rule of law gets undermined, when strongmen start
to create scapegoats. All this happens before persecution

turns severe and Christians start to get killed. Focusing all one's energies, then, on helping the severely persecuted can result in failing to address the very causes of persecution. That's a huge advantage of the broader definition, because it takes into account the roots of persecution as well as its manifestations.

For these reasons, then, I am happiest with the definition that makes persecution a process that reflects the experience of the pursuit of Christ in us from the world and the devil. This enables me to see discrimination, intimidation, and harassment as *types* of persecution rather than prerequisites to it. As that old Chinese pastor used to say, "Remember, though we don't all sit on the same thorn, we do all sit on the same branch."

Of course this definition is not without its hazards. One hesitates to give theological *carte blanche* to many Western Christians who often claim to be persecuted in a way that trivializes the term. Once on a train I watched a young Christian giving out tracts. He approached a Muslim man who refused to accept one. They had an argument, and the Muslim punched the Christian in the shoulder. The young man came back to where I was sitting and we got to chatting. When he saw I was a Christian, he said, "I've just been persecuted for Christ's sake. Did you see it? That Muslim attacked me!"

I bristled at the use of the word *persecution*: "Are you sure you would say his reaction was 'for Christ's sake'?" I felt he was invading everyone's privacy on the train by pushing tracts at them, and when arguing with the Muslim man, he had been quite insulting of his religion. Was the Muslim not just reacting to a bad-mannered presentation of the gospel? Brother Andrew always cautions: "Don't call it persecution until you have done everything you can to bring peace to the situation, and if after all your efforts, you are still hounded, then, yes, you may call that persecution." That is a useful caution. But we must not lay the fault for this "persecution mania" on the more expansive definition of persecution. Frankly, exaggeration of persecution goes on frequently no matter what the definition.[10]

In all my traveling among persecuted Christians, perhaps the most compelling reason for holding the definition that I do came from an elderly Christian who fled North Korea in the terrible famine of 1997. He said, "If you limit persecution to those who are in jail or being beaten or having their property stolen, you are saying that all other Christians are dead. *You see, the best and only way to know you are alive in Christ is when you are persecuted.* The persecution proves Christ is within. I wouldn't take that pleasure away from anyone in the entire world. All Christians must have it!"

The apostle Paul would agree. From a jail cell he writes to the persecuted Philippians that they had been "granted the privilege not only of believing in Christ, but of suffering for him as well" (Phil. 1:29). Remarkable as it may seem, most persecuted Christians do count their sufferings as an honor, because they have been allowed to identify more closely with their Lord. As Xu Yongze recalled when tied to prison gates in an excruciating crucifix position, "I felt a great wave of joy sweep over me from head to toe, and my spirit cried, 'Ah, at last I have been found worthy to suffer a little for Jesus of what He suffered for me.'"

Indeed, it is this experience of the genuinely and severely persecuted that clinches the expansive definition for me. In early 2002 I took three Western friends to a house church in Beijing. This house church always started the meeting with the same question posed to each member: "What are your wounds for Christ this week?" When the Western Christians' turn came, they said, "Oh, we don't really have wounds; we live in free countries, you see." There was a long silence. Then a woman spoke up and, with more innocence than irony, said, "You mean, in free countries you don't fight a spiritual battle?"

The house-church leader thought about all this and then said very gently to her visitors, "Your wounds may not be as gory as ours, but all Christians are asked to carry a cross. That cross will bring you wounds, but take this from us—those wounds will bring you joy. That's the great paradox of persecution: while the wounds will not lose their pain, they will bring Jesus close in a way no other experience can."

I recently saw a witty T-shirt that showed deep down we all know this truth. It read, "Blessed are the cracked, for they let in the light."

Living it out is something else.

If we are all in the ranks of the persecuted to some degree, then from where is this persecution to come? And where is the persecuted church?

*Part Three*

# Where Is the Persecuted Church?

# 6      Sources

*The Four Global Engines
of Persecution Today*

Try this question on for size: in which country was the largest number of Christians killed for their faith in 2004? Audiences today offer a host of different answers. Some people say, "Sudan." Others say, "North Korea, without a doubt." Quite a few say, "China." A number say, "Colombia." Which is it?

If I had asked that question in the 1980s, the answer would have been China or North Korea or the USSR! You took your pick from the three most Communist countries in the world. Atheistic Communism was the biggest persecutor by far. Now, although atheistic Communism still lingers as *a* persecutor, it is no longer the primary persecutor. The nineties saw it joined by other forces.

The question is now extremely difficult to answer. It could still be North Korea, but we don't know for sure. The society is so secret we cannot obtain reliable information. Hundreds could die there each year, and we would never hear of it.

It could be Colombia. Since 1998 more than four hundred Christians have been martyred in Colombia by bandits and guerillas for standing up against corruption and intimidation.

It could even be India, the world's largest democracy. Richard Howell of the Evangelical Fellowship of India told me recently, "The number of Christians killed here could run as high as one hundred a year, but we rarely get to hear about it."

Another guess would be Pakistan. Since the 9/11 attack, Open Doors has been keeping an eye on Christians killed in Pakistan by extremist Muslims and has reckoned the grisly total to be about forty-four Christians killed in the first year following September 11, 2001. The martyrdoms—with a few exceptions—go unreported in the media because Christian family members fear further reprisal if they kick up a public fuss about the death of their loved one.

My best guess for the country where the most Christians were killed in 2004 would now be Nigeria. In March of 2004 eight pastors and fifteen hundred Christians were killed in riots in the northern province of Plateau, mainly as a result of Muslim extremists trying to impose sharia law. But then, many of the Christians were fighting back, so it might be hard to say they were all killed for their faith.

Who knows where the largest number will be this year or the next? But the point is made; the sources of persecution are much more complex and multifarious today than they were in the past.

What we can state with utter certainty is this: *wherever you go in the world today, there is a source of persecution near you!* Four great global sources stalk the world, spawning myriad forms of contemporary persecution of Christians. These are religious nationalism, Islamic extremism, totalitarian insecurity, and secular intolerance.

## Religious Nationalism

Religious nationalism exists where a particular territory or culture is staked out exclusively in religious terms, and the leaders say, for example, "Only Hindus can stay in India," or "Croatia is for Catholics only," or "You are only a true Sri Lankan if you are a Buddhist." In states that define themselves around Hinduism, Buddhism, or Islam, either Christians must accept second-class-citizen status, facing daily discrimination, or worse, they have to get out.

### Unsung Heroes of the Persecuted Church

Robert Seiple, the first American Ambassador-at-large for International Religious Freedom, was well aware that his job would be tough. He knew from his work at World Vision the danger that many face when dealing with suffering Christians—callousness. Not a deliberate callousness; it's just that one encounters so much suffering that the only way to stop being paralyzed by it is to become indifferent to it. His advice was simple: "Always find a face, have a particular person in mind, and remember you're doing it for them." Otherwise it becomes about policies not people.

It is good advice. Scattered throughout the next three chapters are a few faces of the persecuted. Some are famous. Most are not. All are still in situations of danger, so some identities have to be disguised. They are heroes, but their heroism comes from a simple faith that anyone can exercise, even though so many Christians fail to do so. Said the British Catholic politician Baroness Shirley Williams: "Physical courage is common, but moral courage is extremely rare. That's why we need the church—because the exercise of moral courage needs a community that will support it, and no other community will." Through ordinary people, these faces of the persecuted beckon us all to an extraordinary life and teach us to put our wavering courage in God's hands, letting Him make the difference!

The justification for religious nationalism has usually to do with purity, and it is argued that to have other religions in the territory would destroy the special character and unity of the state.

In the 1990s religious nationalism emerged strongly as a prime source of persecution, essentially because atheistic Communism ran out of steam, and a religion-fueled ultranationalism picked up the slack. There were two reasons for this.

First, a whole crop of new nations, spawned by the end of the cold war conflict, looked around for ways to define their identity and expand their boundaries. Religion was quickly seized as justification, and when wedded to mythologies about how populations from other religions were a "plague in their house," the result could often approach genocide.

Sadly, Christianity was implicated in the longest and most violent European war in the second half of the twentieth century—the Bosnian civil war in Yugoslavia. When the Muslim majority region of Bosnia-Herzegovina seceded from Yugoslavia, the minority Orthodox Serbs waged a brutal war from 1992–1995. Mythologies were spun about how utterly distinct these groups were. For example, in Serbia the view was pushed that Serbian Orthodox Christians had suffered under the Turks for centuries and so it was time to establish a greater Serbia and kick the Bosnian Muslims out once and for all. The conflict left 250,000 dead and three million displaced. The chilling phrase "ethnic cleansing" began to enter our vocabulary, although ironically there was nothing ethnic about it in the Balkans at all. Serbian Orthodox, Bosnian Muslim, and Croatian Catholic are all ethnically identical, and until recently all spoke the same language. As Christopher Catherwood writes:

> What made the Serb atrocities worse . . . is that it was often done in the name of a pure Orthodox Serbia, uncontaminated by the pollution of Muslims. While some Serb Orthodox leaders were horrified at the slaughter, others, while never directly condoning it, were not at all displeased with the results: a great increase in Serb-ruled territory and the removal of Muslims from cities where they had lived alongside Serbs for decades.[1]

Croatian Catholics were little better, nor did the Bosnian Muslims preserve clean hands throughout the conflict. Throughout the world a similar pattern began to be seen. In Sudan an extremist Islamic group seized power in 1989. General Omar al-Bashir, the coup's leader, immediately pledged to "purge the country of 'enemies.'" He launched a vicious jihad against the Christian African tribes to the south, including the killing of five hundred thousand Dinka Christians in one of the worst (and most underreported) genocides of modern times.

The second reason religious nationalism became a prime source of persecution is that governments began to realize in the 1990s that religion was an important way to increase their legitimacy. Before the present era, religion was regarded as an unimportant factor. But now political elites saw that religion could be useful either in grabbing power or in maintaining it. In Burma, for example, the unpopular military dictatorship shamelessly promoted Buddhism as the state religion to curry favor with the people, and this has resulted in severe persecution for Christian minority tribes in the hills, such as the Chin.

I remember a Chin pastor telling me how in 2001 the government sent a Buddhist monk to his Christian village. The monk came with five soldiers. Everyone was required to build the monk's house, provide him with rice, give up their children for Buddhist instruction, and erect a Buddhist pagoda in the village. The pastor said, "They tried to coerce us into becoming Buddhists, but when we talked this over with the ethnic Burmese in the plains, they just replied, 'Well, you should be Buddhists if you really want to be Burmese!'"

Even Fidel Castro invited the pope to Cuba in January 1998 to bolster his flagging rule, though in this case it resulted in a better deal for the local Christians. But the general trend is clear—the more religion is regarded as important, the more likely governments are to control it, resulting inevitably in more persecution.

So the Orthodox states are beginning to make life harder for evangelicals; in India Hindu nationalists took power in the 1990s, and for the best part of ten years put thirty million Christians on the defensive. Even Buddhism, which many Westerners consider to be an inoffensive, peace-loving religion, has a vicious nationalist incarnation in Sri Lanka. More than 140 churches have been burned and closed in Sri Lanka in 2003 and 2004, the violence often led by extremist Buddhist monks. Even though Christians have been present in Sri Lanka since 1505, and even today barely muster 8 percent of the population, an extremist Buddhist organization is out to equate being a true Sri Lankan with being a Sinhala Buddhist.

The tactics in Sri Lanka are familiar, and most of them come from the handbook written by the BJP in India to the north. Disinformation and lies are spread about the Christian minority. In the *Buddhist Times*, launched in 2002, it is alleged that Christians support the violent Tamil Tigers, promote pornography and child abuse, and despoil Buddhist statues. The Evangelical Alliance of Sri Lanka exposed a case in 2002 where a sacked church was photographed by the press only after extremists carefully scattered smashed Buddhist relics among the rubble. Lies drive the campaign. On December 12, 2003, a senior Buddhist monk died of a heart attack on a visit to Russia. The extremist Buddhist press reported that he had been assassinated by Christians, and despite an autopsy proving he had died of natural causes, inflamed mobs burned twenty churches on Christmas Eve.

But the extremists do not stop at violence. The Buddhist nationalists formed a political party, which won nine seats in Parliament in January 2004, and set their main political goal as the introduction of an anticonversion law. This law, and the new constitution being drafted, sets out to guarantee Buddhism as the state religion. Article 9 of the constitution under consideration argues that if any other religion seeks to convert Buddhists, the government has an obligation to ensure that the converting religion is deprived of its legal rights to own property and exist. No other proposed constitution is so draconian in penalizing conversion. If it passes, it will take Sri Lanka back to the Dark Ages in terms of religious freedom.

So religious nationalism is a global and potent force. At its mildest, it makes religious minorities feel they no longer belong in their own land. At its worst, it gives a potent justification for genocide. Religion can be a force for good, but in the hands of unscrupulous ultranationalists, it is more often misused as a force for great evil and oppression.

## Islamic Extremism

Some might wonder why Islamic extremism is not included in the religious nationalism category. The reason for separating it is that the dynamics are very different, as we shall see, and ultimately the vision of Islamic extremists is pan-national. They want the whole world to be Islamic. They want all races to become Muslims. The faith is strongly missionary.

Islam as a whole used to be a lot more tolerant. I recall meeting Christians in Cairo in 2001 who said, "Twenty, even ten years ago, we used to visit our Muslim neighbors on religious feast days and wish them well. We would be well received, and they would visit us on our feast days. There was great mutual respect. But that's all gone now. They refuse to associate anymore with us. It's so sad."

Often scholars date the rise of Islamic extremism from January 1979, when the Shah of Iran was toppled by the Ayatollah Khomeini, who began to run a modern state along theological lines. And for various reasons, the tide has run in favor of Islamic extremism since. One reason is that the Saudis use their oil revenues to bankroll it.

A friend teaches the children of asylum seekers in northern England. One day she gave a test to her pupils, asking them to write an essay on the topic "If I had twenty-four hours to live, what would I do?" She had a lot of Muslim boys in the class. All of them wrote the same answer, "I would go to the mosque, say my prayers, then kill my enemies." Astonished, she asked where they were being taught such a fierce doctrine of revenge and discovered it was from a local mosque. She asked a Muslim friend about it, who said, "Those kids did not come from Pakistan as extremist Muslims, but they became that way here. The Saudis built that mosque, installed their own teachers, and spread their narrow, violent vision of Islam, and there's nothing we can do to stop them because they have billions in oil revenues."

The second reason Islamic extremists have been successful in pursuing their vision is that they got a boost in the 1980s when American and other Western powers armed their resistance groups, giving weapons and training in the attempt to stop Communist expansion. The mujahideen in Afghanistan were a case in point. And of course, when the USSR collapsed and the aid stopped, the resistance was furious, as they were deemed surplus to strategic requirements. A breakaway group became the Taliban, who took power and instituted a very extremist Islamic regime that would not have been dislodged unless strategic considerations of a different kind in 2001 resulted in a U.S.-led invasion.

Third, Islamic extremism feeds off a disgust with secularism. The Ayatollah Khomeini once told his critics, "We did not have a revolution in Iran to lower the price of a melon." Western observers are very quick to explain the rise of Islamic fundamentalism in economic terms—a surplus of unemployed young males trying to get a piece of the action. But this is a complete misunderstanding. Islamic fundamentalists share with many Christians a concern that Western civilization has become completely materialistic, even to the extent of banning religious values from all public discussion. They simply do not want that model imposed on them by stealth as economic links increase. I was sad to see in Iraq the first signs of Western decadence appearing on television just a few weeks after the U.S.-British invasion. MTV was the first station to be shown on satellite, with its semipornographic images wedded to explicitly sexual songs. I thought, *I can see why Muslim fundamentalists get so upset.*

### Three Types of Islamic Extremism

But what is Islamic extremism? Are we to think purely in terms of Muslim terrorists or more broadly of Islamic fundamentalism, which has certainly been around since before 1979? The answer is both and more. Paul Marshall warns us to beware of equating Islamic extremism with the actions of Muslim terrorists. Christians are persecuted in three distinct ways by Islamic extremism according to him. The first is *direct state persecution.* This takes place in countries like Saudi Arabia, Sudan, and the Maldives, where it is the government that takes the lead in persecuting Christians. In Saudi Arabia, for example, any non-Islamic or even dissident Islamic religious expression is forbidden. In Sudan, Christians in refugee camps are denied food and water by the authorities unless they convert. The governments in question impose Islam by coercive means, and anyone adhering to Christianity in the midst of that faces an uphill struggle just to survive.

The second category is *communal violence.* Here it is not the Islamic government that is the source of the persecution but the Islamic mob. Whipped up by extremist teachers, the mob often spill out after Friday prayers and target Christians by burning churches and assassinating Muslims who have converted to Christianity. This is widespread in countries like Nigeria, Liberia, Pakistan, Ghana, Indonesia, and even the southern Philippines.

Finally, the third category of persecution is *direct attack by radical Islamic terrorists*. In Algeria, for example, Islamic guerillas target moderate Christians, especially priests, monks, and nuns for assassination. Direct attack is the category that drew a huge foreign policy response from the world's only superpower, the United States, in the wake of the 9/11 tragedy—the most dramatic and far-reaching of the actions of any Islamic terrorist cell.

### Out of Glory

Why do Islamic extremists target Christians for persecution? It is "out of glory." The glory of Islam must be restored. Allah has been affronted by what the Christians have done to the Muslim world, and these reversals must be wiped out so that his glory is seen again. Take, for example, the justification for terrorism that Osama Bin Laden provided in his famous November 3, 2001, videotape. He said, "Following World War One, which ended more than eighty-three years ago, the whole Islamic world fell under the Crusader banner, under the British, French, and Italian governments. They divided the whole world."

That is very significant. Bin Laden is not concerned only about what is happening to Palestinian Muslims but about the humiliation of the Ottoman Islamic empire decades before, when the "infidel" Western powers defeated it and carved up the spoils. For Bin Laden this is an affront that has to be reversed for the glory of God.

The whole issue has been very well put in a small book called *Islam at the Crossroads* by Paul Marshall, Roberta Green, and Lela Gilbert. They write:

> Muhammad was successful as a religious teacher, as a political leader, and as a military leader. They expected to win others to the faith, defeat their enemies in battle, spread throughout the world, and implement divine law over all peoples. Islam has not developed a theology of defeat and suffering, for Muslims have not expected defeat and suffering to be ongoing features of their lives. Of course, they knew there would be occasional defeats and unexpected setbacks, but they expected no permanent loss. They expected to be victorious, and to keep on being victorious.[2]

Muhammad hardly ever lost a battle. He defeated everyone. For a thousand glorious years, Islam spread irresistibly across the world, into Europe, Asia, and Africa. Nothing could stand in its way. The Muslim world stood at the crossroads of the continents and controlled world trade. It was wealthier than its neighbors, its cities more glorious, its scholars unmatched. By contrast Christians were an illiterate, barbarous lot, living in tents in northern Europe, stuck in a dark age.

All that began to change. On September 12, 1683, the date European forces defeated the Ottoman Turks in Vienna, the long defeat of Islam at the hands of the resurgent Christian West began. Because a Muslim has no theology of defeat, to lose territory to a Christian is an affront to Islam. Their God is victorious. There is no possibility of defeat. So that territory has to be taken back, lest God be shamed.

This is hard for Christians to understand, because we do have a theology of defeat. Our whole faith is centered on it. Jesus died on a cross to bring us salvation. Nothing looks more like a defeat than His hanging on a cross, breathing His last. In fact it is a defeat! This redefines how Christians realize God brings victory. We see this in the persecuted church all the time. Think of how down and out the church was at the time of the Cultural Revolution in China. Yet God brought a huge revival out of that seeming defeat.

The idea of redemptive suffering, of God bringing victory in the form of defeat, has no place in Islam. Islamic doctrine cannot admit Jesus died on the cross for that very reason. In Islam, defeat equals disgrace, and honor must be restored, lest Allah be shamed. Whereas for Christians, defeat is so often God's way of accomplishing a victory that would not be possible any other way.

This is the deepest reason why Muslims persecute Christians. They have to take the "territory" back. That is why they cannot lose a person or a land or a tribe to another religion, and since Christianity is the main evangelistic competitor to Islam, there will always be this clash. So when I was visiting Indonesia in March 2003, I was watching with horror some evangelical Christians forming themselves into a huge prayer movement and saying publicly, "We want to make Indonesia 50 percent Christian in twenty-five

## Where Nothing Goes Smoothly!

*The Story of Yousif, a Christian Who*
*Brings Muslims to Christ*

Yousif Matty

Why he stands out is not immediately obvious. Fifties, balding, he looks more like an indulgent uncle than a faith hero. Shake his hand and you wince. And his thick sausage fingers betray a man more used to engineering than evangelism.

But Yousif Matty is very unusual. First, he has a vision that should get him killed—he wants to evangelize Muslims in a totalitarian society. Normally Iraq's church leaders—if they harbor evangelistic ambitions at all—keep them firmly to themselves. Second, unlike most visionaries, he has actually managed to bring many Muslims to Christ. His Kurdistan Evangelical Church, founded in 1992, has hundreds of members, many of them drawn from a Muslim background. Third, and most remarkable of all, he is still in the country; whereas those of vision and effectiveness usually have to flee.

These features set Matty apart in a Middle East known primarily as a place where Christians are fleeing en masse as a result of persecution and discouragement.

How did he manage this? Here are some of the components that go into the making of a faith hero.

*Courage:* The phone rings. Matty reaches for it, hesitates, then steels himself and picks up the receiver. "Why did you hesitate?" I ask him. "Because it may be a death threat," he replies. Matty has received hundreds of death threats as a result of his ministry. He had to hide for four months after being shot at by Islamic extremists and chased by a lynch mob in July 1997. He never opens his front door after 10:00 p.m., knowing that extremists are waiting with rifles to gun him down. Saddam Hussein even paid him the ultimate compliment by dispatching three assassins to Kurdistan, Northern Iraq, to kill him in 2002. All were stopped before they managed to complete their assignment. Two are still at large today, but Matty is not bothered any more about them. "Their paymaster is defunct," he says.

*Tenacity:* "Nothing goes smoothly in Kurdistan for a Christian, even if you have official permission," he says. Matty launched an international school in Dohuk but had to wait a year while Islamic extremists threatened to burn down the premises. They were only dissuaded when the local government offered to build them a mosque around the corner from the school. Matty has four Christian bookshops in four different cities. All have been firebombed. One in Zahko has still not reopened. In Arbil a government minister tried to close down the church's radio ministry. Matty had to take him to court. He won. Every project takes supernatural reserves of tenacity to bring it to fruition or even keep it on track.

*Strategy:* "It takes ten years before you can have a respectful conversation with a Muslim," he says, so his strategy has to be long-term, too long-term sometimes for impatient Western backers. He has founded two international schools, at which more than 250 children of Kurdish leaders learn English. They are the only schools in the whole of Kurdistan where a parent may send their child to receive instruction entirely in English. Kurdish leaders are grateful—at last. One of them actually gave Matty land in Sulemaniyah to build a church. But it took time. And there is no overt attempt to proselytize, though the teaching lessons are often drawn from Bible stories. Once when he told this to Muslim parents, there was an uproar. He thought he was going to be attacked, but when they settled down, one of them explained, "As Muslims, we ought to know the Bible, and we don't want our children coming home with a knowledge of Bible stories that surpasses us. Will you also provide Bible classes for us too?"

*Vision:* Matty wants everyone in his society to encounter Christ, and since he lives in a predominantly Muslim society, he wants them to know Christ too. But in most Middle Eastern countries, Christians are tolerated only in so far as they keep the gospel in their own communities. Matty says, "The way the church has guaranteed its survival in Iraq over the centuries is where we keep the gospel to our own racial groups, that is, the Chaldean Catholics just reach the Catholics; the Assyrian Orthodox reach out only to the Assyrians; and so forth. But this is a racist definition of the gospel. We are not true Christians if we commit ourselves only to keep the gospel to our own racial ghetto."

*Radicalism:* Faith heroes do not accept the status quo. When Matty brought a Muslim convert to his bishop for a secret baptism, the bishop refused. "Do you want to get us all killed?" he hissed. Matty said, "Surely you will do it secretly?" The bishop replied, "Not even in secret will I ever baptize a Muslim—our system does not permit it." Replied Matty, "Then your system is wrong." He turned and left, never to return to the traditional church. He formed his own.

Matty is not the first faith hero to find that the price of being true to the gospel is sometimes to forsake the church.

years." When they make that goal public, it's a red rag to a bull. If they succeed in making converts on that scale, there will be carnage on a similar scale. The Muslims will feel compelled to force the Christian converts back into the Islamic fold. Despite the cordial relations between mainstream Christian and Muslim leaders there, the Muslim leaders have warned them privately, "We will tolerate you, but don't attempt to evangelize us."

To prevent Christians from always assuming a doomsday scenario, we always have to add this important qualifier: Muslims the world over are always made up of three groups—a frightened majority, a liberalizing elite, and a fanatical fringe. Most majorities in Muslim countries would not vote for sharia law given the chance, though they find it impossible to oppose it formally, as they would look like bad Muslims. Yet they did so in Indonesia. We must never tire of saying this: *more Muslims suffer at the hands of Islamic extremists than Christians.*

The small but influential liberalizing elite would say of Christians and Jews: "You are people of the Book, so you will come to heaven with us." It is the fanatical fringe that forms the driving heart of Islamic extremism, and they exert an influence out of all proportion to their numbers. With weapons of mass destruction (particularly of a chemical and biological nature) now able to be procured and launched by virtually anyone, we can see why countries as powerful as the United States are so worried about maintaining security and stability in the twenty-first century.

### Totalitarian Insecurity

A totalitarian state is one in which the political leaders dominate every aspect of society. No one is allowed to organize outside of state control. Ironically, despite all this power, it is fear in these states that motivates the persecution of Christians. Christians are a threat to any totalitarian state simply because they refuse to be dominated. States like this include what is left of the Communist bloc: Cuba, and the four Communist states of Asia—China, Vietnam, Laos, and North Korea. These countries have a quarter of the world's population.

### The Chinese Example

This fear of the church among the Communist bloc is ancient and modern. The ancient version goes back to Marx and his suspicion of religion as the opium of the people. The modern version goes back to 1989, when one of China's top leaders happened to be visiting Romania at the time of the fall of Ceausescu. He became rapidly aware that a Hungarian Reformed pastor, Laszlo Tokes, had inspired the resistance movement. When Ceausescu fell, this Chinese leader made haste back to China and reported to the leadership: "These Christians are subversive. We might have thought they were harmless, but we have to realize they could be dangerous." It was at that meeting that the infamous statement was made: "We will have to strangle the baby while it is still in the manger."

So in the 1990s there was a lot more interference again in the Chinese church, and the short golden era of freedom in the late 1980s was over. But the broadside against the church was more subtle: squeeze don't smash. Smash the church, and you merely drive it underground, away from state control. Squeeze it, and you keep it where you can influence it and apply the pressure gradually so that it becomes a tool of the state, rather than an organ of resistance.

A particularly clever tactic has been to label house churches that refuse to register as "cults" and attack them under laws that allow the state to treat them as dangerous political extremists. This gives the government an excuse to refute human rights criticism by saying, "Oh no, it's nothing to do with their religious affiliation. We are closing down this group because they are a threat to social stability." Gone are the days in China when thousands of leaders were in prison for their faith.

When a high-level delegation visited China recently, I was charged with compiling a list of Christians in prison that the delegates could bring up with China's leaders, and I had a job finding fifty names that I was sure were in prison for their faith. Now there are more than fifty, but it's hard to prove. So Christianity is tolerated but controlled, so that its radical elements may not emerge. A house church may be left alone if it just sings hymns and studies the Bible. But if they start agitating for better treatment for AIDS sufferers or see their Christian duty as organizing the unemployed into unions, then watch the government spring into action with terrifying force.

### Atheism and Power

Notice I have not mentioned atheism as an engine of persecution. This would have been true twenty or thirty years ago, but Communism as an ideology has withered on the vine. All that is left is the totalitarian structure, which holds on to the rhetoric of Communism for convenience, and persecution becomes understandable in terms of the basic power dynamics of totalitarian leaders and states. The essence of a totalitarian state is that the government has to know everything everyone is up to. Paranoia goes with the territory. Everything is dominated by the state. The leadership has to be served. Anyone who demurs—no matter what the motive—is automatically an enemy.

Christians are a subversive bunch—that is why they get into so much trouble in totalitarian situations. They don't worship anybody but God! And this plays out in any situation where someone holds all the power. It need not even be in an actual state. All over Latin America are territories controlled by *caciques*, local gangsters who run drugs and rule local populations through intimidation and extortion, often with the government turning a blind eye or taking a payoff to stay clear. If a pastor in Columbia refuses to allow the young women of the church to be seized as the sex slaves of the bandits, he is persecuted. No one must be allowed to stand up to the bandits. If one person does not cooperate, then others might not too. So the *caciques* rush to make an example of him out of fear that his fearless spirit would catch on.

Location-wise, most Christians who suffer under this source of persecution are based in the tribal dictatorships of Africa, the bandit-controlled territories of Latin America, and the Communist regimes of Asia.

## Secular Intolerance

I don't think we talk enough about secular intolerance, perhaps because it doesn't have a roll call of martyrs yet, but it is an up-and-coming source of persecution for sure. Frankly the democratic Western bloc is becoming more intolerant of evangelistic religions. Words like *evangelistic campaign* and *proselytization* are becoming loaded terms, conjuring up images of narrow-minded fundamentalists who want to "shove religion down our throats."

There is a town near where I live in the United Kingdom where an Anglican church received a government grant to refurbish some of their church premises. The arrangement was to have a café that would serve as a resource to the town. The vicar said airily one day, "Of course, to get the money I had to sign that we would refrain from evangelizing on the premises." It's amazing that he seemed to think there was nothing wrong with the agreement. He just signed away a vital religious right—to share his faith—and a Western government asked him to! Now the church members cannot pray in their own café.

Why would this particular government department give money only on the condition that Christians refrain from evangelism? Because they have bought the line of the Dalai Lama, who says, "Everyone should stick to the religion they were born in—that's the only way we can ensure social harmony." Secular intolerance maintains that we all have different beliefs, and we had better accept that everyone is just as right as the next person, or else!

The definition of religious tolerance has been subtly changed to bring this about. Originally, religious tolerance was introduced to limit the power of the state, not the church. The state was not allowed to prefer one religion or religious party over another. For example, in England the toleration laws meant that non-Anglicans could attend university, because the state's power to discriminate against those of differing beliefs was taken away. This was also, in some cultures, called the separation of church and state principle, and it was most powerfully applied in the United States.

But now a new definition of tolerance is being applied, this time not to the state but to the individual, who is told, in effect, "You must accept that all religious beliefs really just amount to the same thing." The secular state has recently abandoned its historic neutrality and is seeking to impose its own version of religious truth on everyone. In other words, if you don't buy the secular understanding of religion, then you are going to find it increasingly difficult to practice your own. The secular belief is that religious differences are trivial. Polish Catholic philosopher Leszek Kolakowski exposes this trend. He writes:

> It is important to notice, however, that when tolerance is enjoined upon us nowadays, it is often in the sense of indifference: we are asked, in effect, to refrain from expressing—or indeed holding—any opinion, and sometimes even to condone every conceivable type of behaviour or opinion in others. This kind of tolerance is something entirely different, and demanding it is part of our hedonistic culture, in which nothing really matters to us; it is a philosophy of life without responsibility and without beliefs. It is encouraged by a variety of philosophies in fashion today, which teach us that there is no such thing as truth in the traditional sense, and therefore that when we persist in our beliefs, even if we do so without aggression, we are *ipso facto* sinning against tolerance.[3]

Argentinean evangelist Luis Palau was interviewed on BBC radio recently in Britain. He was conducting a campaign in a British city that was full of Muslims. "Are you wanting to make Christian converts among Muslims?" asked the interviewer. There was a palpable hesitation on Palau's part, and I could see why. If he said yes, then that would seem a very incendiary and arrogant attitude. Who is he to think that Muslims should become Christians? In the end he hemmed and hawed, saying, "Well, not really. Muslims can decide for themselves how to respond to the gospel." But it illustrates the new climate. If we admit that we would like Muslims to know Christ and convert to Christianity, we are called arrogant and bigoted by a secular culture, because all religions are the same.

But the arrogance is all on the secular side. Where did they get their unexamined assumption that all religions are the same? Who are they to tell me that when I pray to Jesus Christ, it's just the same as a Zen Buddhist meditating or a Muslim prostrating toward Mecca? Who are they to tell me that my Scriptures are really just saying the same thing as the *Bhagavad Gita*, the Qur'an, or the writings of Sai Baba? That is a position of colossal arrogance, especially as it is a generalization made from ignorance about the vital differences between religions.

Bishop Lesslie Newbigin, in his magisterial *Foolishness to the Greeks*,[4] reckons that the source of this secular generalization can be traced back to the intellectual movement called the Enlightenment, which occurred in the late 1700s and early 1800s. At that time a distinction between so-called "facts"—things that could be proved scientifically—and "values"—things that could not be proved scientifically—came into common currency. Religion was lumped into the "values" category. After all, you cannot prove that God exists. So "values" are just opinions that cannot be proved, unlike "facts," which have to be believed. Thus religious truth became downgraded into the realm of subjective opinion, and since opinions are not facts, there is no rationally compelling mechanism for holding one strongly as opposed to another.

The tragedy was that however much this generalization may hold for some religions, it is a complete misunderstanding of Christianity, which claims that God's activity is placed into the world of facts. God intervened in history time and again to save His people in the exodus and ultimately in the incarnation and resurrection of His Son. Christianity claims the resurrection as a fact, not a value.

This fatal distinction eventually leads to persecution. For one thing, it stops free speech dead in its tracks. For example, if I claim that the Muslim faith lacks a concept of forgiveness, this is not taken as an attempt to compare one religious truth with another; rather, it is labeled "Islamophobia," and that label increasingly has legal consequences. Or if the church maintains that homosexuality is not a God-pleasing lifestyle, it is not asked to give the justification for the Bible and Christian teaching forbidding it, but rather the church is immediately accused of "homophobia." The secular mind-set refuses to accept that religious language has a truth component. It is all lumped into the realm of values. For *values*, read *prejudices*.

Another consequence of the distinction is that it privatizes faith. If your religious truth is really just "your truth," then you have no right to argue for it to be included in laws or ask social scientists to take it into account. According to the secularist, faith is individual, private, and intensely personal and is ruled out automatically from the public sphere, which is left to be run on—guess what—entirely secular values.

The hypocrisy of this stance is obvious, since the assumptions underpinning secularism, such as "life must be explained only by biological cause-and-effect factors and not by outside agents" are also faith positions. And so secularism attains, by stealth, a quasi-religious status. Why then must secularism be allowed in schools and not theism, if both are, in effect, faith positions? Also it follows that if you privatize religion intellectually, it's a small step to politically marginalize it too. This is what has happened in the last fifty years, to the alarm of many Christians who are only now waking up to the fight for the culture. There is a secular elite that is out to scour religion from the public square entirely. In the United States this fight has received the highest profile, especially since in 1947 the Supreme Court decided to interpret the Constitution through an absolute interpretation of the phrase "separation of church and state." Henceforth, instead of the state ensuring that it was even-handed in its dealings with religion, it now decided that the state must separate all spheres of government from religion. As Paul Marshall writes: "In modern politics, since the state tends to get involved with all aspects of human life, this invariably means that religion must give way to governmental concern in every aspect of life. When the state gets in, religion is supposed to get out."[5] Thus Christians have watched in recent decades their banishment from the realm of education, policy making, and even lawmaking on morality. In recent years the state is even extending its powers to internal church affairs.

This means there will be in Western societies a greater cost to speaking out for Christ. This is the battle for the Western church. In some places it has started legally. The French anticult law of

May 2001 is so badly worded it may allow for the state to call any evangelical who is caught evangelizing a *cult member*. It has not happened yet, but the mechanism is in place.

These are the great global engines that are preventing more than a billion Christians from experiencing—in its legal form—the benefits of religious liberty, that is the right to practice, share, and change their religion without coercion. These global engines result in more than two hundred million Christians experiencing severe persecution, including beatings, jailings, and violence. They also mean that spiritually every Christian has to fight against at least one source of persecution. Wherever you go in the world today, there is a source of persecution near you!

So where are you? It's time to take a ride around the continents and examine these sources in action.

# 7 The Persecuted Church—Part One

*Latin America,*
*Middle East, Africa*

Buckle up, because you are about to take a ride that will make your eyes pop and your blood boil. These two facts alone will do it.

1. Christians are the largest single group in the world who are being denied their rights on the basis of their faith.
2. Very few people know this, and those who know seem to do very little about it.

It remains amazing to me that a single community of three hundred million people could be systematically repressed, marginalized, and discriminated against, and yet in a world bristling with stop-at-nothing investigative journalists, this story rarely shows up in a daily newspaper or magazine. It is, however, too big a story to ignore completely, and occasionally the global plight of persecuted Christians intrudes on the front pages.

Earlier this year I was going to address a crowd at a Christian conference in England when someone ran up to me and said, "Have you seen the latest issue of the *Spectator*?" He handed me the magazine, and the headline was "Why Christians Are Still Persecuted." The author was a self-professed atheist, yet he had uncovered a story that troubled him deeply. He wrote:

> I am no Christian . . . I may not believe in the man with the white beard, but I do believe that all persecution is wrong. The trouble is that the trendies who normally champion human rights seem to think persecution is fine, so long as it's only against Christians. While Muslims openly help other Muslims, Christians helping Christians has become as taboo as jingoistic nationalism.[1]

The author went on to puzzle why, according to his calculations, 200 million Christians face violence and 350 million face discrimination, and no one seems to know or care. He ended his article with a pursed lip: "The guilt-ridden West is ignoring people because of their religion. If non-Christians like me can sense the nonsense, how does it make Christians feel?"

Answer—it makes Christians feel sick and angry. Yet I held up the magazine to an audience of two thousand people that night and said, "What's wrong with this picture? You are getting more information from an atheist in a secular magazine about your brothers and sisters who are suffering all over the world than you will receive from all the scores of meetings you will attend at this conference all week." The persecuted church was just not on the agenda. Even the Christians seemed to have stopped caring!

Well, let's start by changing that. Let's get the facts before we intervene. And as we go, we'll take time to fix some of the faces in our minds as well. Persecution is not an abstract tragedy. Persecution is always an individual tragedy first, and then it becomes a universal tragedy as the worldwide body shares and cares for the victim.

As we dive into information about the persecuted church on each continent, keep three major facts in mind:

1. *Christianity is the world's most successful evangelistic religion.*
   According to the *World Christian Encyclopedia* (WCE), by 2000
   the world Christian population numbered 1.9 billion, or 33
   percent of the world's population, making it the world's largest
   faith.[2] In second place were Muslims at 19.6 percent, and 13.4
   percent were Hindus. The trouble is, this 33 percent statistic
   includes everyone who self-identifies as a Christian, or just
   someone who lives in a country with a Christian heritage. In
   response to this, the editors of the WCE came up with a category
   called "Great Commission Christians," essentially those who
   care enough about their faith to spread it. This group, which
   really is the core of world Christianity, numbered 647 million in
   2000, leaving an inactive Christian population of more than 1.3
   billion.[3] But since Christians are the most numerous religious
   community, it follows that they are likely to form the largest
   percentage of those persecuted for their faith.

2. *Christianity is no longer primarily a Western religion but a Southern
   religion.*
   In 1900, 81 percent of all Christians were white. By 2005 this
   had dropped to 43 percent, reflecting the massive growth of
   the church in Africa and Asia. Christianity, for the first time in
   many hundreds of years, is no longer a Western religion. Today
   the largest Christian communities are found in Latin America
   and in Africa. The numerical balance of power within Christianity has shifted to the South, and the church continues to
   experience remarkable growth almost everywhere except the
   West. So if you want to find the persecuted today, you have to
   look at where the church is growing—the plains of northern
   Nigeria, the jungles of Colombia, the rice fields of China. It is
   the growing church that is the persecuted church.[4]

3. *A majority of active Christians today no longer have any relationship
   with the historic churches.*
   According to the WCE there are now 386 million Christians
   in the world today who have no interest in and no use for
   historic denominationalist Christianity. That's 19 percent of
   all nominal Christians and well over half of all active or witnessing Christians. Much of this postdenominational growth

has come from the charismatic explosion. The most successful social movement of the twentieth century is Pentecostalism, which had no adherents before 1900 and numbered 115 million in 2000, according to *Operation World*,[5] and if you add in the charismatics, the number rises to 345 million. As a rough guess, it is the more independent, often Pentecostal-charismatic Christians that form the majority of persecution cases, because they are spreading the faith in new areas, away from the safer compounds patrolled by the historic churches. Also the severely persecuted church itself accounts for a big slice of this trend, especially with the growth of the Chinese house churches, possibly growing at the rate of ten thousand a day, according to the WCE. Clearly, in a persecuted context, loose-knit, noninstitutional churches that are not dependent on a rigid ordained priesthood are better adapted to the operating conditions underground.[6]

With slightly more modest figures than the WCE, the *World Churches Handbook* puts the Christian total at 1.7 billion today. In terms of continents, this is the breakdown:[7]

Asia: 262.7 million or 16 percent
Africa: 243.8 million or 15 percent
Europe: 434.9 million or 27 percent
North America: 347.2 million or 22 percent
South America: 308.1 million or 19 percent
Oceania: 18.7 million or 1 percent

This looks odd at first glance. In Europe 434.9 million people is 60 percent of the population. Can 60 percent of the population of Europe really be Christian? Well, they are, but only in the most generous sense. For example, in the United Kingdom 64 percent of the population say they are Christians, but only 12 percent hold membership in a Christian church, and the number attending a service regularly is probably nearer 7 percent.

Also for our purposes, Asia and Africa are a bit too unwieldy as descriptive areas, since the Muslim Middle East gets lost in between them. For example, is Egypt to be dealt with under Africa or as part of the Muslim Middle East? The most important thing for us to discover is where the church is growing, because this is usually where it is persecuted. Where it is not growing, no one needs to bother.

With these facts in mind, away we go to visit the persecuted church on each continent.

## Latin America—Too Many Martyrs!

How can the world's most Christian continent have so much persecution? That's the conundrum that defines this huge area of five hundred million people scattered throughout fifty or so countries from the baking deserts of Mexico in the north to rugged Cape Horn at the southern tip of Argentina, and not forgetting the sun-soaked beaches of the Caribbean states. No other continent boasts such a high percentage of Christians; none other produces so many martyrs! Since 1995 more than one hundred pastors have lost their lives for Christ in Colombia alone. In Peru the death toll of pastors between 1980 and 1991 was 529, mostly at the hands of the extremist guerilla group Shining Path.

Virtually everyone in South America would say they are Christian. This is largely due to the dominance of the Roman Catholic Church. Colombia is 96 percent Catholic, Venezuela 95 percent, Peru 93 percent, and Argentina 92 percent. But this dominance is not actual. Catholic leaders bravely commissioned a devastating survey of their membership in the nineties and concluded that only between 10 and 14 percent of the population of Latin America were practicing Catholics.

More startling is the fact that the number of evangelicals is only slightly lower than the number of practicing Catholics. Mostly Pentecostals, they come in at between 10 and 12 percent and are the twentieth century's biggest church-growth story. A miniscule 0.01 percent of the continent's population in 1900, huge revivals in Brazil, Chile, and Argentina in the fifties and sixties catapulted them into prominence. Indeed, in some ways they are more influential than the Catholics because they are more dispersed. Evangelicals have three hundred thousand congregations throughout the region to the Catholics' thirty thousand. Nowhere have they made more headway than in giant Brazil, where the nominal percentage of Catholics fell from over 90 percent to 76 percent in 1995—thanks to the inroads made by the Pentecostals.

But if Africa is the continent the Western world forgot, then Latin America is the continent it left behind. Between 1968 and 1973 a wave of socialist-inclined governments came to power across the continent, then after 1973 more authoritarian, anti-Marxist regimes took over, relinquishing power reluctantly in the eighties. Ever since, progress to liberal democracy has been slow. Despite a wealth of natural resources, most countries are crippled by debt, often due to rampant corruption. The poor pay the most for the chaos, growing in such numbers that inequality is a boiling political and theological issue.

The governments of Latin America seem to be utterly ineffectual ones. In 1999 the UN declared Colombia "the world's most violent state," with 50 percent of the world's kidnappings happening on its soil.

On many occasions the United States has expressed frustration at the inability of Latin American leaders to stop the huge drug-running industry. This frustration boiled over with the invasion and removal of Panama's General Noriega in December 1989. The image many Westerners have of Latin America is of corrupt politicians in the pocket of greedy drug barons, who run their country with their own private armies, or of steely dictators like Chile's Pinochet who sent death squads to round up thousands of dissenters.

*Sources of Violence*

It is the essential lawlessness of Latin America that results in so much persecution, as a vibrant church stands up against it (something the evangelicals were not so good at doing until recently). The all-pervasive nature of the violence results in multiple sources of persecution. Richard Luna, former director of Latin America for Open Doors, lists six for starters:

1. *Caciques:* These are local mafioso who control small regions through terror. Often bandits linked to drug lords, they see Christians, who refuse—after becoming converted—to buy alcohol and drugs, as a threat to their economic stranglehold on the community.

2. *Revolutionaries:* This was the continent where the iconic Che Guevara fought and died, and the hills are still full of vicious Maoist insurgents. Christians peddle the "opium of the people" and must be stopped. The Shining Path guerillas of Peru were the most notorious, killing Romolo Saune in 1992, a famous Quecha convert and a recipient of the WEF Religious Liberty Award. Miraculously, Saune's death proved to be a dramatic turning point in the war against Shining Path, now reduced to a ragtag band in the mountains.

3. *Religious extremists:* Many rural areas are run by religious extremists who deny evangelicals their legal rights as citizens. It's sad that most of these extremists tend to be Catholics, and some persecute evangelicals out of jealousy at their growth, which comes at the expense of the Catholic Church.

4. *Paramilitary groups:* These are privately funded armed groups, often acting for powerful landlords or drug lords. They coerce thousands of peasants to leave the land and are guilty of many massacres of Christian villages.

5. *Governments:* Many military and police personnel are out to get Christians, especially when they think they are complicit in harboring or supporting insurgents, or even in just supporting the poor. A famous Catholic priest said, "When I give money to the poor, they call me a saint. When I ask, 'Why are the poor so poor?' they call me a Communist."

6. *Witches and Satanists:* Fifty Colombian pastors are known to be on a Satanist hit list, and three pastors were killed in 1999 and 2000 by Satanist assassins. Also many nominal Catholics are involved in spiritualist movements. In Brazil, for example, it is thought that more than a third of Catholics belong to a

mediumistic religion called Umbanda. Often these extreme sects are under the control of demonic influences hostile to Christians.

### The Hot Spots—Two to Watch

#### COLOMBIA

"Is your God stronger than my gun?" asked the eight-year-old paramilitary of an Open Doors worker recently. Thousands of insurgents think they know the answer to this question. Colombia's 45.6 million people are constantly terrorized by men—and even children—of violence, men like Pastor Fausto, who said that before he became a Christian, "Killing was as easy as drinking a glass of water." He was killed on September 6, 1999, probably by someone with the same attitude as he once had.

The death toll from the violence makes grim reading. Forty-seven pastors killed in 2003, eighteen more in 2005, and more than four hundred since 1998. More than four hundred churches have been forcibly closed, with two million people displaced by the fighting, a half million evangelicals among them. Evangelicals number five million, and more than one million live in conflict areas where life is very cheap.

These conflict areas form 40 percent of the country, where the government army cannot enforce law and order and the paramilitaries and guerilla armies wage a deadly war that engulfs everyone. Christians in these areas are caught in a familiar pincer movement. If they help the poor with charitable work or negotiate with guerillas to secure peace deals, the paramilitary armies assassinate them for "sympathizing with Marxists." Yet if they refuse to join the violent activities of guerillas, they are assassinated or harassed in turn for being "antirevolutionary."

The recent conflict stems back to the mid-1960s, when two Marxist movements, inspired by the Cuban revolution, sprang up to make Colombia a socialist state. Soon ideology withered away, and the guerillas turned to the more lucrative trade of drug running, extortion, and kidnapping. The oldest and largest group among the left-wing rebels is the Revolutionary Armed Forces of Colombia

## An Endangered Peacemaker

*Ricardo Esquivia Risks His Life to Obey Jesus in War-Ravaged Colombia*

Ricardo Esquivia

Ricardo Esquivia expects to be arrested or assassinated in Montes de Maria. Despite his international reputation as a consultant on conflict resolution—he will meet this year with government officials and human rights experts in Brazil, Belgium, Holland, Canada, and the United States—Esquivia's life is very much at risk in the "red zones" of his native Colombia.

"Life there is very complicated," says Esquivia, fifty-seven. "People look at me with suspicion. Some consider me an enemy. I think the danger for me is increasing."

Colombia, South America, has been mired in civil war for decades. The mayhem has penetrated every corner of the country. More than two million displaced persons forced to flee their homes live with fear, hunger, and poverty. Meanwhile, warring factions and criminals rake in billions of dollars from drug trafficking, kidnapping, and killer-for-hire industries. Christians and church leaders are among the innocent civilians who get caught in the crossfire.

Amid the mindless violence, this one man has an audacious plan to empower ordinary Christians to end the war through the gospel of peace. Esquivia is the founding director of the Commission on Restoration, Life and Peace of the Evangelical Alliance of Colombia (CEDECOL). In May 2004 Esquivia resigned his day job in Bogotá and moved to Sincelejo, a city in northern Colombia near the mountainous Montes de Maria region. As in other red zones, law and order has disappeared as rival armed groups vie with one another for control of the area.

Montes de Maria has a large evangelical Christian community, especially among the estimated seventy thousand displaced persons living in refugee communities on the outskirts of Sincelejo.

Esquivia plans to continue work he began more than fifteen years ago to promote peace through the teachings of Christ. His twenty-five-year-old son, Gerardo, is part of a team Esquivia is assembling to carry out a project he calls Sustainable Holistic Peace and Human Development through

Churches. The project aims to mobilize evangelical Christians to improve the lives of those both inside and outside the church. Reducing the suffering the civil war has caused will help bring peace to troubled Colombia.

The ultimate aim of Sustainable Holistic Peace and Human Development is for Christians to use their gifts and talents as primary resources to teach fellow believers trades, which would lead to the creation of jobs and small businesses.

"We have doctors, we have engineers, we have lawyers, we have farmers, we have shoemakers, we have bakers," Esquivia says. The project will help people depend on themselves, "not on the state or outsiders," he says. "People here must understand that God has blessed us with resources and that we can support ourselves."

Esquivia and his team also offer training in conflict resolution to advance peace. A key element in the plan involves mobilizing thousands of youth under twenty-five who don't have work and can't afford college tuition. "Many of them don't see a future, so we're organizing through this work so that they see a light on their path," Esquivia says.

He hopes to see the model reproduced all over Colombia because he believes the only hope to end Colombia's unrelenting civil war is the gospel. He talks of "people power"—nonviolent resistance to armed groups in the name of Christ—as a strategy for peacemaking. So far, about one hundred local church associations have networked thirty-five hundred people to take part in the program.

Funding from the Colombian government and the development programs of the European Union and United Nations has helped get the project rolling, but Esquivia wants to see Sustainable Holistic Peace and Human Development eventually pay its own way.

"Ricardo is definitely up to it, and I'm glad he's doing it," says Adam Isacson, program director for the Washington, D.C.–based Center for International Policy. "He's one of very few who could pull it off.

"These peace labs set up all over the country are key ways of helping Colombia out of conflict," says Isacson, whose group promotes demilitarization, human rights, and international cooperation. Prayer chains have been organized to intercede for the danger-plagued project.

Esquivia conceived the concept of peace through nonviolence and sustainable development in the 1960s while studying for a law career. In 1986 he moved his family to the northern Colombian town of San Jacinto, where he bought a farm and taught peasant farmers about nonviolent social action. An army general, however, accused him of being allied with a subversive guerrilla army. Fearing for his life, Esquivia went into hiding. In 1989 he learned the army had falsely accused him of killing forty-two foreigners and a Catholic priest. He fled Colombia before authorities could detain him.

Churches around the world rallied to his defense and, with help from Amnesty International, persuaded government officials to appoint a commission to look into the charges. As a result, the military retracted all accusations.

In 2004 the same army general accused him of acting as the ideological chief of the 37th Front of the Revolutionary Armed Forces of Colombia (FARC). Peasants told Esquivia that military officers had been questioning them about him and his work.

Esquivia's friends and co-workers alerted Christians around the world to the threat, and the international community of faith responded with a letter-writing campaign to Colombian officials. The campaign led to a meeting between Esquivia and military commanders, which satisfied them that Esquivia has no ties to any subversive group. The charges were again dropped.

Esquivia says the remarkable level of Christians' response made his plight impossible for the government to ignore. The incident offered a compelling lesson in how the body of Christ can make a difference in complex world affairs and in guaranteeing the safety of Christians on the front lines of building peace and proclaiming the gospel.

"The international faith community is the key; it's the only thing that can guarantee our well-being," he wrote in a March letter to supporters. "We have seen how it is possible to create a wall of international protection that surrounds and, to a certain extent, guarantees the freedom of a human rights and peace worker."

When asked if he would prefer to make peace from a safe distance, he shrugs. "I have to be with my people. That's what gives flavor to life.

"I believe I'm doing God's will," he adds. "I've felt a call to be here and I'm prepared for whatever comes."

(FARC), with an army of fifteen thousand, all of them better paid than their counterparts in the Colombian army. In the eighties and nineties, groups of paramilitary units were formed by a whole array of private businessmen, drug barons, and even multinational corporations to fight the guerillas with force. The state virtually took a backseat, and despite peace talks, the violence continues unabated, with consequences that spread far beyond the Colombian border. For example, 90 percent of all the cocaine sold on the streets of the United States is grown in Colombian fields.

Yet this conflict is played out against a backdrop of even darker violence. This is a state where more than five thousand people each year die violent deaths. Every day one person disappears without a trace, and three people fall victim to an execution-style killing. Yet what is not so well-known is this: only 15 percent of this violence is due to the armed conflict. Colombia is simply the most violent state in the world and would be even if the war were not going on within it. The unacceptable level of violence in daily life goes back to the period called *La Violencia*, when from 1948 to 1962 a brutal civil war between conservatives and liberals claimed three hundred thousand lives. Colombians have never known a time when life was respected, the rule of law observed, and justice enacted.

The country's only hope is the church, which alone can model the kind of peaceful reconciliation that resolves social conflict without destroying society in the process. With peace talks stuttering, Ricardo Esquivia, a Mennonite church leader, says, "I work from the principle that peace cannot simply be signed on a paper, nor is it the product of a military victory. The Bible says that to have peace you have to work for justice from the ground up. You have to rebuild trust, repair bonds broken by violence." Such a stance comes at a price. He bought land in guerilla-controlled territory and farmed among a community that had embraced violence. Over time he won many back to a path of peace, then abruptly had to flee the country when assassins threatened. He is now back taking daily risks for reconciliation.

And in the midst of the horrors, God works miracles. One day a guerilla went to lob a grenade into a church. Crouching outside the window, he prepared to throw, then hesitated. A song was being sung by a young woman. The song reminded him of his childhood. His grandma taught it to him as she bounced him on her knee. Smitten with grief at the recollection of such joy, he led his troop back into the hills. Two days of spiritual torment followed until he slipped away, found the local pastor, pointed a gun at his chest, and said, "Will you help me become a Christian?" Soon after he was baptized, and he stayed so long underwater the pastor began to fear for his life. But the guerilla was divesting himself of all his weapons. He rose up to proclaim his new, risen life with Christ; his rusting instruments of death buried with his old life—as powerful a symbol of real baptism as one can find.

Converted guerilla leaders formed an AGAPE movement in 2003, which stands for the Association of Repentant Guerillas Preaching the Gospel, and which by the end of 2004 has resulted in three thousand guerillas and paramilitaries handing in their weapons. In this land drenched with blood, the church defiantly shakes the fist of peace. It brings persecution and reconciliation at the same time!

### Mexico

Despite being right on America's doorstep—or perhaps because of it—suffering Christians in Mexico are seldom mentioned. Persecution is concentrated in the southern state of Chiapas, where 250,000 Indians of four tribes, all related to the ancient Mayan people, live in poverty. Nearly half are Christians, and in the last ten years a staggering 35,000 of them have been illegally driven off their land by bullying *caciques*, angry that Christians are no longer consuming the native alcohol, *posh*, on which their racket depends. These local landlords have the nerve to publish unofficial laws forbidding the building of churches and meeting with other believers, even in homes, and demanding that Christians continue to participate in pagan sacrifices. The candles, flowers, and animals used in the rituals are all available at an outrageous price from—you guessed it—the *caciques*!

To make matters worse, some of the Indian population formed themselves into a fighting unit called the Zapatistas in 1994. Although their grievances are genuine, sadly they chose as their model the coercive revolutionary armies of Latin America, and they preserve a "join, leave, or die" philosophy. They fight the *caciques* with force and resent any Christian who refuses to take arms and bring about "liberation."

Again the Christians are caught in a pincer movement. The local corrupt authorities hate them because they are too ethical; the local revolutionaries hate them because they are too gentle. Open Doors reckons the total number of strongly persecuted Christians in Mexico's 100 million population to be 120 thousand, also due to extremist Catholics and spiritualists who are resentful of evangelical growth.

Chiapas is the site of one of the highest-profile miscarriages of justice in the recent history of religious liberty. On December 22, 1997, six men, twenty-one women, and eighteen children were gunned down in a Catholic hermitage in the village of Acteal. Exactly who did the shooting and why are still a mystery, but in the ensuing manhunt, eighty farmers were picked up and accused of the massacre. Sadly, they were picked up by police acting on tip-offs from members of a Catholic community group called Las Abejas, many of whom were in land disputes with evangelical farmers. Among the eighty accused were thirty-four evangelical peasant farmers from Presbyterian, Assemblies of God, and other Pentecostal churches, and they have languished in jail ever since, with many of them receiving jail sentences of thirty-six years. A government review begun in 2004, on which many pinned their hopes, came to nothing in late 2005 as all sentences were maintained. Despite evidence that many of the accused were thirty miles away at the time of the massacre, they continue to face the rest of their lives behind bars. Their plight reveals the complexity of persecution today, highlighting the politics of land grabbing and substandard legal procedures that are the constant bane of the harassed Latin American believer.

## The Middle East—The Case of the Disappearing Church

Christians are disappearing fast from the Middle East, and persecution has a lot to do with it. It's incredible! How can Christians be an endangered species in the very region where Christ walked, talked, died, and was resurrected; where the flames of Pentecost licked down to spread the church all over the known world in a

## To Suffer Is Beautiful

*The Story of Domingo, an Indigenous Indian Who
Changed His Profession for Christ*

Domingo Lopez and his wife, Anacleta Martínez Alvarez

Before his conversion to evangelical Christianity sixteen years ago, Domingo Lopez dedicated his time to producing *posh*, the potent homemade liquor that indigenous Indians in Chiapas drink at traditional religious festivals. Domingo's encounter with Christ obliged him to change his profession. He also had to change his address. Why? Because *caciques*, the community leaders who dominate religion and economics in the Chiapas highlands, do not like people to give up the old ways to follow Christ. *Caciques* expelled Domingo, then thirty years old, and his family from their ancestral home in Aguacatenango after they converted.

Their story is common in Chiapas, where an estimated thirty-five thousand Tzotzil- and Tzeltal-speaking Christians live in exile because of their faith. *Caciques* have used threats, beatings, arson, and murder to drive out Christian families like the Lopezes from their homes.

The *caciques* are afraid the evangelicals will infect their neighbors with their beliefs, causing them also to spurn religious festivals, *posh* drinking, and other customs that earn the *caciques* a lot of money. Simply put, Christians are bad for business.

Despite the unrelenting pressure, Christianity has grown steadily throughout the indigenous communities of the Chiapas highlands. According to government census figures, 35 percent of the state population adheres to evangelicalism. Chiapas now has more Protestants per capita than any state in Mexico. This is possible because Domingo Lopez and hundreds of humble believers like him have not allowed the pressure to stop them from sharing their faith in Christ.

Today Domingo lives with his wife and five children in Teopisca, where he pastors the Jesus the Good Shepherd Church, a Tzeltal-speaking congregation he founded. He also distributes Bibles and trains pastors and church leaders to evangelize rural communities throughout the Chiapas highlands.

Domingo has become so well-known for his ministry that he eventually changed his name. To the many Tzeltal believers who know him, including a new group of Christians in his hometown of Aguacatenango, Domingo is known as "Juan de Teopisca."

The *caciques* know him too. Lopez receives regular threats on his life, like the time two years ago when anonymous callers told him that if he visited the believers in Aguacatenango one more time, they would be waiting to abduct him and see that he died a slow and painful death. The same fate awaited Pedro Cosh, a member of Domingo's evangelistic team, they said.

Lopez and Cosh continued their regular preaching visits to Aguacatenango, and so far no one has carried out the threat. And in the meantime, more Tzeltals have accepted Christ. For example, a local *curandera* (witch doctor) became seriously ill and could not cure herself. She made several visits to other *curanderos* in the community, all to no avail. Desperate, she remembered hearing that Juan de Teopisca and his evangelistic team had experienced some success with healings, so she decided to consult them. They spoke to her of Jesus and she accepted Him as her Savior. Afterward, the evangelists prayed for her healing. The *curandera* miraculously recovered from the illness and became a powerful witness in her village to the power of God.

Incidents like this are why Domingo Lopez is busy in several villages around Teopisca organizing groups of new believers into congregations and helping them construct simple buildings in which to worship. He will continue his evangelistic work despite the threats, beatings, and other forms of harassment he faces.

"To suffer is beautiful," he says. "It hurts your body but fortifies your spirit."

single generation; and where the supreme Emperor Constantine corralled the entire population of the Mediterranean basin into vast basilicas to worship God and hear giant preachers like Chrysostom, Augustine, and Athanasius?

The answer is Islam! Islam was irresistible almost as soon as it got going in 622, because, as church historian Kenneth Latourette wrote, it was the "ideal warrior religion," promising a special, instant paradise to those who died in battle. Also, conquered Christian populations were quick to seize the tax advantages offered to them by astute Muslim conquerors if they converted. The clincher was to set the severest penalty—death—for leaving the Muslim faith for another. Even so, a large Christian remnant remained. In 1900 there were forty million Muslims in the Middle East, and 6.5 million Christians. But the twentieth century has seen the most dramatic decline of all. Now there are three hundred million Muslims and only twelve million Christians, a percentage drop of Christians from 15 to 4 percent. In individual countries, this decline is even more catastrophic. Turkey was 30 percent Christian in 1900; now Christians number only two hundred thousand, out of a population of sixty-two million. In Lebanon the Christian population dived from 75 to 35 percent over the same time period.

Population pyramids and a persecution-caused exodus are the two reasons for this decline, according to the persecution analyst on this region for Open Doors. "First, Muslims have tended to have much larger families than the Christians, often with six or seven children each. Second, persecution in the last century has forced Christians to emigrate in vast numbers." In his book *From the Holy Mountain*, William Dalrymple tells of his visits to most of the Middle East's Christian population and concluded sadly that, with the exception of Syria, there is no place where traditional Christian people seem happy or have a sense of hope for the future.[8]

If the last hundred years have been the saddest ones for Christians, the last thirty have been the hardest. Islamic extremism got its greatest boost in 1979 when Muslim clerics toppled the seemingly invincible Shah of Iran and set up the world's first theocratic state since medieval times. If, in the eyes of Westerners, such an arrangement seemed out of place in the modern world, to many Muslims the world over, it seemed just what was needed to replace a decadent and declining civilization. Fundamentalist movements, often with a militant agenda, sprang up in virtually all Islamic countries, and the practice of Islam enjoyed a massive revival. A Beirut-based journalist (who values his anonymity) once explained to me why the extremists enjoy such a good hearing: "After the humiliation of Arab armies by Israel in 1967 and 1973, there was much soul searching. The Islamists came along and said, 'Well, you lost because you are not practicing Islam well enough. If you will only come back to Islam properly, then you will have success. Blessings follow faithfulness.' And of course, when the extremists triumphed in Iran against all the odds, they had almost irresistible arguments from then on."

The upshot is that Christian minorities are increasingly marginalized, and converts from Islam increasingly terrorized. Sometimes the militants organize into jihad units that target Christians. The shameful massacre of thirteen Coptic Christians in Daryut, Egypt, in May 1992 was carried out by a carefully orchestrated mob of ten thousand. But most Christians experience the intolerance in daily life. Brother Y, a fifty-five-year-old Egyptian believer, recalls: "In my childhood Christians and Muslims got on well together. We respected each other's feasts, and even participated in them. Now if we wear a cross in the street we are spat upon, and we never dare to give our children Christian names or we damn them to a life of social exclusion."

### Persecution Profile of the Region

Since we are using "Middle East" in quite an expansive way, starting from Egypt and going up through the Gulf all the way east to Pakistan, we'll divide it up into four zones, each containing a different persecution scenario.

#### WHERE SHARIA REIGNS

The area where sharia reigns includes the Arabic-speaking nations of the Gulf, dominated by Saudi Arabia. *Sharia* is the revealed law of Islam, and obedience to it is here enforced by the state and becomes the basis of all state laws. Ask locals in these countries, and they answer, "There might be Christians but only among the expatriate communities." This is not always true, though it would be dangerous to give details, for this is a most repressive region. This is because sharia forbids apostasy, or conversion from Islam to another religion. Saudi's leaders declare it is forbidden for anyone to practice any religion except Islam on Saudi soil, even privately. There are no churches in the land. Home meetings, even among expatriate Christians, are discouraged. In some cases the fanatical religious police have even stopped the giving of Christmas cards. Foreign Christians visiting the country today often have to plead with customs officials to be allowed to take in their personal Bibles.

If you become a Christian in Saudi Arabia, you had better move away—fast! The state will hunt you down and prosecute you severely. In Yemen the family unit will do the same. There are chinks of light in the region, however, such as Qatar, with a population of seven hundred thousand, of which three-quarters is expatriate. At the end of 1999 the emir gave permission for the sixty thousand Roman Catholics to build a church there—the only one of its kind in the Gulf.

### Where Liberalism Reigns

The other Arabic-speaking countries of the Middle East, including Egypt, Jordan, Lebanon, Palestine, Syria, and Iraq make up the area where liberalism reigns. Here the policy is a little more relaxed, mainly because a sizable and historic Christian minority already exists in these countries. The Christian minority is tolerated after a fashion, and they are free to hold services and maintain their numbers. The leaders of these countries are rarely practicing Muslims and preserve a complicated suspicion toward Islamic extremists. Sometimes they hunt them down. Sometimes they appease them. In either season, though, Christians suffer. For example, in Egypt, when Muslim extremists are rounded up, Christian leaders will also be arrested in groups just so the police can pretend to seem evenhanded.

Some Christian minorities are very large, most notably in Lebanon and Egypt, which gives them some clout. But spreading the gospel is a very incendiary act. In Egypt a Muslim is not even allowed to enter a Coptic church. Democratic structures and rights are in place, so it is possible to appeal against mistreatment, but the system tends to be manipulated by Machiavellian strongmen, and justice is rarely the outcome. In most of these states (Egypt, for example, is an exception), it is illegal to convert to another religion from Islam.

### Where Extremists Reign

Extremists reign in places like Iran and, until recently, Pakistan. Like the Gulf States, they are all Islamic republics, but in contrast, here it is the extremists that exert the greatest influence on government policy. In Iran extremist clerics *are* the government! Consequently, in addition to being marginalized by galloping Islamization, Christians are frequently the target of mob violence, especially in Pakistan, where family honor codes insist that anyone who converts must be killed. It is here that fathers have killed their daughters with sickening regularity. A ridiculous blasphemy law also applies, where a Muslim can make an anonymous accusation against a Christian for slandering the Prophet, and police have to jail the Christian purely because an accusation has been made. In both Pakistan and Iran, the death penalty for apostasy is mandated. In Pakistan and Afghanistan, Islamic extremists no longer hold the highest offices of state, but extremists are so numerous that their influence remains all-pervasive.

### Where Secularism Reigns

It's not surprising that Christians are treated the best in countries where secularism reigns, but since Turkey is the only strongly secularist state (Indonesia is another, but that will be covered in Asia), it is disappointing that there are so few Christians in the country to benefit from it. President Kemal Atatürk, who ruled Turkey from 1923 to 1938 introduced the secularist policy. His stance became a virtual religion of its own. Said a Christian journalist who lives in Istanbul, "Make a call for an Islamic state here and you will get thrown in jail." Extremists are not absent of course, and a democratization process gives them a higher profile, but if a Turkish Muslim becomes a Christian, it is unlikely the family would feel it their duty to kill him or her. Ostracism rather than execution is the usual penalty for conversion here.

One might lump the newly independent Central Asian republics into this category. Until recently under Russian occupation, their governments retain a more secular, indeed atheistic, attitude toward religion. Despite the populations of these nations being overwhelmingly Muslim, none of them are Islamic states, and in the last few years the tiny Christian populations in them have grown fast. In Turkmenistan there are now more evangelical Christians than in Turkey. However, that does not mean all is well. Most of these states have retained the same rules as Russia on religious freedom—register under government control or be illegal! Islamic fundamentalist movements are powerful here, with fascist-type leaders anxious to stamp out these movements. Christians often get caught in the middle, ensnared in the same laws designed to stop Islamic extremists.

### Two to Watch

#### PAKISTAN

Pakistan's 3.6 million Christians are at their wits' end. Surrounded by more than 150 million Muslims, they can be sent to jail at the whim of even a child who takes it into his or her head to accuse them of insulting Islam. The Catholic bishop of Faisalabad, John Joseph, was so fed up that he committed suicide on May 6, 1998, in protest against the intolerable laws that caused such fear in the Christian community. If the world looked on in sympathy, the Pakistani government continued to ignore Christian concerns.

Bishop Joseph committed suicide nine days after a thirty-two-year-old Christian man, Ayub Masih, was sentenced to death by hanging for blaspheming Islam. A controversial blasphemy law prescribes a mandatory death sentence for anyone found to slander Muhammad and life imprisonment for slandering Islam. To activate this, all one needs to do is make an accusation. One is not required to provide details. The accused must be immediately arrested, and if found guilty, be put to death. So ridiculous is the law that when the court asks, "What did the accused say?" the accuser will answer, "I can't repeat it because it would be blaspheming." Courts connive in this. On June 4, 2001, twenty-six-year-old Shabbaz Masih was charged under this law for tearing up tracts that contained Qur'anic verses. He was mentally disabled, but the court continued to prosecute, even though Pakistani law prohibits the conviction of a person of "unsound mind."

So often the law is used as a pretext. Ayub Masih was accused because some mullahs were after his land. Thirty-year-old Anwar Masih was accused of blasphemy by a former neighbor, Naseer Ahmad, whom he had met after a two-year absence. An innocent inquiry about his friend's beard led to the charge that he was slandering the Prophet who mandated the wearing of beards. But Naseer was only settling an old score. Anwar had encouraged a Christian to register a complaint after Naseer had beaten him.

Instead of the court throwing out the case against Anwar, he spent nearly two years in jail, and on his release on June 4, 2004, his first act was to gather his wife and four children and go into hiding to avoid the extremists who have sworn to kill them. Although the blasphemy law has not been carried out in recent years, it remains a potent weapon of intimidation.

This odd law has actually been on the statute book since the founding of Pakistan in 1949 but was only activated by President Zia in the 1980s. The more liberal government of Benazir Bhutto tried to modify it. When the justice minister announced the modifications (in Ireland, at a safe distance), a prominent sheik at a public rally in Karachi put a bounty of forty thousand dollars on the minister's head for anyone who would assassinate him. Such is the power of extremism here that the sheik was never even cautioned, and the proposal—needless to say—never implemented. Although General Pervez Musharraf took power in 1999, ousting an extremist government, he nevertheless has to appease the Majlis Muttahida-e-Amal (MMA)—an alliance of six anti-Western, pro-Taliban, pro-sharia Islamic parties—who hold the balance of power still. He has not challenged their Islamist agenda, and his attempt to amend the blasphemy law failed.

Though the blasphemy law dominates the headlines, we hear less about Christians killed every year in Pakistan by Muslim extremists. Families of the slain Christians tend to keep the deaths quiet for fear of further reprisals. The killings we do hear about are often only the tip of the iceberg. A recent atrocity was the gunning down of Pastor Harbour Samsoun, his driver, and fellow evangelist Daniel Emmanuel in their vehicle on April 7, 2004. Police were quick to blame the killings on a family dispute, but the two men were targets of extremists, receiving phone threats demanding they stop their Christian work.

The culture, even without the aid of extremists, takes its toll. Ninety percent of Pakistan's Christians are illiterate. The rest clean the streets or toilets of public buildings if they do not work for a church. Converts are disinherited by law and hounded by relatives, who sometimes employ terrorist cells to track down and kill converts who flee to foreign countries. In the countryside the kidnapping of young Christian girls and their raping by Muslim zealots is an all too common outrage. Indeed, it is the youth of the Christian community who are a particular target and face daily the threat of being kidnapped and forcibly entered into the madrassas (Islamic schools).

Zeeshan Gill, a sixteen-year-old Pakistani Christian, was walking back from his school on November 7, 2003, in the town of Sargodha, in Pakistan's Punjab Province.[9] He was approached by an electrician named Amjad Warriach who had done some work in the boy's home. He took him to the Jamia al Qasim al Almoom madrassa, which was attached to the local mosque, and his nightmare began.

Kept under guard, he was beaten and threatened, and then forced to recite the Islamic creed, which in their view made him a Muslim. He was told if he ran away, he would be killed. They began training him in the use of guns and grenades and told him that he was to be sent to fight in the Muslim holy war in Kashmir, where he would "spread Islam at the speed of seventy miles an hour."

For three days he was missing, and his mother, Raza, was beside herself. Her husband had died twelve years earlier, and she struggled to provide for her two sons as a medical technician. Zeeshan was probably targeted because there was no male elder in the family.

Eventually she learned that her son was being held at the mosque. She was not allowed to see him. She engaged a bailiff and together with a local police officer went to the mosque. In the presence of his captors, Zeeshan said he had become a Muslim, but his mother knew he was lying.

A court summons was ordered, and on November 14 Zeeshan appeared with his madrassa leader and again made the same declaration, saying he would return to his mother only if she became a Muslim. She asked the judge if she could speak to her son privately, but the judge declared that her son was "a sensible boy" and had the right to convert. She was unable to see him.

Zeeshan came back to the house on November 20 to collect his effects, but under the watchful eye of a Muslim bodyguard. Four days later he was told to report for final training at Raiwand Islamic center to be sent to Kashmir, but first he was allowed to return home unaccompanied.

Of course he told his mother what had happened. Seeing how frightened and distressed he was, Raza Gill fled with her two sons to the home of relatives many miles away. Finding a secure hiding place for Zeeshan, however, will be hard, as assassins may have been dispatched.

As so often happens in the affairs of the kingdom of God, it took a disaster to bring blessing to the Christians. That disaster was 9/11. "Up until then," said a Pakistani Christian leader, "this country was being rapidly Talibanized, and the Christian community was under constant attack. After 9/11, the U.S. government began to support Musharrif in order to quash Islamic extremist at the source, and it has been better for Christians ever since." Yet it remains to be seen whether Musharrif can really change the society into a more tolerant one, and extremist mob violence remains an all-too-constant threat in this backward state.

## "God, Is There No Christian Who Can Teach Me the Bible?"

*A Pakistani Evangelist's Quest to Know the Truth*

A typical Pakistani evangelist (not Christopher)

A row of simple metal doors lay at the end of potholed roads and alleys accessible only by foot. Yacoob tapped on one. Moments later, a teenage girl opened the door a crack, spoke to Yacoob in whispers, and invited him into the home. A group of Christians from the West entered with him.

Girls ranging in age from six to twelve scurried about the living room, excited about their visitors. They were daughters and nieces of a man whose father, an imam, had named him Mohammed. The visitors listened as his story unfolded.

As a young man, Mohammed became a lay scholar of Islam. His brother became a mullah, also called a *maulvi*, or mosque leader. After a lifelong spiritual search, Mohammed, thirty-five, came to personal faith in Christ six years ago. He changed his name to Christopher—"Christ-bearer"—and has devoted his life to spreading the gospel to Muslims and others who, like him, hunger for truth.

Meanwhile, his extended family is searching for him. When he told his father of his decision to follow Christ, his father threw him out of the family. Three days later, his father died of a heart attack.

Christopher's wife, Maria, demanded a divorce. His mother-in-law brought a renowned Islamic apologist to his home to convince him to return to Islam. For six hours, Christopher used references from the Qur'an and the Bible to prove to the apologist the truths of Christ. When Christopher's brothers visited and found Christopher steadfast in his newfound faith, they told him he should die.

He moved his wife and five children far from his relatives.

Christopher is bold in his witness, which has extended to his co-workers and bosses at his government job. He was jailed for converting to Christianity. Three months later he was miraculously released and, again miraculously, allowed to keep his job.

He shares the gospel wherever he goes and gives away copies of a comparative study of the Bible and the Qur'an, a study that was key to his own conversion.

Christopher believes God called him from an early age. As a seven-year-old boy, he told his aunt that he was a Christian, even though he knew no Christians, had never heard the gospel, and didn't live near a church.

As an eighth-grader, Christopher answered an ad for a Bible correspondence class, which he completed. His brother, however, intercepted the course's completion certificate, ripped it in pieces, and beat him.

Over the next few years, he had several interactions with Christians, including a street sweeper who shared the gospel with him. That reinforced his desire to know more about Christianity.

One pastor, however, was so afraid to talk to a Muslim about Christ that when Christopher asked to learn from him about Christianity, the pastor simply handed him a Bible, said it would teach him, and shut the door in Christopher's face.

When he learned that a shopkeeper he had met was a Christian and asked the man if he could refer him to a pastor who could teach him the Bible, the shopkeeper put Christopher off for days before telling him, "Sorry, but because you are a Muslim, I am afraid of providing you a pastor." Desperate, Christopher prayed, "Oh, God, is there no Christian who can teach me the Bible?"

Nine months later, Christopher went to a homeopathy shop to get medicine for his wife's backache. He told a man in the store about his wife. "He prayed and gave me some medicines and blessed me in a way that Christians do," Christopher said. The man refused to take Christopher's money for the medicine. When Christopher asked the man who he was, "He told me he was a Christian who loved his Lord Jesus Christ," Christopher said.

The homeopath found an engineer named Pablo willing to teach Christopher the Bible. Their detailed discussion about the Son of God, however, didn't fully satisfy Christopher, so Pablo took him to a church shortly after that. The pastor's sermon topic was "Jesus Christ is the Son of God," which he proved from the Bible, history, the Qur'an, and the *Ahadees* (sayings of the prophet Muhammad).

"This was the first time I listened to this topic presented so logically and with full explanation," Christopher said. "This was the very first time I became convinced that Jesus Christ is really the Son of God."

Soon afterward, God reinforced Christopher's conviction with supernatural signs, including a bright light that filled his room as he studied the book of Jeremiah and the miraculous healing of his daughter from a high-grade fever that threatened her life. Maria, who was home with the toddler while Christopher was at church, told him at what time the child's fever broke. It was the precise moment he prayed for her healing.

Months later Christopher was baptized. Over the course of the next three years, Christopher's wife, eleven members of her family, and several other acquaintances have come to faith in Christ through his testimony.

Christopher is now an ordained pastor and evangelist. "We want to do a great job for the glory of God among the Muslims as well as in nominal Christians. Along with this, my in-laws' family and also my family and I are feeling unsafe in these circumstances," he said. Many churches and Christian leaders are afraid to help the family because of the country's strict Islamic society. An "accident" could end their lives and ministry. "So please lift your hand in prayer to the Lord for this valuable ministry and for these precious people of God," he said.

When asked if the cause of Christ was worth the suffering and constant danger, Maria said, "Christianity means persecution. We have no fear of death because Jesus loves us. We are preaching him because we believe in eternal life." She added, "I want to give the message to other Muslims to come to the cross and understand the Holy Scripture and encourage Christians to reach out to Muslims."

SAUDI ARABIA

There are six million expatriates in Saudi Arabia, the superrich state of 25.6 million people. Six hundred thousand of them are Christians; many are part of the half-million-strong Filipino community. Yet this state allows no worship except that of Islam on its soil. Christians are not allowed to build churches, hold services, wear crosses, or even send Christmas cards. Worse, the state is the taproot of global Muslim intolerance, spending billions from its oil revenues each year erecting mosques throughout the world and staffing them with extremist clerics.

This double standard greatly annoys Christians. In April of 2004 forty Pakistani Christians were worshiping in a private house in the capital, Riyadh, when several carloads of *muttawa* (Islamic religious police) burst in, stopped the sermon, and began to beat the worshipers. Said a Pakistani church leader, "We are very upset over this. Why do Saudi Muslims have the right all over the world to build mosques and worship in them, when they refuse to designate places of worship for Christians who are guest workers in Saudi Arabia?"

The intolerance within the state is the result of an agreement between a warrior and a holy man that could be right out of the pages of the Old Testament. In the eighteenth century Arabia was full of warring tribes. Muhammed ibn Saud was the leader of the tribe of Saud. Wanting his campaign for hegemony blessed, he approached a famous religious scholar, Abd al-Wahhab, who promised him military success over his rivals on the condition that the victorious House of Saud must protect his strict doctrinal rule from opponents. The House of Saud triumphed, just as the holy man predicted. And the King of Saud was as good as his word—he made Wahhabism the main form of Islam in Saudi Arabia. The problem is that Wahhabism is the most puritanical form of Sunni Islam. The Ottoman Turks had no love for this extremist version of Islam and deposed the House of Saud.

All of that happened a long time ago, but in 1932 King Abd-al-Aziz regained the throne for the tribe of Saud, and Wahhabism was back in business. Thanks to the oil revenues discovered at the same time, this brand of Islam could be exported without regard to the cost.

In practice the religious policy is not quite as oppressive as in principle. In embassies and foreign compounds, some Christians do meet discreetly in small groups for Bible studies and are unmolested. But the rules are vague, and freedom often depends on social status. The Saudis may hesitate to arrest Europeans or Americans, but they care little about harassing Filipino, Indian, or African Christians. Every year Christians are harassed and deported, simply for the crime of worshiping together in homes. Saudi's Ministry of the Interior has a fanatical element that will stop at nothing. When fifteen Filipino Christians were arrested on January 7, 2000, for holding services in the house of Art and Sabalista Abreu, the police even pressured the young children in the one-hundred-strong congregation to divulge details of the prayer lives of their parents.

Yet such is the wealth of Saudi Arabia, and its status as a military ally of the United States, that the mistreatment of Christians went ignored by the State Department charged to expose religious liberty abuses. This attitude began to change when most of the 9/11 suicide bombers were seen to be disaffected Saudis, radicalized in the subsidized religious schools of the land.

Extremism breeds extremism. One of the great untold stories of persecution today is that much of the Muslim-Christian violence that has caused such mayhem in Nigeria and the Sudan, and even in Western Europe, is traceable to Saudi-built and Saudi-staffed mosques in these places. Extremism for export may well be the reason that in 2004 Saudi Arabia was listed as a "country of particular concern" by the U.S. State Department. The ailing elderly men that run the country, however, make gestures to ward off criticism. They reined in a thousand clerics in 2003. But as a Riyadh Christian said, "There are forty-nine thousand more clerics in the country that will keep the extremist message alive." The only good news to report is that, although the law requires Muslim converts to Christianity to be killed, none have been killed in recent years.

## Africa—the Continent We Love to Forget

"Poor Africa," we often say. Western images of Africa are invariably negative ones, and with good reason. Four apocalyptic horsemen gallop to and fro across the deserts, jungles, and velds of this vast continent, spreading death to the eight hundred million people that live in the fifty-six countries making up modern Africa. These horsemen are war, famine, plagues, and poverty.

Arguably the greatest of these scourges is war, especially since famine, plague, and poverty are often the consequences of war. More than two million people died in civil wars in the 1990s—half of them in Rwanda alone in 1994. Abiding images include Belgian and French troops evacuating those with foreign passports, then scuttling away to leave the Tutsi civilian population defenseless in the hands of the merciless Hutus. Grainy television images from long-range lenses showed people kneeling beside piles of corpses on the street, begging youthful gang members for their lives, only to be chopped to death with machetes. Vacationers taking a dip in Lake Victoria, one hundred kilometers away from the Rwandan border, were horrified to find bloody and bloated bodies floating into the lake at the rate of eighty an hour.

While Hutu leaders eclipsed Hitler, Pol Pot, and Stalin in carrying out the century's fastest extermination campaign, the UN Security Council was deliberately altering official cables from the capital, Kigali, that used the word *genocide*. Substituting the word *massacre*, they managed to ensure that no military intervention would be organized. Said one official, anonymously, "After the Jewish holocaust, we could not use the word *genocide* and do nothing, because the UN was set up to stop such things, but we had to make the alteration because no one wanted to send troops to their deaths to sort that mess out." Ironically Rwanda had a seat on the fifteen-member Security Council at the time and denied the killing was taking place. Not a single member dared to challenge the lies they knew they were hearing.

While the West may share some complicity in Africa's poverty, famine, and plagues, this is undoubtedly the world's most misgoverned continent. While millions die of famine, an estimated 40 percent of food is lost due to inadequate transportation and storage. AIDS has reached pandemic proportions in countries such as Uganda and South Africa partly because governments have refused to acknowledge the true scale of the problem. In South Africa, for example, fifteen hundred people contract AIDS every day. One in nine of the population is HIV-positive, and if little continues to be done, ten million will have died by 2010. Though Africa has produced Mandela, more often it produces Bokassas, Amins, and Abaches—men who raid their own country's coffers without shame.

If Africa is poorer than it was forty years ago after the great "freedom" year of 1960, when seventeen nations threw off the colonial yoke, it is far richer spiritually. Almost four hundred million people on the continent are Christian, and the church grows at a rocketing four thousand people per day. Evangelicals form 15 percent of the total population. It is precisely this growth that has led to a sharp increase in persecution.

### Conflict between Christians and Muslims

Persecution in Africa occurs primarily where the two dominant religions of Christianity and Islam butt up against each other. This conflict is comparatively recent and strongly localized in the sub-Saharan belt. The northern nations of Africa are Islamic, with a tiny Christian presence if any. The southern nations are overwhelmingly Christian. Both these religions have revived over the past fifty years, but they have made their converts primarily among the animist groups in their regions. Their respective revivals have pushed Islam south and Christianity north, so that in the last twenty years where they have met has become the main arena of persecution. With Christians comprising 48.4 percent of Africans, and Muslims 41 percent, it is the battle of the giants concentrated in small areas where Muslims and Christians overlap and compete to convert the few remaining animists. They are like elephants and tigers trying to drink from the same dwindling waterhole.

This conflict arena is also known as the Sahel Belt, composed of countries such as Sudan, Nigeria, Ethiopia, Chad, Burkina Faso,

Senegal, Zambia, and Djibouti. Many of Africa's persecuted live in those countries. In Sudan the extremist Muslim government seems bent on the genocide of non-Muslims. In northern Nigeria hundreds of churches are burned and leaders imprisoned even while the president, a Christian, wrings his hands far to the south. On the whole the problem is that these countries or regions within countries are in the hands of Islamic leaders who feel bound to turn their areas into religious republics after the pattern of Iran, and this may be in states where up to half their people are not Muslim.

Not all persecution comes from militant Islam of course. Sad to say, in Rwanda Christian practiced genocide against Christian, and in states such as Mozambique and Namibia, believers are often targeted by insurgents for failing to fight. In countries such as Ethiopia the traditional Orthodox Church has a militant wing that persecutes independent evangelicals. But African Christians are not complaining. According to Dr. Tokunboh Adeyemo, president of the Africa Evangelical Association, "Our strong churches today are to be located in places of political hostility, religious intoleration, and cultural intimidation." The ultimate illustration of this was Uganda under the terrible reign of Idi Amin. Adds Dr. Adeyemo, "The church of Uganda has never sent out ministers of the gospel like Bishop Festo Kivengere in large numbers as it did under the tyrannical reign of Idi Amin."

*Two to Watch*

#### Nigeria

Africa's most populous country of 137 million has a wonderful constitution that allows for complete freedom of religion and even the right to proselytize. The problem is that many Muslim regions within the country are ignoring the constitution, introducing Islamic law into society, and even issuing bans on Christian evangelism. Nigeria's reputation for religious tolerance has taken a battering since 2000, when Christian minorities in the northern states that introduced sharia law were attacked while making peaceful protests. Twenty pastors were martyred in February of that year in Kaduna state alone.

## God Should Have Taken Me

*The Story of the Widow of a Martyred Church Leader*

Tsige and her two sons,
Zelalem and Dawit

"God should have taken me, not Dantew," says Tsige, the widow of an Ethiopian church leader martyred in a vicious attack in July 2002. "Dantew would have been of much more worth for God's kingdom here on earth than I could ever be."

But instead, it was her husband who laid down his life at age thirty-nine, and Tsige is left alone to provide for their two teenage sons.

Her isolation is very real. She is the sole evangelical Christian living in Bikolo Abye village, just ten miles from where her husband was murdered in the town of Merawi, northwestern Ethiopia.

All her neighbors and acquaintances know that she is an outcaste "Pente," or Pentecostal, the derisive term for evangelical Christians who have abandoned the ancient Ethiopian Orthodox "mother" church to join the growing number of Protestant fellowships springing up across the country.

And they know that her pastor husband was hacked to death by rampaging Orthodox priests and their followers. He was targeted because he was helping build an evangelical church in Merawi. Although some forty suspects were arrested after his murder, none were charged, and all were eventually released.

Tsige lives in a small rented room of a village compound, earning a modest salary as an Amharic language teacher at the local middle school. It's a far cry from previous years, when she and her husband owned their own home in Merawi and had two teaching incomes to cover their family expenses. But by stretching, she makes ends meet for herself and her sons.

Still, she faces the loneliness of being separated from both of them, as well as from all her extended family. Both of the boys are living apart from their mother now to complete their schooling.

Every Sunday she boards a local bus for the hour-and-a-half trip to Bahir Dar to worship and fellowship with an evangelical congregation there. It's also her one chance each week to see her older son, Dawit, who is studying civil engineering at the university in Bahir Dar. She manages to rent a room for him there and also covers the expenses for her younger son, Zelalem, who is staying with a Christian family two hundred miles to the south in Addis Ababa to attend high school.

But her deepest concern is for her sons' spiritual and emotional state as they recover from the traumatic shock of watching their father die while his enemies ridiculed him.

A noisy mob had surrounded their home in the dark on the night of the fateful attack, shouting and banging on metal pans and heaving stones at the house. After Tsige was hit in the face by a large rock thrown through the window, Dantew begged her to escape through the back door and summon the police. Although reluctant to leave him and their sons, she finally slipped out the back while the attackers were breaking down the front gate to their home. To her dismay, she found the police station unmanned, and she ran through the streets in near hysteria, unable to find any help.

In a matter of minutes the attackers broke into the house, smashing doors and windows and partially destroying the roof in the process. They made straight for Dantew, felling him with two axe blows to his head. After dragging out his sons, who were found hiding under the bed with a house servant, they released the servant and then set a guard around the house. Meanwhile, they shouted crude remarks against Dantew.

"Why don't you die?" they mocked him. "What kind of soul do you have? Is it like that of a cat?"

With his two gaping wounds bleeding steadily, his life slowly ebbed away through the night, while the boys watched and listened, helpless. The attackers refused offers from a doctor living nearby who pleaded with them to let her treat Dantew's wounds. When the police finally arrived, the vigilantes shot off their guns to keep the police force from approaching.

After the guards withdrew, Tsige returned in the early hours of the morning to find Dantew barely alive. By the time she got him to Merawi's medical clinic, they could not even find a vein to give him a blood transfusion, and he died en route to the hospital in Bahir Dar.

Because of the savage death that had taken place in their home, Tsige tried in vain to find tenants who would rent the house once she had it repaired. After eight months she was forced to sell the house at a substantial loss.

Tsige has a good relationship with Dantew's family, who live in the Bahir Dar region and all remain traditional Orthodox church members. "They accept me, and they are very kind to me and the boys," she says.

Tsige's own family members in Addis Ababa, where she was born and raised, have urged her since Dantew's death to move back to the capital. It's a compelling option for her, since all of them are also evangelical Christians and one of her sons is already studying there.

And admittedly, she continues to experience some hostility from the traditional Orthodox population in her village and the Bahir Dar region. "I'm not scared," Tsige says. "But I don't want to move back to Addis Ababa and leave Dawit behind in this very hostile area." Dawit's application to transfer his studies to Addis Ababa University has been denied.

"I'm not sure of God's will yet," she says. "So for now, I'm staying here, until God confirms to me what He has in mind for me to do."

Nigeria's population is 50 percent Muslim and 40 percent Christian, so it is important that the communities tolerate each other. The trouble has come from the north, however, where the Muslim Hausa and Fulani dominate, though sizable Christian minorities exist. Ahmed Sani Yerima, governor of Zamfara state, was one of the culprits. His state adopted sharia law in its entirety in January 2000.[10] Other states began to follow suit despite the rioting and a ruling by the federal government that implementing sharia was unconstitutional. Now a total of eleven states have adopted parts of sharia law.

Christians in these states were dismayed. Although sharia law should not apply to them, the law has social provisions that in effect turn them into second-class citizens. Such provisions include separation of sexes in buses, clinics, and churches, and compulsory Muslim education in schools. And when one governor declared, "Only people with beards will win government contracts," the writing was clearly on the wall for all non-Muslims.

An extremist element is leading the push for sharia, backed by groups of organized thugs. It is thought that ten thousand Muslim mercenaries have been recruited from Niger and Chad to invade Christian villages. The violence is merciless. When Beatrice Agana heard of the riots on the streets of Kaduna, she rushed to school to pick up her son. She arrived only to hear his voice raised in terror. Muslim fanatics were surrounding him, and he was pleading with them to spare his life. As she ran toward him, a dagger blade flashed in the sunlight, and they butchered him in front of her eyes. "Kill me too," she screamed at them. They would have obliged if a military unit had not arrived and forced them to scatter.

More and more northern states seem determined to impose sharia, despite the chaos it brings. Christian leaders contend that its introduction is politically motivated, and they talk of a "hidden agenda" that uses sharia as a cloak to drive the Christian population out of the predominantly Muslim states. More than eight hundred churches were burned and twenty pastors martyred in 2000. Shocking riots erupted in September 2001 in Jos, leaving more than one thousand dead, and then in March of 2004 another dreadful conflict took place in the Christian majority Plateau state, with mobs killing fifteen hundred Christians and leaving 175 thousand displaced. There are now nine thousand Christian children orphaned by the fighting.

It may be fair to state that more Christian martyrdoms have occurred in northern Nigeria in recent years than in any other country in the world today. It is probably fair to say also that no other conflict has been so internationally ignored. Yet the situation only gets worse. Rebecca Kefas, from Yelwa, is a church worker who has survived three attacks from Islamic mobs. She says of the first time:

> About six o'clock in the morning, we heard the Islamists shouting, *"Allahu Akbar,"* the signal for fighting. Unknown to us, we were already surrounded. When the Christians began to run away, the Islamists told us to gather in the church where we would be safe. Shortly before seven o'clock, soldiers in fake uniforms arrived, then the Islamists climbed into the church premises and killed all the Christian men. By ten o'clock, all the church and surrounding buildings were destroyed and fifty people had been killed. I am a living witness to this.[11]

Another time during an attack, she hid in the church toilet. Peering out through a crack in the door, she saw three men from her congregation killed in front of her eyes. She was found by the attackers, who said, "We kill only men." She fled out of the church compound and managed to get into a car with seven other Christian men in it. The driver was shot with an arrow, and the car stopped. The Muslim mob dragged the driver from the car, gouging out his eyes. Rebecca was a "worthless woman" and again allowed to flee. Her last sight of the scene was to see petrol being poured over all the men, and they were burned to death.

Rebecca was fortunate, however. Many Muslim mobs do not spare women. Archbishop Peter Akinole, primate of the Anglican Church and president of the Christian Association of Nigeria (CAN) said, "How can anyone explain the reason for invading a church where women, children, and men were worshipping, asking them to surrender and lie face down, and then proceed to machete and axe them to death in their house of worship?"[12]

But the government does too little too late to stop the violence, and when the governor of Yobe state, Alhaji Bukar Abba Ibrahim, declares, "Civil war is an acceptable price to pay for the implementation of sharia," the outlook for the next five years looks bleak for Christians. Many fear that the Christians will have to organize defense militias in the future, taking the civil war to a new level. Still, the church grows. In the village of Bogoro all the men were slaughtered, including Pastor Bukar. His son saw his father slaughtered. When they came to kill the son, he received a machete cut to the head and fell flat, pretending to be dead. The only male survivor of the village, his first words were, "I must follow in my father's footsteps and become a pastor also."

### Eritrea

The fact that one of Africa's smallest countries contains the largest proven number of Christians in jail in the world must rank as the most surprising fact in the world of persecution today.[13] A staggering total of 1,778 Christians, including twenty-eight pastors, sit in jail here, some of them literally cooking to death in suffocating metal shipping containers parked in jungles.[14]

This situation is all the more surprising because this crackdown on Christians came out of the blue. Until May 2002 there was relatively little persecution in this impoverished land of 4.4 million people, who are virtually half Christian and half Muslim. For once, the sudden persecution had nothing to do with interreligious tension. Just what it is due to is still something of a mystery.

The facts are that the Eritrean government in May 2002 declared that any Christian who did not belong to the three approved denominations—Orthodox, Catholic, and Lutheran—should stop worshiping, register with the government, or face immediate arrest. Leaders of the twenty thousand or so evangelicals in Pentecostal or independent churches hastened to register but soon realized that the government had no intention of registering anyone, and the spate of jailings began.

A recent survey of arrests gives some idea of the crackdown. On December 31, 2004, sixty members of the Rhema Charismatic Church were arrested for having a New Year's Eve celebration in the pastor's home. On January 9, 2005, sixty-seven evangelicals were arrested during a wedding. On March 13 sixteen Christians were watching a teaching video in a home when police burst in, arresting them all. On March 22 Pastor Kidane Weldou was stopped while driving his pickup truck and arrested. No one knew for four days what had happened to him. On May 28 a Christian wedding was stopped and all 250 guests hauled off to the police station. Seventy guests were quickly released because they claimed to be either Orthodox, Lutheran, or Catholic. The remaining 180 remain in prison. Clearly, if you belong to a church that is independent, you cannot even meet in a home for prayer without being spied on and liable to arrest and detention.

Each time the arrested are told, "If you sign a pledge never to attend an unregistered meeting again, you will be released." Sadly, many do sign. Another sad feature is that the leaders of the approved denominations, with the exception of some Catholic leaders, have not used their voice to protest the treatment of their fellow Christians.

It's maddening that no one is actually told in specific terms what his or her crime is. Police lecture the prisoners, saying that they are "engaged in activities that the government does not approve" or that their worship is "a threat to national security." To date, no arrested Christian has been put on trial. They all are detained without charge.

The reason this campaign was launched is an object of speculation. Jonah Fisher, the BBC correspondent expelled from the country, said that the government seemed to be "afraid that people who consider their highest allegiance to be [to] God, at some point may not be patriotic and follow the state's instructions."[15] Others think that the targeting of nonconformist churches reflects a fear that these Christians have a propensity to refuse to serve in the military. But it could just be increasing paranoia among an essentially Marxist government that is resisting all calls for democracy. This seems confirmed by the fact that throughout 2005, Orthodox clerics also began to be jailed. Isayas Afewerki, president since independence in 1993, offered to hold elections in 1998 but never delivered. In the past three years, thousands of dissidents have been rounded up and jailed also without trial. Paranoia did seem to be a factor when Girma Asmeron, the Eritrean ambassador to the United States, called Pentecostal churches the Christian equivalent of Al-Qaeda in an interview with the Voice of America.

So the weary dance continues. The government refuses to admit that there is any persecution, while hundreds of Christians—including children and grandparents—suffer in dreadful prisons and camps. In these camps, they are brutalized by guards, forced to work arduous hours, fed only two pieces of bread weighing 80 grams a day, and when they are injured or sick, are told that the prison hospitals are "not for Christian prisoners."

Are you angry yet? Are you upset? Do you want to do something about all this? Hold on, we're only halfway through our persecution big dipper ride that bestrides the planet.

# 8 The Persecuted Church—Part Two

*Asia and the West*

## Christianity's Biggest Challenge of the Third Millennium

Asia was designated by Pope John Paul II as "the land of the coming millennium" in 2000 on a visit to India. He meant that the region would be the main focus for Christian mission activity for the next one thousand years. It's not hard to see why:

- Eighty-five percent of the world's non-Christians live in Asia. The first millennium saw the evangelization of Europe. The second saw the evangelization of the Americas and Africa. The third sees Asia as the final frontier. It's Asia's turn!

- Seventy-five percent of the world's population lives in Asia. The continent contains the world's only billion-population states—China and India. You can fit the entire populations of Africa and Latin America into China alone.

- Fifty percent of Asia's population is under twenty-five years old. Asia will go on to form an increasing percentage of the world's population, especially since the youth portion of Western societies is shrinking rapidly.

But behind the statistics lies another reason for Asia's missionary priority—embarrassment! Christianity has left barely a dent in the continent. Writes Dr. Saphir Athyal: "Though there was a Christian presence in Asia for two millennia, and there were active missionary efforts by the Roman Catholics for five centuries, and by Protestant missions for half that period . . . Christianity constitutes only about 7 percent of Asia's population."[1]

Christianity came to India as soon as it arrived in Europe in the first century. It arrived in China in the seventh century. Yet it never dislodged the established religions of Hinduism and Buddhism. If we define Asia as beginning east of Pakistan and traveling all the way to the Pacific, only the Philippines has a mainly Christian population.

Most Asian states are predominantly Buddhist, with the exception of India and Nepal, which are Hindu. Muslims are dominant in four states—Indonesia, Malaysia, Bangladesh, and the tiny Maldives islands. China remains an exception, since its religious proclivity is a unique blend of Daoism, Buddhism, and folk religion, although it's hard to know how much of the population still practices it.

Much has been written on the reasons Christianity has fared so poorly. Cardinal Jozef Tomko, prefect of the Congregation for the Evangelization of Peoples, answers this theologically: "It is, all told, the scandal of Christianity that grates on the cultures of Asia." Asians are used to universal religions and find it hard to relate to a faith that says there is one God and one way: His Son and no other.

Others tend to look to more historical factors, such as Christianity being seen as the colonizers' religion, especially when missionaries followed behind resented armies and administrations, little realizing that their message was tainted by association. Still more look at contemporary factors, pointing the finger in particular at Christianity's failure to stand with the poor of Asia, who constitute 99 percent of the continent.

Yet the mystery remains, as each reason falls short. Asians have embraced some absolute faiths and ideologies quite happily, just not Christianity. Communism is the main example. Then one has to realize that colonizers in many countries actually attempted to stop the missionaries from coming in. And the role of the other religions at articulating the voice of the poor is perhaps less impressive than the Christian one.

All we are left with is the fact that only one in thirteen people in Asia would describe themselves as Christian, as opposed to one in three in Africa, and three out of four in North America, and no one knows why!

It's not all bad news, of course. If the *World Churches Handbook* is right in estimating that just over fifty thousand people per day trust Christ, at least half of those new converts are from Asia.[2] Indeed, some argue that half of them are from China alone. Prior to that, Christianity's strongest revival took place in South Korea in the fifties. Christians now number nearly a third of the forty-seven million people in South Korea, sending more than ten thousand missionaries throughout the world. And even with the church being such a small percentage in Asia (3.5 percent), Asian Christians still constitute 10 percent of Christendom.

### Four Persecution Zones

Asia is very diverse, and to break the countries into blocs has limited usefulness. One can call India and Nepal the Hindu zone, but 130 million Muslims live in India—more than in any Middle Eastern state. Laos and Vietnam are predominantly Buddhist, but they are also ruled by Communist regimes. Should they be classified as part of the Communist or Buddhist bloc? Despite the obvious oversimplifications, a grouping of the Asia Pacific region into four "religious" zones may provide a useful insight into the nature of persecution in each zone.

#### THE BUDDHIST ZONE

The Buddhist zone includes Burma, also known as Myanmar (87 percent Buddhist), Bhutan (99.9 percent), Sri Lanka (70.3 percent), Cambodia (87 percent), and Thailand (94 percent), the countries where Buddhism holds sway over the bulk of the population. In fact, in Bhutan, Sri Lanka, and Thailand, it is the state religion.

In this zone Christians form small minorities in each society. They are at their largest in Sri Lanka (7.6 percent Christian of 19 million) and Burma (6.3 percent of 42 million). In the rest of the zone, they are 1 percent or less. In Bhutan, Christians number only a few score.

Sri Lanka, Bhutan, and Burma worry persecution watchers. It's not so much that Buddhism has a fundamentalist movement that attacks Christians for "sheep stealing," but local Buddhist priests will occasionally incite attacks against churches that are too successful in evangelism. Sometimes the state tries to stop the attacks, as in Sri Lanka; sometimes the state sponsors the attacks, as in Burma.

In Sri Lanka more than 120 churches in 2003 and 2004 were closed due to the intimidation of violent mobs, often led by Buddhist monks. These extremist monks are essentially nationalists who believe that a true Sri Lankan must be Buddhist. However, they cannot make blatant nationalism their rallying cry, so they use the "forced conversion" charge as a smoke screen. They have even moved into politics and extracted a promise from a government that should know better than to pass anti-conversion legislation. "Because we are Christians, we are accused of being foreigners . . . in our own land," says pastor Ajith Fernandez.

On the whole, though, Buddhism lacks a fundamentalist movement comparable to Islam. Extremists are not absent from the ranks of Buddhists, though they are not yet a force like their Islamic and Hindu cousins.

Perhaps Tibetan Buddhism is the only movement that has the potential to make life harsh for Christians. The image of toleration peddled by the Dalai Lama abroad is belied by life for Christians in Tibet, where Tibetan Buddhist leaders have committed some shocking atrocities against ethnic Tibetans who dare to become Christians.

### THE HINDU ZONE

Around thirty million Christians live among the one-billion-plus Hindus in India and Nepal, which makes it astonishing that Hindu

## From Riches to Rags

*The Story of Karim, a Teenager Who Left*
*an Opulent Lifestyle to Follow Christ*

An Indian teenager not unlike Karim

Before his conversion, Karim* says he was completely naive about the cost of his decision to follow Jesus. "I didn't know the difference between Islam and Christianity was so deep. I thought, because my father respects and loves me, if I said I wanted to become a Christian, he would just say, 'Okay.'"

Karim's father, a wealthy industrialist in India, provided a lavish lifestyle for his five children. The family lived in a twenty-two-room mansion with dozens of servants to cook, clean, and maintain gardens, a swimming pool, and a fleet of automobiles. Growing up, Karim enjoyed his own suite at home to entertain friends, one thousand dollars a month spending money, and frequent holidays with the family in Europe and the Persian Gulf.

When he was a teenager, Karim's life began to change. He tells the story while sitting cross-legged on the cement floor of his modest apartment:

> I was a sincere Muslim but not religious. One night I heard a voice saying, "Come and follow me." The next morning, I shared this with my father. "Maybe you could go to the Holy cities of Islam and spend some time," he said. So I did.
>
> I returned five to six months later and felt I had peace. But then I began to feel a restlessness building in me. This continued until 1992, when my car broke down three times in front of a church I used to pass every day.
>
> The third time it broke down, I walked into the church and told the pastor I wanted to know what he believed. I shared with him that I heard a voice saying, "Come to me and I will give you rest." He turned to Matthew 11:28 and asked me if it was the same voice or just similar. I read it again and again. It was exactly the same.
>
> He gave me a New Testament. "If you have any questions, you can come any time and ask them," he said.
>
> Things began to get tense between me and my family. I was always reading the New Testament and eventually told my father

that I was thinking of becoming a Christian. I showed him the book I was reading. He threw it away and said, "No more reading."

After a few months, I told the pastor that I wanted to become a follower of Christ. He said, "Okay, but you have to get permission from your father."

I asked my father for permission. He said, "You have to decide: either your family or your new religion. Choose one."

The struggle to make that decision lasted four or five months. I honestly didn't know what real life was about. The only thing I knew was that you could draw money from the bank whenever you wanted to buy whatever you wanted. But as I was reading through the New Testament, I started thinking about Matthew 6:33: "But seek first the kingdom of God and his righteousness, and all these things will be added unto you."

I went to my father and said I wanted to become a Christian.

He said, "You have to leave the house." So I packed all my possessions, including my bankbooks. When I was about to go, my father said, "Leave all these things here. You have no right to take anything with you."

It was another tough decision. But I felt something telling me, "It's okay; go ahead."

So I walked out with what I was wearing, one pair of pants and one shirt. I asked my father for ten rupees for bus fare.

I went to the church and told the pastor my story. He was shocked. He told me I should not have done what I did.

The next day I boarded a train to go live in an orphanage where some believers had a ministry to drug addicts. Each morning we would bring children in from the street, give them baths, and teach them to count or memorize the alphabet. We called it the Pavement Club.

I lived there for almost six months. I still had only the pants and shirt I wore when I left home. Whenever they needed laundering, I would take them off at night, wrap a bed sheet around myself, wash the clothes and hang them to dry until morning.

But you know what? I think the street kids were attracted to me because I wore the same clothes every day, like they did. In the six months I was there, the Pavement Club grew from 15 to 135 children.

Later I served in a church for some time, and they sent me to Bible college. Then I did rural missionary work for a year before entering seminary. I am now married. My wife and I both want to go to north India and start some kind of business, or whatever the Lord leads us to do, to bring people to Christ. That is our focus.

When asked if he misses the opulent lifestyle he left a decade ago to follow Christ, or if he thinks he might want to go back to it someday, Karim takes a moment to ponder his answer.

"Who can say? I'm only human," he shrugs. "But I don't think so. I'm getting along fine."

*Real name withheld by request.

extremists are so frightened of the church they persecute so fiercely. The 1990s were a hard decade for India's Christians, although for the four hundred thousand Nepalese Christians, the nineties were better than the eighties.

The main source of persecution in India comes from Hindu extremists, fanatics who have convinced themselves that the Hindu edifice is about to crumble because Christians have illegally converted lower caste and animistic tribes.

The fear has some basis in fact, as the lower castes (Dalits) are becoming very disenchanted with the oppressive elitism of Hinduism. But the argument that tribes have converted en masse to Christianity because of inducements is nonsense. Indeed, it is a remaining scandal under Indian law that when a low-caste Hindu becomes a Christian, he or she loses privileges, such as state educational assistance; whereas if a person becomes a Buddhist or Muslim, the privileges remain.

Many Christians in India face ongoing discrimination. In the case of a poor Christian, this can result in massive inconvenience. For example, in southern India, a Christian tribe was refused the right to use the well in the village where another, higher caste also lived. Water had to be drawn from a well eight miles away, and because so many of the tribe had to take this long walk, their ability to work was compromised. Some even died of starvation. But that kind of persecution rarely hits the headlines. It's too subtle and occurs in villages where forms of communication are primitive.

The main type of publicized persecution concerns atrocities perpetrated by Hindu extremists. These range from rapes of nuns; killings of missionaries, such as Australian Graham Staines; beatings; church burnings; intimidation; and general thuggery.

### THE COMMUNIST ZONE

Despite the fall of the Berlin Wall in 1989, millions of Asia's Christians still languish under an ideology that proved to be the greatest persecutor of the twentieth century—Communism.

In China more than sixty million Christians (6 percent of the population) face daily discrimination and pressure to register and come under invasive government control. In Vietnam the Christian Protestant community has rocketed up to 1.3 million (from 137 thousand in 1975), with 6.5 million Roman Catholics. In Laos, a tiny state of 4.5 million, Christians number barely 1.8 percent of the population. No one knows how many Christians are left in Stalinist North Korea, whose total population may have fallen from twenty-two to twenty million in recent years due to catastrophic floods and famine partially caused by agricultural mismanagement. Not surprisingly, estimates vary from ten thousand to a very wishful five hundred thousand for Christians left in this state.

Yet it is only in North Korea that the Stalinist model of persecution remains. As far as is known, the Korean Christian Federation—the only legal church in the country—is a complete farce. It's supposed to have ten thousand members, but visitors to Pyongyang in 2002 found the church closed on Easter Sunday. Whenever a service is held, visitors get the eerie feeling that the entire service is just an act.

Christians do exist in North Korea, since some escape into China across frozen rivers. They tell of very small house churches, organized along family lines but deep underground. Dreadful stories abound of scores of Christians in Auschwitz-type concentration camps, there for no reason other than their professed allegiance to Christ. They are even forbidden to look upward.

Mao is long dead, and the Chinese church may no longer produce martyrs by the dozen each year, but due to its size (sixty million plus), the Chinese church still remains the largest single persecuted community in the world. It is not the most persecuted, however. There are probably no more than a few hundred house church leaders in jail at any one time, and most of them are released after paying fines. Sentences are still handed out, though not with the same alacrity as in years past.

The legal printing of forty-six million Bibles since 1988 has greatly alleviated the Bible shortage in the cities, though some shortages remain in the rural areas. Relaxation of publishing laws has resulted in a spate of religious books going on sale in government bookstores. In the universities, it is "cool" to study Christianity, and young people pack the official churches in search of God.

Nevertheless, the government remains frightened of Christianity, especially of house churches that organize into networks without permission. A refusal to register is often taken as confirmation of being a cult. Most house churches in cities tend to cap their numbers between fifty and seventy; otherwise, they are forced to close and join local Three Self churches. The underground nature of these churches' existence makes the urgent task of discipling the two million–plus converts each year almost impossible. And the more organized they become, the more the government clamps down.

The official church offers some support at a local level, although its national leadership—handpicked for loyalty—see their job primarily as ensuring that overseas Christians believe there is no persecution continuing in China, thereby ensuring that overseas aid comes solely through official channels. Evangelism outside church premises is still forbidden.

As in China, the Protestant church in Vietnam has seen explosive growth under Communism, especially among the tribals of the central highlands who now constitute 75 percent of the evangelical total. They tend to bear the brunt of government hostility. Scores of evangelists remain in prison for their faith there.

In the more relaxed south of Vietnam, in Ho Chi Minh City, house churches face intermittent police harassment, as do congregations from the officially recognized Evangelical Church of Vietnam.

In Laos there are one hundred thousand evangelical believers, roughly half from the Khmu minority people. Persecution has been severe in certain areas, especially near Luang Prabang. Because of their mini-Christian revival, the object of the government's wrath has been the Khmu people. More than ten Khmu Christians are thought to be in prison, and many others have come under pressure to recant their faith. The Bru Christians in the south have also been hounded from village to village.

### The Muslim Zone

The predominantly Muslim countries are Indonesia (85 percent Muslim of 212 million), Bangladesh (87 percent of 140 million), Malaysia (55 percent of 22.5 million), Brunei (71 percent of 300 thousand), and the tiny Maldives, whose 248 thousand people are said to be 100 percent Muslim. It is the smallest and largest of these states that compels the attention of persecution watchers.

The Maldives may be an island paradise to some, but its sandy beaches and waving coconut palms mask a steely religious intolerance. President Gayoom declared on July 3, 2000, that the country was an Islam-only zone. There is a dark background to his remarks.

In 1998 the only known Maldivian Christians—about thirty of them—were rounded up and subjected to around-the-clock interrogation to recant their faith. Even President Gayoom visited them. Apparently, they all have "returned" to Islam.

The saddest feature of the whole saga was that one of the original Christian converts, a woman, was betrayed to the authorities by her twelve-year-old son. A week later, they all were in jail. Not even a campaign from some Christian organizations to stop tourists from visiting the Maldives could induce the country's leadership to admit their heavy-handedness.

In Indonesia, since the late nineties, the news has been dominated by gory headlines of ethnic Christians and Muslims massacring each other in the Maluku Islands. More than eight thousand have died from the conflict, which erupted in January 1999, leaving two hundred thousand refugees. Though the conflict has abated somewhat, relations between the two communities remain tense.

Muslim extremists in this vast state are especially frustrated because their political parties, which issue a call for Islamic law to be applied to all Indonesian Muslims, get resoundingly rejected at the polls. They have never been able to get more than 15 percent of the popular vote. Thus far Indonesia's leaders have held firm in refusing to countenance Islam as a state religion, and they preserve a studious neutrality between the various religions as required by a long-standing policy of *pancasila*, a vague unifying ideology that enjoins every citizen to espouse five principles—belief in one supreme God, humanism, nationalism, popular sovereignty, and social justice. Indonesia has always had powerful moderate Muslims, such as the cleric Abdurrahman Wahid, who was president from 1999 to 2001. These moderate voices defend a policy of religious tolerance and are most insistent that Islam should not become the state religion.

At the moment, most Muslims appear to agree. This comes as a great relief to the fifteen to twenty-five million Christians of Indonesia, who in many areas, especially on the island of Java, have experienced greater freedom in the post-Suharto era. But thirty years of dictatorship have left many old scores to settle, and though extremists are minorities, they are still numerous. As the Jakarta-based Jesuit expert, Franz Magnis-Suseno says, "Even if only 1 percent of the population are extremists, that's still an army of two million people." Indonesia will do well to keep religious and ethnic strife from derailing the progress of the largest Muslim-dominated liberal democracy in the world.

Two incidents in 2005 shook the Christians of Indonesia again. Three Christian housewives who ran a Sunday school were jailed for three years on September 1. A case had been brought against them by the Muslim Clerics Council when it became known that Muslim children were attending their Sunday school. Despite the women ensuring that permission was received from their parents, a troubling verdict—perhaps swayed by angry courtroom mobs—was handed down that they had violated the Child Protection Act, which prevents "deception, lies, or enticement" to cause a child to convert, even though no child had actually converted. Many Christians believe the Indonesian judiciary—especially after the Supreme Court rejected their appeal on February 7, 2006—has disgraced itself.

In October of 2005, Muslim militants in Poso, central Sulawesi, assaulted four teenage Christian girls walking on the street. Three of the girls were beheaded, and the heads were displayed in plastic bags with the message, "We will murder one hundred more Christian teenagers, and their heads will be presented as presents." To their credit, the Christian community has refused to be baited into violence, but the provocation could get even more savage in forthcoming years.

### Vulnerable Christians

Thus Asia's Christian community—despite staggering growth in many countries—remains an isolated minority. This minority status is what worries many persecution watchers.

Christians are vulnerable. In Indonesia, if militant Islam gets going, then Christians can do little to stop genocide from occurring. Said a pastor in Situbondo, when his church was burned in 1997, "We had literally nowhere to run, because the whole country is basically Islamic."

Even in China, where church growth has been astonishing, Christians number barely 6 percent in a sea of folk religion. In India Christians number less than 3 percent in a sea of Hinduism, and in smaller countries, such as the Maldives and Bhutan, they muster just a single struggling congregation or two.

The candle burns brightly, but the cave is vast and dark.

*Two to Watch*

CHINA

The world's longest continuous civilization continues to present a series of baffling paradoxes to the observer. This is the land run by the Communist Party that urges rampant capitalism on the populace, erecting posters that blare, "To Get Rich Is Glorious." Mao portraits and statues remain the focal point of many Chinese cities, but when dusk falls the most prominent sights are the glowing neon of McDonald's arches or the face of Colonel Sanders. There is more westernization and more nationalism, more unemployment and more prosperity, more repression and more openness than ever before.

Paradoxes also pile up when considering persecution. This is the country that welcomed Dr. Billy Graham in 1988 while at the same time arresting a house church leader known as "The Billy Graham of China," Xu Yongze. This is the land where an underground Catholic priest—Father Jiang Sunian—received a six-year sentence in 2000 for printing the Bible, while a vast printing press in Nanjing prints millions of Bibles each year. This is the place where the vast majority of believers worship underground, yet any visitor can worship freely with fellow Christians in open churches in the cities. And in March of 2005 the government adopted new regulations on religious affairs that issued an olive branch to house churches to register, yet followed that up on May 22 with the largest mass arrest of house-church workers in recent years, detaining six hundred Christians in Changchun, Jilin Province. The future scenario is probably also paradoxical; there will be more freedom and more persecution in China in the next few years!

No one can ignore China. It will join America as a world super-power in the twenty-first century for certain. In 2010 its economy will be the world's largest in GNP terms. Its domestic market of three hundred million households already is. Its Christian community is already the world's second largest, at sixty-nine million, according to *Operation World*.[3] So rapid is the expansion of Christian belief in this country, especially among the educated and political elite, that David Aikman, in his book *Jesus in Beijing,* was moved to claim in 2003 that "it is possible that Christians will constitute 20 to 30 percent of China's population within three decades."[4] This could result, he adds, in the incalculable blessing of China becoming a superpower operating out of a Christian worldview. Aikman is shrewd enough to balance this speculation by noting that China could also be an aggressive global menace.

The Chinese revival is still under forty years old, but it is the larg-est and longest in the history of Christendom. In 1949 when Mao took power, there were three million Catholics and seven hundred thousand Protestants. They were soon to be put through the fire, as Mao's Cultural Revolution swept all institutional vestiges away. Yet out of this crucible of suffering, during which thousands of Chris-tians died, the church resurrected from the late seventies so that there are thought to be as many as eighty million Christians today.[5] More than eighteen million Protestants and five million Catholics belong to their respective state churches, but tens of millions more Protestants and at least ten million Catholics keep their distance, organizing in so-called house churches, determined to stay clear of the state. The more organized house churches, and especially those with outside links, face continual harassment from the government. This rarely results in martyrdoms, though police brutality has con-tributed to a number of deaths in custody. Arrests of leaders run in the hundreds each year, though most are fined and held only for short periods. Those guilty of underground printing of religious materials, however, do tend to be tried and sentenced.

## Double Persecution

*The Story of Mamat, a Young Uygur Christian*

Many young Uygur Christians face double persecution—first from family and religious leaders when they abandon the Muslim faith; and then from the Chinese government, which sees the Uygur minority as a dangerous separatist group. *Note*: for security reasons, the face of Mamat cannot be shown; the young man in the photo is another Uygur from Xinjiang Province.

"That will be Mamat now," Helen said when she heard the faint knock on the door of the apartment. Moments later she led him into the room. The twentysomething young man in gray trousers and a brown knitted sweater was twisting his Uygur (pronounced WEE-ger) cap in his hands as he entered.

Helen led him to a seat and offered him tea. "English or Chinese?"

"Oh, may I try English tea?" he asked very gently, still twisting the cap in his hands. He knew very well that if he was discovered sitting in the apartment of a foreign Christian, the consequences could be serious. Yet he was willing to meet with us and share his experience of life as a Muslim convert in one of the most restricted parts of China.

Mamat was from a Muslim family. His two brothers would always join the older men in the house on prayer mats as the Muslim call to prayer rang out through the streets. Mamat said in those days he was eager to defend Islam. He would often hit his sister if her skirts were too short or if she went out with boys without supervision.

When he was seventeen years old, a friend gave him a tape to listen to. Mamat took it home, popped it in the stereo that was on the family's mantelpiece, and listened, only to discover that the tape was political, urging Uygurs to rise up against the government and declare an independent homeland. He listened to the tape out of loyalty to his friend but didn't agree with the opinions expressed.

Just a few days later, officers from China's Public Security Bureau arrested the friend who had given him the tape. Ten days later, they arrested Mamat. At the police station Mamat was put through an interrogation. "Yes, I did listen to the tape," he told them, "but I didn't understand it. Please forgive me. I won't do it again!" But in spite of his pleas of innocence, he was charged and sentenced to forty days in prison.

He was thrown into a concrete cell crowded with twenty men. Conditions were very sparse, with thin mats on the cement floors for bedding. The men were fed water and steamed bread for breakfast, water at lunchtime, and another piece of steamed bread for their evening meal. Mamat soon felt weak and dizzy when he tried to stand up.

Most of the men in that room were hardened criminals, but they became very devout once they entered the prison. As the call to prayer rang out over the city, they would kneel and pray, touching their heads to the floor, as if pleading with Allah for deliverance. Mamat remembers watching them, thinking about the hypocrisy of their actions, knowing that these men would return to a life of crime as soon as they were released.

After his release, Mamat knelt every day on his prayer mat at work. However, the prison experience had stirred his heart. He hungered for something more than the ritual of those empty prayers.

Every couple of months after that, Mamat was called into the police station and asked to sign a form declaring that he was no longer attending the mosque. The Chinese authorities were doing their best to stamp out the Muslim faith, along with Christianity.

Eventually Mamat quit his job at the factory and moved to a university in a large city in China where he hoped to study English. At the university a classmate shared the story of Jesus with him. He listened, again out of politeness, remembering a time when another "political" message not popular with the Chinese government had landed him in prison.

There was a strong pull in these new stories about a God-man named Jesus, so eventually Mamat agreed to go along to a restaurant and meet a foreigner who was sharing the Jesus story with a small group of Chinese students.

At that meeting the foreigner invited Mamat to meet with him at his home once a week to read and discuss the Bible. Mamat was so hungry for truth that he agreed. He met faithfully with the teacher for a full year, touched by his faithfulness and friendship. Nevertheless, Mamat was fully aware that a commitment to this new religion would bring almost unbearable changes to his life.

During that year, Mamat studied the history of the Uygur people and realized to his surprise that Islam was not their original faith. He had heard of the Swedish missionary martyrs of the 1930s and the first Uygur converts who were martyred along with them. Those stories were in the Uygur history books, but he had never paid much attention to them. He also knew about Jesus, because he was taught as a child that Jesus was a prophet, albeit an obviously lesser prophet than Muhammad.

Finally, Mamat realized that if people had believed in Jesus for two thousand years, and if Jesus had that much influence throughout history, then the message of the gospel must be true. After twelve months of deep soul-searching, he committed his life to Christ.

At the time, he was sharing a dormitory with five other young men, all of them Uygurs. The foreign Christian had given him a partial translation of the Uygur Bible, which he kept hidden under his pillow. He would bring it out at night when nobody else was in the room. He also had one or two other small teaching books in Uygur that explained the basic principles of the Christian faith.

Then one or two of his fellow students saw him reading the Bible and asked questions. The problem is, they were very difficult questions, ones for which Mamat had no answers.

As we sat drinking English tea (Mamat seemed to like it), we gave him a book in Uygur that answered questions on faith. As he leafed through its pages, Mamat's face lit up. "This book is exactly what I needed," he told us, "a real answer to prayer!"

Uygur Christians face double persecution. They are persecuted by their Muslim families, neighbors, and imams (religious leaders) who believe conversion to another faith is a rejection of the Uygur culture and everything it stands for.

Persecution comes from the Chinese government, as well. Authorities are wary of the Uygur people because of their drive for an independent homeland in northwest China. A Uygur who becomes a Christian is immediately marked as a double traitor to the People's Republic. Combine religion and the cry for human rights and you have an enemy that must be subdued.

Knowing the risks, Mamat continues to share his faith with his fellow students. A few months ago he started an English conversational group that meets in a tea shop outside the university. There they discuss the issues of faith and the meaning of life, often reading passages from the Bible.

That day over our cups of English tea, Mamat asked us to pray for wisdom for the future. Life back in his hometown is very difficult because his friends remain true to Islam and don't understand why Mamat no longer attends prayers at the mosque. He feels safer in a large city, where he is no longer under the constant scrutiny of local officials.

Mamat says that many of the Uygur people became disillusioned with Islam after the September 11, 2001, terrorist attacks and are now searching for answers elsewhere. His prayer is that God will show him the way to reach his own people.

The Uygurs are searching for an earthly kingdom. What better solution to their search than to point them to a heavenly kingdom that will answer every cry of their hearts!

Four crises unite to create increasing tension between the church and the government of China. The first two crises are in the culture at large; the second two have to do with the churches specifically.

The first two are the *political legitimacy crisis* and the *social instability crisis.*

The *political legitimacy crisis* affects the government itself. At some point it is going to look absurd to everyone (if it does not already) that a government consisting of a Communist Party with an ideology requiring a planned economy is directing an economic revolution toward a market, capitalist economy. The clichés of ideology that are still in place will wear increasingly thin, and the government must reinvent itself to stay in power.

The upshot is that the Communist Party as an institution will become increasingly insecure, and this is dangerous to anyone who falls outside government control. Paranoia will increase, and Protestant house-church believers must be major targets, since they constitute the largest "underground" group in the country.

As a Shanghai pastor explains: "We are the objects of great suspicion by the government simply because we keep our distance from them. To stay clear is to show dissent in this country, and so they come after you. The only way to be left alone is to join them and pretend to go along with them. But we will not play such games."

Feeding this insecurity will be a *social instability crisis.* China joined the World Trade Organization (WTO) in 2000, and the social ramifications of this are enormous. More than 50 million workers from heavy industry are being laid off, and 100 million peasants currently on the land will lose their incomes, joining the 150 million migrant workers already on the move from village to town. In other words, China may have an internally displaced population of more than 300 million in the next ten years. The potential for social chaos is high.

Managing the fastest and largest industrialization in human history is bound to stretch the resources of the Communist Party. Even now the threat of urban terrorism from disaffected workers is high, with bombings of factories on the rise.

As these twin crises develop in the culture, the house-church movements will react to them. Many house-church leaders anticipate a *new discipleship crisis*, which will come as a result of the social instability crisis.

Urban and rural house-church movements are consciously targeting the migrant population, and although evangelization efforts are just beginning, they are finding the migrants a receptive group. Some leaders now talk of a "second convert boom," where the numbers of Christians explode like they did in the 1980s.

Certainly there seems little doubt that refugee populations are more susceptible to embracing new religious beliefs, especially as they are insecure in a new environment and newly able to differentiate themselves from the beliefs of their old environment. But this "boom" in convert numbers will reinforce the existing discipleship crisis, which was defined by a leader of a house-church network in Henan Province as "when people become Christians at such a rate that it overwhelms the ability of the church to disciple them adequately in the faith."

The persecution implications are these. If the house church booms again, then its profile rises higher and higher, threatening an already insecure government by the sheer scale of its numbers.

Furthermore, to cope with the need to disciple the new converts, house-church movements will seek greater assistance from the Western churches, especially in requesting more teachers to come and help. And since the government criminalizes the offering of outside help to the house churches, much of this assistance will have to be illegal. Thus we can expect more training seminars to be broken up by police, more deportations of foreign teachers, and more arrests of local leaders.

The fourth crisis is a *social involvement crisis*. As Chinese society gets more unstable and as social needs become more glaring, we will begin to see the house-church millions develop a social consciousness.

Already there are indications from the leaders of the larger network house-church movements that they wish they had more theological input in the area of how to get involved in meeting society's needs. Traditionally house churches have kept clear of any social work, since the government has claimed a monopoly on such action. But as the potential for social chaos grows, and a larger and larger underclass emerges from the breakneck speed of capitalism, house churches will feel an increasing responsibility to get involved.

In Lanzhou there is a house church of thirty-two individuals who became concerned about the number of AIDS sufferers in their city. At first they welcomed a couple and cared for their needs, but about a year ago the leader of the group said, "We have to tackle the roots of this problem—there are hundreds of AIDS sufferers here, and we cannot help them unless we build up some expertise in caring and assist at a policy level."

Three of the house-church members were doctors, and they offered their services free to a government agency. The official who received them was grateful but cautious. He said, "If you are all Christians, then we need a clear understanding of what you are allowed to do and what you are not." The negotiations are still continuing a year later.

These Christians are not finding it easy to deal suddenly with government agencies after years of keeping clear, nor are they sure how their faith allows them to care at this macro level. For example, should they sanction the dispensing of condoms?

A sharper edge to this scenario may come from the more intellectual house churches in the big cities. Already one group in Beijing is talking of organizing workers' unions. This would bring a swift clash with government forces. Also as the WTO reforms take effect, new professional castes will emerge, creating new identities. For example, some will see themselves as "Christian lawyers" or "Christian economists," and entirely new networks of influence could be created.

At the moment, however, it would be wrong to say that the house churches are all anxiously discussing ways to get more socially involved. But the trickle of concern in this area may become a flood, especially if Chinese society at the grassroots level starts to unravel.

It will lead to a clash with the government. Says a high-ranking leader with the Little Flock house-church movement in Fuchou:

"There are two things the government fears with the house churches: one, that they unite and become a solid bloc of influence; two, that they become politically active and begin to affect the social system."

These four crises can be viewed as four corners of a box pulling in toward the center, shrinking the space and bringing an insecure government, an unraveling social system, an expanding house church, and a socially awakening house church into what may be a deadly proximity. It does not have to happen this way. Government policy could relax. The house churches may not experience the expected surge in convert numbers. But based on present evidence, the convergence of these crises seems to be a more than likely scenario.

It would be a mistake to pretend that all persecution comes from the state and can be eliminated. A Chinese Christian is often more likely to experience persecution from a family member or a bigoted folk religion priest than from a state official. Indeed, on a recent trip, I counted five arrests and no less than thirty-six instances of Christian women being badly beaten by non-Christian husbands on hearing of their conversion. So even if government policy becomes more tolerant, persecution will remain a phenomenon, since there is an "eternal term" in view, according to many of China's Bible teachers, in which the "world" is opposed to Christ, an antagonism that will never recede.

Thus persecution will recede, intensify, and always remain! Another puzzle worthy of the world's most complicated culture!

### Sri Lanka

It is far too easy to close down a church in Sri Lanka today. On Saturday, August 6, 2005, the pastor of the Four Square Gospel Church in a village called Horana, Kalutara district, was informed that a mob, which had disrupted his service the previous Sunday, was intending to do the same the next day. The pastor requested police protection. It never came, but the mob did—fifty of them, led by a Buddhist monk. They demanded that the twelve believers leave the church and never return.

The situation began to get worse, and the pastor called the police station. The police came and let both sides talk. The Buddhist monk

## We Have Gone through This Because of Christ

*Prema, a Young Evangelist in Sri Lanka, Demonstrates the Meaning of Faith under Fire*

Prema

Prema's smile was genuine, but beneath the sparkling eyes her heart was heavy. The friends who introduced us drew us aside and said that she seemed discouraged that day, not quite herself.

Because of death threats, the young evangelist has been forced to abandon any work during daylight hours. Prema meets under cover of darkness with small groups of "baby" believers who sing and pray in whispers to avoid being overheard.

She customarily arrives for meetings sometime after 9:00 p.m., along with others who trickle in by ones and twos. They typically spend time in prayer and worship before sharing a meal, then reconvene in the early hours of the morning for Bible study. After the believers slip away into the night, Prema will sleep for a few hours and leave before dawn to avoid being seen by hostile neighbors.

The call to share the message, which changed her life when she was thirteen years old, still burns in her heart.

Prema recalled the day when her aunt, a former Buddhist, became a Christian and rushed over to share the news with Prema and her younger brother.

"At first when I heard about Jesus, I wasn't that interested," Prema admitted. "But at that time I was very sick, and when my aunt prayed for me, I was healed. So I knew she had found something real."

Her Buddhist parents were not impressed when she accepted Christ, but after observing the change in her life, the whole family became Christians, one by one, over the next eight years. No church existed in the village, so they attended a service held in a school once every three months. It was barely enough to feed their hunger for teaching and fellowship with other Christians.

The force of that hunger led Prema to become an evangelist. When she finished secondary school, she enrolled at a Bible college in a nearby city. She graduated in 2000 and felt strongly that God had called her to take the gospel of Jesus to a certain area of the country she had often visited with a friend from Bible school.

The two of them rented a room in a private house and began knocking on doors. Six or seven new converts were soon meeting in Prema's room for weekly Bible study and prayer.

When the monks at the local Buddhist temple discovered what was happening, they were furious.

"One night two young men came to the door and asked us to go with them to a meeting," Prema explained. "We were made to sit on a mat on the floor while the monks scolded us. We didn't feel any fear. But they also called the house owner to the meeting and asked her to stop renting the room to us."

This happened several times over the next year. Each time that the girls established a small group of new believers in a new village, they were evicted and forced to find new lodgings.

Prema remembers a Buddhist festival day in 2001 when they were once again made to move to a new village. Undaunted, they were soon holding services in the kitchen of their rented house with thirty-three believers in attendance. The kitchen was so small that people sat in the cupboards! Prema asked permission from the landlord to build a small thatched shelter outside the house for meetings.

A neighbor who became a Christian gave Prema the keys to her house when she left town. In late 2003 the girls moved into the house and spent the next two days building a fence around a small plot of land nearby. They had managed to raise enough money to purchase the lot and hoped to build a house and church of their own on it.

It didn't take long for news to reach the ears of the local Buddhist monks. On the second day one of the monks came and warned them to leave the area, "or else." The girls lodged a complaint with the police and kept building the fence.

That night as they went to bed, Prema warned the others not to change into their nightclothes. She had a feeling that something unusual might happen. They went to bed, exhausted from two days of hard physical labor, but awoke not long afterward to loud shouts. They watched a mob of thirty people break down the fence they had just built.

"The moonlight was very bright that night, so they had no torches, but they were carrying things in their hands to break the fence," said Prema.

The crowd then rushed the house.

"My immediate thought was, *Lord, you have to look after us,*" Prema said. "One of the girls hid under the bed. The other girl couldn't fit, so I covered her with my body. Then the crowd broke the doors and came in shouting, using dirty language. They were calling us prostitutes, threatening to kill us.

"Eventually a man found me in the dark. I struggled with him and managed to stand up. The girl under the bed kept quiet, but when I was caught, she began to scream. Then the men caught the other girl who was with me. I think God gave me supernatural strength, because I dragged some people to the door and tried to push them out. But they hit me with their fists."

Prema was silent for a moment before adding, "I want to thank God that He protected us. None of us were harmed. We really felt the presence of God with us. I can't describe it."

The crowd dragged the girls outside, forced them onto their knees, and ordered them to repeat the words "Buddha is Lord."

"But of course we couldn't do it," Prema said. "Instead, we got up and sat on the fence posts, which they had torn down. I remembered the story of Shadrach, Meshach, and Abednego in the Bible, and how they stood firm when they were persecuted, so I didn't give in."

The mob dragged the girls down the road into the center of the village, kicking and punching them violently until they arrived at the police station. All three girls were held overnight and released the following morning. Prema was immediately taken to the hospital for treatment.

The monks mounted a poster campaign, warning villagers to report to authorities if the girls came back to the village. The new believers received anonymous letters warning them that if they continued to follow Jesus, they would "lose their arms and legs."

But Prema refuses to give up. "I'm convinced that God called me to this area. If this is God's will, I am willing to sacrifice my life, although not foolishly.

"Now I go to visit believers in several villages after it is dark. We have only a few people gather at one time, and after going to one place, I don't go back there for several weeks."

What are Prema's feelings toward God after these hardships?

"I know He is close to me, but in reality I don't know what to do. These days I am going through a sorrowful time because I can't spend time with the believers. But one good thing has happened. For a long time we prayed for the salvation of people in this area. Because of this trouble, now most of them know what we believe. They know we have gone through this because of Christ."

Prema's new plan is to establish a church in a larger town close to the villages where she has gathered cells of new believers. Her prayer request is for them. "Please pray that God will allow us to meet together again, and please pray that the believers will stand firm."

claimed that Christians had no right to start a church in a village that was 99 percent Buddhist. The Christians claimed a constitutional right to freedom of worship. The inspector of police listened, then ruled that since a disturbance of the peace had already occurred, the pastor was to stop meeting for worship.

How clever, and how unjust! The mob had come and created the disturbance of the peace, but the police saw the source of the disturbance as the existence of the church that provoked the mob. The police want things stable and will take the path of least resistance. "Close the church down for now. Sure you have your rights, but in the present climate, it's just unwise," they often say. As we have seen, mobs triumph when the police fail to stand up for the law.

The problem is that in the past few years, the police have been failing to stand up for the law more often than not, reflecting a new attitude in Sri Lankan culture that Christians are troublemakers who should be repressed. This island paradise off the southern tip of India is well-known for its dreadful civil war, which has claimed sixty thousand lives since the 1960s, as the northern Hindu Tamil Tigers battle against the majority Sinhala Buddhists for autonomy.

In the last decade, nationalism and Buddhism have fused spectacularly. To be a true Sri Lankan, they argue, you must be a Sinhala Buddhist. Christians, who number 8 percent (7 percent Catholic and 1 percent Protestant) of the nineteen million population, are in the firing line because they refuse to construct their religion along racial lines, and they draw converts from both the Hindu Tamils and Sinhala Buddhists. There is also an economic dimension. Most new churches are planted in villages where an offering is often given to the local Buddhist priests. Christians no longer give this gift, resulting in a loss of status and resources for the Buddhist priest.

Extremist Buddhists began to organize in the late nineties, and taking their cue from the tactics of India's Hindu extremists, soon launched a propaganda offensive portraying the Christian community as an enemy of Sri Lankan culture who were growing through "unethical conversions." The lies are blatant. The *Buddhist Times* reported the work of World Vision under the headline: "Buddhist Children on Christian Auction Block." At a conference of the

Evangelical Alliance in September 2004, Buddhist monks claimed that "Christian fundamentalists were offering Rs. [rupees] 25,000 to convert." They claim that Christians promote pornography, support the Tamil terrorists, and desecrate Buddhist holy sites.

Their hate campaign moved into high gear in December 2003, when a popular Buddhist monk, Ven. Soma Thero, died of a heart attack on a visit to Russia. Despite a postmortem confirming heart failure, a media and poster campaign was launched claiming Christians had murdered the monk. Religious riots erupted throughout the country. That Christmas, twenty churches were attacked or torched. The hate wave was exploited by the extremists' newly formed political party, the Jathika Hela Urumaya (JHU), which won nine parliamentary seats in 2004 and lost no time drafting the "Prohibition of Forcible Conversion" bill. The government is running scared of the Buddhist extremists and is set to cave in to their demands. The bill, if passed, will result in "legalized discrimination" against Christians, according to Evangelical Alliance leader Godfrey Yogarajah.

Yet the church grows not just in spite of, but often because of, the persecution. Perhaps if the Buddhist extremists were to meet one woman, Sister Lalani, they would realize how hopeless their cause was. Sister Lalani is the widow of Pastor Lionel Jayasinghe, shot to death before her eyes while she was cooking dinner on March 25, 1988. He was a former Buddhist monk and had started a church in the deep south of Sri Lanka in the village of Tissamaharma. A cross marks his grave. At the time it was placed there, it was the only cross in an area of fifty square miles, inhabited by nearly a million people famed for their resistance to the gospel.

His wife was counseled to leave the village. She came back from the funeral and said, "I will take up where he left off." She never wiped off the stains of her husband's blood from the walls of her home. She said, "Every time I see them, each stain gives me courage to stay on and continue the vision for which he gave his life."

So Sister Lalani has continued the work while raising their one-year-old child. She has been issued death threats. The church was set on fire, destroying the roof. Five bombs were placed in the church, but most did not go off. Her house was continually surrounded by mobs and stoned, often throughout the night.

She stayed. Now the church has three hundred believers, and there are a thousand more believers in the surrounding areas. In a region utterly unevangelized before, this woman has planted literally scores of churches in the face of the most vicious opposition.

The God of Sister Lalani has glorified His name, and although more persecution appears on the way for Sri Lanka's Christians, so too does more fruit.

## The West

"Come over to [Europe] and help us," pleaded the Christian in the apostle Paul's dream (Acts 16:9). Paul heard the cry, and Europe became the crucible of Christianity and the most influential continent on the globe. But now, the "glory has departed," as Europe's churches empty out and in the West generally the Christian worldview is in high retreat. As an African Christian said recently, "The world church is having a feast, but the West hasn't turned up at the table." Philip Yancey offers a stark observation: "God goes where he's wanted."

Why is God not wanted in the West anymore? No one quite knows, but the facts are that not just in Europe but in the entire West, churches are hemorrhaging members. Throughout Europe, Canada, Australia, and New Zealand, church influence, membership, and attendance have been in sharp decline for several decades. In the fifty-two countries of Europe (including Russia) with a combined population of 729.8 million in 2000, 71 percent identify themselves as Christian, yet less than 10 percent in most countries attend a church regularly. In other words, there are possibly more people worshiping on a Sunday morning in China than in the whole of Europe!

The decline is worrying enough; the rate of decline is more alarming still. Since the end of the Second World War, church attendance has roughly halved, and the under-thirty generation is hardly bothering with church at all. In England, for example, in

1979, 5.4 million people attended church. By 1998 that number had fallen to 3.7 million—a decline of 35 percent, and that during a time when the population increased by 5 million. Future projections are also bleak. A Christian Research Report for the UK released in September 2005 predicted that the church would shrink by a further two-thirds by 2040. Average churchgoers would be in their sixties and seventies, and older denominations, such as the Church of Scotland, could disappear entirely. Even in the United States, which has bucked this trend with church attendance remaining fairly constant at between 30 to 40 percent of the population, there is no room for complacency as the mainline churches also have lost 50 percent of their members (offset by the growth of the new churches) and, like Europe, find the younger generation exhibiting a determined indifference to church life.

Behind the dire statistics, of course, it is not all doom and gloom. Perhaps the decline of institutionalized forms of Christianity and the departure of nominal Christians are not bad things for a kingdom that is generally repressed rather than expressed by plodding, moribund institutions. Others point to the paradox that although *belonging* to churches has declined, *believing* in Christian or spiritual truth has not. In Western Europe, where 29 percent say they attend a church once a week, 70 percent say they believe in God, 57 percent in the concept of sin, and 33 percent in the resurrection of the dead. Yet the "believing without belonging" brigade seems to exhibit a spiritual openness that indiscriminately embraces all types of religious truth, such as New Age, and happily uncouple religious experience from moral responsibility. One wonders whether it is really just selfishness with religious tinges.

Europe is unquestionably the West's center of gravity, at least historically, since America was a product of European events. Religiously speaking, Europe divides into three zones: an Orthodox east, a Catholic south, and a Protestant north. The Orthodox east came into being in the eighth century when Russia embraced the Orthodox faith, and countries like Romania, Bulgaria, and Greece followed suit. The Catholic-Protestant divide occurred as a result of Martin Luther's actions on October 31, 1517, when he nailed ninety-five theses attacking the corruption of the Catholic Church on a church door in Wittenberg, Germany. Generally speaking, the southern states, such as Italy, Spain, Portugal, and France, stayed Catholic, and more northern countries, such as Britain, the Netherlands, and the Scandinavian lands, became more Protestant (the exceptions being Ireland and Poland). These three divides are still there, though in some countries, Catholic and Protestant communities have become equally significant, such as in Holland, Britain, Hungary, and Germany.

This tale of division is, unfortunately, the place to begin the story of persecution. An American Catholic commentator, looking at Europe, marveled in 2004: "European man has convinced himself that in order to be modern and free, he must be radically secular."[6] There is a very simple reason for this—in Europe freedom and peace were attained only by banishing religion from the public sphere.

While the Reformation aimed to bring spiritual renewal to the church, in reality it brought a hundred years of needless, pointless, bloody warfare between Catholic and Protestant states. Finally, in the mid-seventeenth century, exhausted from the fighting, European leaders decided that the only way forward to ensure peace was to emancipate the culture from the shackles of religion. In an intellectual period called the Enlightenment, which sought to replace religion with reason, faith became privatized, where it could no longer start wars between states. In a sense, the church deserved it. And even today, it is still paying the price. Among many European politicians, their secularism runs deep, and they assume automatically that personal liberation exists in proportion to the distance gained from institutional Christianity.

America was different. Sociologist of religion Grace Davie attempts to distill it:

> In Europe, and particularly in France, the Enlightenment became a movement interpreted as freedom from religion . . . if you like, from the benighted nature of religious views. If you look at the American Enlightenment, this is entirely different. Instead of freedom from belief, in America the Enlightenment has mutated into a freedom to believe.[7]

Indeed, the whole country was born out of the desire for religious tolerance. It dates back to 1534, when Henry VIII decreed England was henceforth Protestant. This pleased some Puritans, who continued to work for the demotion of what they felt was Catholic ritual and doctrine in the new church. But a more radical group of Puritans held that this reform agenda was doomed to failure. They became separatists, even teaching that the monarch could not be the head of the church. This was sedition in the sixteenth century, and eventually in 1620 they set sail for North America on the Mayflower. Not that they were models of tolerance when they landed. New England Puritans drove all other types of Christians away and even put the Quaker missionary Mary Dyer to death in Boston in 1660. It fell to Baptists like Roger Williams and Quakers like William Penn to give to the colonies a distinctive doctrine of the radical reformation—in contrast to Europe—namely, the separation of church and state. And so in the United States of America, at least until recently, the state's studied position of neutrality in religion was not seen as a mandate to hound religion out of public life.

## Marginalization of Christianity

Despite the differences, both American and European cultures share the same two problems that led to the marginalization of Christianity in the West.

### A PRIVATE AFFAIR

The idea that religion is a private affair is a two-hundred-year-old problem. Ironically, a devout Christian, the British philosopher John Locke (1632–1704), gave us the idea. Although he succeeded in doing much to bring tolerance to the West, he also left us an unfortunate distinction that has remained part of the fabric of religious tolerance ever since. Locke said that religion was "a public irrelevance." Religion had to do with the state of one's individual soul and one's future in heaven, he taught. As such, it had no connection to social life. The advantage was that the state was henceforth forbidden to interfere with religion in this private sphere.

The disadvantage was that the state got control over public life. The privatization of religion had begun.

The simple fact was that Locke did not understand the true nature of belief, let alone religion. Any belief always finds its way into action whether religious or not. We are social creatures, and our interactions with others are always governed by our values and beliefs. Eventually all private beliefs have a public expression, so long as we leave our houses in the morning. But if Christians are forbidden to express their faith in the social realm, all that means is that the public square is controlled by those of different beliefs who are not excluded, namely, the secularists.

To be fair, Locke had no idea that over time, religion would be eased out of the public square through the exploitation of this loophole. But it results today in a devout Catholic cabinet minister in the United Kingdom declaring, "I have a private spiritual life and I have a faith. It is a private spiritual life and I don't think it is relevant to my job."[8] This was Ruth Kelly. Her job? The education secretary. How on earth can her Christian faith *not* be relevant to the education of a nation's children? The tragedy is that even Christians have bought into this bogus distinction, and they hide their faith.

### A MATTER OF TASTE

If the two-hundred-year-old problem *privatizes* religion as a result of the toleration revolution, a fifty-year-old problem *relativizes* religion as a result of the human rights revolution. This makes faith a matter of taste.

Again, this revolution started well and continues to have beneficial effects. The aftermath of the Second World War saw the founding of the United Nations and the drafting of charters protecting individuals from the expansion of state power in everyday life. Human rights has now become the dominant language of political discourse in the West. However, the human rights revolution has evolved alongside pluralistic and postmodern cultures, which have removed the moral underpinnings of individual rights. At a recent human rights conference, I was trying to argue that Christianity was a contributor to the modern notion of tolerance. A friend from Amnesty International took me aside and said, "You don't get it do you?" When I looked puzzled, he said, "There is no rational discourse anymore. The group that shouts the loudest and organizes the best gets the rights. That's how the game works."

What is not realized is that human rights is a zero sum game. Harvard Law professor Mary Ann Glendon exposes the shallowness of this approach:

> A tendency to frame nearly every social controversy in terms of a clash of rights (a woman's right to her own body vs. a fetus's right to life) impedes compromise, mutual understanding, and the discovery of common ground. A penchant for absolute formulations ("I have the right to do whatever I want with my property") promotes unrealistic expectations and ignores both social costs and the rights of others.[9]

This impacts religion. If the pro-gay lobby is successful, then, for example, the Roman Catholic Church can be found in breach of a person's sexual human rights because of that institution's unwillingness to ordain practicing homosexuals to the clergy.

The negative tendencies of both these revolutions have provoked a civilization crisis in the West that, so far, only its prophets have exposed. Two of these prophets are former White House aide turned Christian Charles Colson and the Russian novelist Aleksandr Solzhenitsyn. Colson points out that belief is no longer truth but "your private belief." Truth has lost its absolute dimension to undergird and guide society. He writes:

> If truth is merely private, then trying to convince others of one's opinion is seen as a power play—an attempt to impose one's private morality onto someone else. And once people make up their minds that it is merely a power issue, then why even bother trying to persuade others? The only thing left is force. That's why the watershed issue of our day is truth—the biblical teaching that truth is not private but transcendent and deeply rooted in ultimate reality . . . the casualty [if Christians do not succeed in making this clear] will be America's democratic freedom.[10]

Solzhenitsyn takes this a step further. If the average Westerner has no moral reason to be good, then all that is left to keep a person good is the law. Westerners have reduced morality to keeping on the right side of the law. But laws, says Solzhenitsyn, have to be observed with a certain spirit that makes them effective. Take that moral spirit away, and all you have left is a barren legalism that will try to get away with any behavior that does not land you in jail. As he told the graduating class of Harvard University in 1983: "Wherever the tissue of life is woven of legalistic relationships, this creates an atmosphere of spiritual mediocrity that paralyzes man's noblest impulses."[11] When Westerners replace the question "What is truth?" with "Is it legal?" the writing is on the wall.

### Forms of Persecution

At present, persecution in the West is coming from three main sources:

1. Anti-minority churches—nationalistic churches that are bullying religious minorities
2. Anti-Christian elites—secular political elites who are determined to sideline Christianity
3. Anti-absolutes culture—a materialistic culture that is increasingly confident in repressing Christian morality

#### ANTI-MINORITY CHURCHES

Nationalistic churches that are bullying religious minorities are mainly a European problem, where links between church and state are very close. Just over half of the current twenty-five European Union (EU) members have state churches. This is not a problem in itself, but often these churches express a narrow nationalism and press the state to discriminate against Christians of a different, "rival" denomination. Protestant evangelicals, for example, are the object of slander campaigns from the Russian and Greek Orthodox churches. Willie Fautre, a Brussels-based scholar specializing in religious liberty, says, "There has been a tendency for leaders of majority churches to stoke up a paranoia about evangelicals by calling them 'cults,' and that panics some political elites into premature and poorly thought-out laws that entrench discrimination."

On September 26, 1997, Russia passed a law that placed restrictions on any religious group that had less than a fifteen-year presence in the country to organize, own property, and engage in missionary work. Many saw in this the hand of the Russian Orthodox hierarchy, threatened by the missionary efforts of the new foreign evangelicals. Instead of making their own churches more attractive to the Christians, the Russian Orthodox hierarchy prefer to get the government to oust the "opposition." In 2005 Anneta Vyssotskaia, coordinator for the International Day of Prayer in Russia, released a report documenting a deteriorating security situation for evangelicals. Protestant charismatic churches particularly were facing pickets led by priests, and even mob violence, and slander from a media branding them as "sects" and "contaminators of Russian culture."[12]

### ANTI-CHRISTIAN ELITES

Professor Rocco Buttliglione called the move of secular political elites to sideline Christianity a "neo-secular inquisition." He was referring to his rejection as justice commissioner by the European Parliament in 2004. A devout Catholic, he was being grilled by a parliamentary committee on his private views about homosexuality. He said he considered it a sin but added that it would not stop him from upholding the civil rights of homosexuals. He was barred from EU office. The scandal of his rejection sent shockwaves around Europe because it exposed the double standard of the secular elite. Their actions sent this signal: we will trust a professing homosexual who is an atheist to protect the human rights of Christians, but Christians will not be trusted to protect the rights of homosexuals. Some, like the new Pope Benedict, label this "Christophobia" because it is *only* Christians that are the target of this secular elite. They would not have dared to oppose a Muslim candidate with similar private views on homosexual activity.

Secular political elites vary in anti-Christian intensity, but they all share and spread a caricature that Christianity is an intolerant, negative religion. Often the anti-Christian campaigns are spread by extremist gay rights lobbies. Sometimes the secularism is stealthier, with subtle changes of interpretation of law, as in the United States, that restrict the practice of Christianity.

Some people are trying to interfere with the internal workings of religious communities, not content with banishing them from the public. Other political elites, mainly due to their ignorance of how religion actually works, end up restricting the rights of Christians in the mistaken attempt to create more religious freedom. In 2005 the UK government, in an attempt to buy back Muslim votes after the Iraq War, tried to rush through a bill outlawing incitement of religious hatred. Despite warnings from the Christian community, the law was so vaguely worded that it effectively criminalized the stating of Christian truth, should someone find that truth insulting. Fortunately, the measure was successfully watered down enough in its final Parliamentary reading in early 2006 to lose its sinister potency.

To be sure, the fight is on, and by no means lost from the Christian side. The 1990s saw in America the return of evangelicals to the political mainstream, and even in more secular Europe, there are signs of hope. In May 2004 ten new countries joined the EU; eight of them were former Communist countries. They bring a more positive understanding of Christianity. In countries like Poland, for example, the way dissent was expressed was through going to church. Christianity was a means of resisting and overcoming Communism. This understanding challenges the more Western European view that Christianity is a negative force that will only break up societies. When a seventy-thousand-word constitution was proposed in 2004 and no mention of God was made in a historical preamble, it was the Poles who were outraged and forced the French to back down.

### Anti-Absolutes Culture

In June 2005 the Co-Operative Bank of the United Kingdom gave an evangelical Christian lobby group called Christian Voice thirty days to close its account of three years. Their explanation was terse: "It has come to the bank's attention that Christian Voice is engaged in discriminatory pronouncements based on the grounds of sexual orientation."

The astonished lobby group, who held to a conservative position on the issue, asked the bank's leaders for clarification. One of the leaders stated that they considered the group "homophobic" and, crucially, claimed that their stance was incompatible with the UN Declaration of Human Rights (UNHR). Yet the declaration says nothing about sexual orientation. What is astonishing is the confidence the bank felt that its entirely new interpretation of human rights law was correct. It reveals a belief within the culture that moral absolutes coming from the Christian faith should be utterly repudiated.

Stephen Green, the director of Christian Voice, wrote that the bank "should renounce all claims to support the UNHR and plainly state on their home page that they do not want any business from Bible-believing Christians including Evangelicals, Catholics, orthodox Jews and Muslims or anyone who does not share their passion for gay rights."[13] In retaliation, the so-called ethical bank bounced the checks of the Christian Voice in the thirty-day period, even though there were sufficient funds.

The incident may illustrate that the prevailing mainstream culture in the West is becoming more hostile toward religions with uncompromising ethical beliefs. There is a new anti-absolutes militancy around. Indeed, there are parts of the secular culture that no longer respect the right to have certain religious views, even in private. Christian values are under attack from a materialistic, pluralistic worldview that considers biblical morality bigoted.

Charles Colson calls on Christians to challenge seven lies that are pushed in popular culture:

Lie 1: We have the freedom of choice to be who we want and to do what we want.

Lie 2: Marriage can be between any two people, and it lasts only as long as both are happy.

Lie 3: We'll live in harmony if we tolerate the beliefs of others.

Lie 4: Art should break traditional norms and challenge outworn beliefs.

Lie 5: Christian beliefs are a private matter.

Lie 6: Entertainment is a vehicle to help us fulfill personal desires.

Lie 7: God accepts us as we are, and there are many ways to him.[14]

Challenge these lies in the West today, and it will not be tolerance the Christian will experience, but persecution! But challenge them we must. The future of Western civilization depends on it. As the Catholic philosopher Henri de Lubac warned: "It is not true, as is sometimes said, that man cannot organize the world without God. What is true is that, without God, he can only organize it against man."

### Two to Watch

#### FRANCE

France is virtually unique in Europe for developing a doctrine of the secular state to such an extent that it effectively functions as a surrogate religion. The seeds were sown in the atheistic anger of the 1789 French Revolution, and now France, with its sixty million people, remains one of the most secular countries in Europe. Ironically, the distinctive doctrine of *laitice*,[15] dating from a 1905 law to strictly separate church and state, started off as a good thing and was viewed positively by Protestants, as it stopped Catholic meddling in national affairs. But over time the doctrine has been reinterpreted to mean that the state must actively expunge all religion from its functions. President Chirac was the only European head of state to insist that any reference to Europe's Christian heritage be removed from the preamble of the proposed European Union constitution. "France is a lay state and as such she does not have a habit of calling for insertions of a religious nature into constitutional texts," he declared grandly in September 2003.[16]

The constitution's main architect was former French President Valéry Giscard d'Estaing, who only worsened the situation by trying to explain, "Europeans live in a purely secular political system, where religion does not play an important role."[17] His comments served to reveal two features of French secularism—how strong it is and how ignorant it is. D'Estaing seemed unaware that more than half of the EU population live in countries that support established churches or formally acknowledge God in their constitutions.

Even other democracies have condemned this aggressive secularism. In December 2003 when the French government banned the wearing in state-run schools of Muslim scarves and other "conspicuous religious symbols," such as large crosses, the liberal *New York Times* demurred. In a leader it stated, "Banning believers from following the discipline of their religion is, in fact, state-imposed secular fundamentalism."[18] The U.S. State Department condemned the decision also.

This action was primarily aimed at Muslims who number nearly six million in France, probably a larger number than practicing Christians in this nominally Catholic country. But French Christians had their own brush with "secular fundamentalism" during the passage of Europe's toughest anticult legislation. In the late 1990s secularists became concerned about the activities of cult movements, such as the Church of Scientology and the suicidal Order of the Solar Temple. Although this feeling was Europe-wide, only French secularists rushed to enact an anticult law, which in the drafting process was so vaguely worded that France's four hundred thousand evangelicals began to fear their own classification as a "dangerous cult." In many cases the fact that they were not Catholics rendered them objects of suspicion, and they became stigmatized by a media that began to see evidence of cultish activity everywhere.

Article 9 of the proposed law established a new crime of "mental manipulation," defined so vaguely that Rev. Jean-Arnold de Clermont, president of the French Protestant Federation, protested: "Where is the limit between the persuasive speech, the passionate sermon, and the mental manipulation? In fact all the religious movements must feel threatened by the anticult fight. Is it possible that one day I will be suspected too?"[19] The law passed on May 30, 2001, although that controversial article was removed.

To date no prosecutions have been brought under the law, which may prove unworkable in practice, but the act has had two unfortunate effects. First, many newer evangelical congregations feel that they cannot exercise their full religious freedom, especially as some of them are on a government black list as dangerous cults. Pastor Samuel Peterschmitt testified that he was hesitant to practice "the laying on of hands" while praying for the sick in his church in Mulhouse, Alsace, for fear of accusations of illegally practicing medicine. He said, "If you do that and say you heal people, then you risk being prosecuted."[20] Second, other governments throughout the world have taken inspiration from the French law to pass more stringent anticult legislation, which catches many genuine Christian churches in its dragnet. China particularly makes a defense of its draconian laws by appealing to the French precedent.

For all its faults, however, France does stand as one of the few European cultures genuinely wrestling with the issue of how to preserve the coherence of a national culture with the very different values of religious minorities, particularly non-Christian minorities. Other democracies, such as the United Kingdom, have given up on trying to preserve a single national culture. But this is being rethought in the shattering aftermath of 7/7. On that date in 2005, four homegrown British Muslims detonated themselves in central London, killing fifty-two of their fellow citizens. British politicians are wondering whether their multicultural society is really working and, although they would never admit it publicly, are casting a glance over at France for ideas on a way forward. If French Christians can genuinely be dialogue partners in the new debate of how to make national culture and religion coexist, they could make a positive difference that would benefit not only France but the whole of the West.

### The United States

American Christians form the world's largest, richest church, with 134 million members out of a population of 278 million in 2000. In this country presidents and politicians talk openly about their faith, religious broadcasting is ubiquitous, evangelists are A-list celebrities, and prominent evangelicals broker key political alliances that can even swing elections. This is the land where Dr. Billy Graham prays with presidents, where Rev. Martin Luther King Jr. led the Civil Rights Movement, and top box office film stars like Mel Gibson and Rene Russo share their Christian faith openly. No wonder America is the only Western democracy self-confident enough to export its own values. It is inconceivable to think of any European government passing legislation like the 1998 International Religious Freedom Act, which mandated the world's most powerful government to examine every other country's religious liberty record and, if it falls short, to use the machinery of the state to improve it.

However, although American Christians may be the envy of their European counterparts who live in far more secularized countries, there is a growing feeling among them that they are being excluded from their own culture, and that unrepresentative secular elites are expanding the reach of the state and driving Christian principles from public life to the detriment of democracy. David Limbaugh's book *Persecution: How Liberals Are Waging War against Christianity*—a title that says it all—clearly struck a chord by shooting onto the bestseller lists in 2003 and 2004. While most reviewers appeared to agree with his argument that "anti-Christian discrimination occurs in a variety of contexts throughout our culture, from the public sector to the private sector, in the mainstream media and in Hollywood, in the public education system and in our universities,"[21] many felt the extent and even the strength of the secular hostility was overstated.

Richard Mouw, president of Fuller Theological Seminary, the largest evangelical seminary in the country, urged Limbaugh to "lighten up a bit." He argued, "It is a little difficult to accept the picture of traditional Christians as a beleaguered minority when the beliefs that are taken to be under attack are shared openly by some of the most prominent leaders in public life."[22] But there is no contesting the widespread unease, and even writers as nuanced as Stephen L. Carter confirm it:

> Many people of deep religious commitment, especially but not exclusively evangelical Christians, look at the nation today and see a place that is run in ways that make it harder for them to practice their religion, and harder for them to pass it on to their children . . . one can scarcely be surprised . . . if they feel driven to the point of thinking that the nation is actively at war with them.[23]

There are two "wars" that American Christians are particularly worried about: cultural wars and constitutional wars. The first war is similar to that in Europe. Many Christians believe that an influential minority of fanatical secularists is out to replace Christian values with liberal values in the culture at large, by force if necessary. Although this group is small, its actions have rated headlines. The evangelical magazine *Christianity Today* carried the story "Corporate Thought Police," detailing the plight of Christian employees who refused to sign the "sexual nondiscrimination" agreements of their companies.[24] One employee of AT&T Broadband refused to sign a certificate pledging to "fully recognize, respect and value the differences among all of us, including sexual orientation." The Christian employee told his supervisors that he would certainly never discriminate against a homosexual but could not sign a statement that required him to accept homosexual activity as an equally valid sexual lifestyle. He was fired. He is not alone. The coercive nature of this is disturbing. Not only are Christians *not* allowed to hold private views at odds with the mainstream, they are being asked to replace their Christian values with liberal ones or else!

Education is another area where some Christians find themselves under siege from "politically correct" activists. The Williamsburg Charter Survey of Religion and Public Life reported in 1988 that one in three academics held that evangelicals were a "threat to democracy."[25]

The second war is more particularly American—constitutional wars. Here it is felt that some in the judiciary seem intent on reworking the relationship between church and state, to the detriment of the church. Judicial elites exercise far more power in America's political system than in any other modern democracy, and although few argue that the judiciary is full of fanatical secularists, there is a concern that there is nevertheless an agenda to push religion out of the public sphere, perhaps due more to an ignorance of religion's contribution than a hostility to it.

The relationship between state and church is controlled by a so-called "establishment clause" in the first amendment to the U.S. Constitution, which states, "Congress shall make no law respecting an establishment of religion." Up until the 1940s, this was interpreted to mean that the government should be evenhanded in its cooperation with religious bodies. In other words, it could not favor, for example, the Presbyterian Church over the Catholic Church. There was no suggestion, however, that the state should have no relationship at all with religion. The clause assumed that there would be one and was a guide to how the relationship should proceed. However, in 1947 Supreme Court Justice Hugo Black changed the way this clause was interpreted. He claimed that it had to be interpreted through Jefferson's phrase "separation of church and state," and he ruled that the government had an obligation not only to be evenhanded but to eschew any action that might "aid" religion in general.

Paul Marshall puts his finger on the confusion that the ruling was to bring:

> Black's attempt to use "separation" *itself* as the means of clarification of the relation of "church and state" confused the entire issue. The First Amendment was meant to give a solution to the problem of the relation of the distinct institutions of "church and state," not merely to state the problem once again. Black's formulation lost the answer provided by the First Amendment and left the problem open-ended. This open-endedness has allowed many other non-constitutional views of church and state to intrude.[26]

This arbitrary ruling has led the Supreme Court to attempt to keep the business of government away from religion, which is disastrous because, as the state expands, religion must get out. This leaves the field clear for the secular worldview to receive state support at the expense of a religious worldview. It has also led to the most bizarre rulings. In the 2004 case of *Locke v. Davey*, the Supreme Court gave its blessing to official religious discrimination, permitting the state of Washington to offer educational subsidies for underprivileged students to study any subject *except* theology. The unfairness is clear. As a friend of the court brief stated:

> The irony of Washington State's discrimination-infected legal structure is this: devotees of Marxism may use Promise Scholarships to pursue degrees in accredited departments that school students in the

idea that "religion is the opiate of the masses." Under current law
. . . scholarships may be used to study religion from a standpoint of
agnosticism, skepticism, condescension, or hostility . . . except [from]
the most traditional, commonplace standpoint down through the
ages—the standpoint of faith.[27]

Another debacle was the confusing ruling in June 2005 that allowed displays of the Ten Commandments on state land but banned
them from courtrooms. Harvard law professor Mary Ann Glendon
has no illusions about the direction the American legal system is
taking: "If present legal trends continue, it is not fanciful to suppose
that the situation of religious believers in secular America will come
to resemble *dhimmitude*—the status of non-Muslims in a number
of Islamic countries."[28]

This new interpretation of the separation of church and state has
turned into a mandate to drive religion from public life and ends up
favoring an atheistic culture over a religious one. This is damaging
to democracy. As Stephen Carter points out, if religion had been
kept out of public life in the history of America, then there never
would have been the abolition of slavery in the nineteenth century,
the protection of workers from exploitation in the early twentieth
century, or the Civil Rights Movement of the late twentieth century—three epochs in the building of American democracy that
were led by church initiatives.[29]

Yet there is a strong ray of hope here. The state has overreached
itself. As we have seen, while it preaches the doctrine of the separation of church and state, it is also its greatest violator. As Michael
Horowitz puts it:

> There is a wall between the state and the church. Christians used to
> do what they liked behind that wall, and let the state do what it liked
> beyond it. But now the state has leapt over the wall, and is trying to
> restrict the free exercise of religion. The effect has been that American
> Christians have had to fight back, and as they do so, are beginning
> to say, *if these are the new rules, there must be no more walls.*[30]

You can't have walls to keep Christianity out of public life if you
refuse to erect the same walls to keep out alternative, nonreligious

worldviews. So American Christians are organizing and have moved back into the public arena in significant numbers in the last two decades. Evangelical naïveté at the political table is still common because evangelicals are so new to it. Also an extremist and voluble fringe within evangelicalism continues to add fuel to the secularist agenda every time they open their mouths. For example, evangelist Pat Robertson's August 2005 remarks beseeching the U.S. government to assassinate the Venezuelan president makes it harder to defang secularists convinced that Christians are antidemocratic. Nevertheless, among evangelicals particularly there is a determination to fight their way back into the public sphere where they can have an equal say in the development of their culture and country. Whether they succeed or not will have enormous implications for the fight against persecution worldwide, especially as America will continue to contain—for the short term at least—the world's most influential Christian community, and the world's most influential government.

We've met the church. We've seen the fierce waves of oppression lapping over the world. We've seen the dilemmas for the church on each continent. We've seen the faces of the heroes. Now our task is to help them. How do we help in such a way that will serve and not use, bless and not harm? The persecuted deserve our best effort. How do we give it?

# Part Four

# How Do We Help the Persecuted?

# 9

## The Tricky Business of Doing More Good than Harm

Helping the persecuted ought to be a simple, straightforward business. After all, as a friend in the intelligence community said, "Surely it's just about getting the right information, finding the money, and then implementing the correct strategy, right?"

Right in principle. Dead wrong in practice.

In reality, helping the persecuted is messy, controversial, and confusing. What's worse, even with the best intentions, not everyone who sets out to help the persecuted actually ends up doing so. Take a simple example. It's a fact that Christians in southern Sudan are a persecuted community. When extremist Muslims seized power in 1989, the largely Christian tribes of the south became targets for bombings, massacres, and raids. More than five hundred thousand have died. How do we help them?

"We help them by buying back slaves," said certain Christian organizations in the late 1990s. Shocking evidence was presented that thousands of Christians, especially children, were being kidnapped by Muslim traders, forcibly converted, and sold as slaves. Many of those who wanted to help believed the only way was to go to the Muslim traders and hand over cash to buy them back. Crude maybe, but necessary! Soon a huge campaign was under way, with celebrities making media appeals to government leaders, and children in American churches and schools setting up lemonade stands to raise funds for slave redemption schemes. One organization even said that for eighty dollars you could buy back a Christian slave and receive their photograph and a letter of thanks.

And so the great slave redemption campaign got going. Some organizations redeemed more than fifty thousand slaves apiece. The tactic was direct, drastic, and definitely successful in raising awareness of the dire plight of Christians in Sudan.

But donors were confused. While a few Christian organizations engaged in slave redemption, more refused to do so. Some referred to it as "the great slave scam." Newspaper journalists uncovered evidence that many so-called slave traders were bogus, often collecting the cash by corralling illiterate villagers to meet foreigners flying in with money. Afterward, everyone got their cut, while the well-meaning foreigners flew back on the plane writing more fundraising copy on how more Christians had just been freed, when in fact they had just been had.[1] One journalist, Declan Walsh, claimed to have evidence that when one ministry spent more than three hundred thousand dollars in a week, the corrupt commander earned enough from his cut to buy forty wives. But this didn't clear up the confusion. Were these journalistic reports based on incidents that were exceptional rather than typical?

Other Christian organizations took a different tack. They admitted slavery did go on but said that slave redemption was a misguided tactic that only fueled the very trade it was trying to stop, especially when one ministry handed over two million dollars to one of the world's most economically deprived areas, thereby making slave trading—in the eyes of some—the only viable business in the entire country.

Still other Christian organizations claimed that to make slave redemption the cornerstone of one's strategy represented a failure to understand and connect with the larger, greater, more urgent needs of the Christians of southern Sudan. Said Clive Calver, director of World Relief, "We jump up and down about the forcible Islamization of a child who has been kidnapped and taken into slavery, while we sit back and watch as half a dozen children starve to death."[2] His organization complained that while maybe fifty thousand Christians were under threat of slavery, 2.4 million were dying of starvation.

## A Multifaceted Problem

From this example, then, we can see that helping the persecuted boils down to three questions, which in practice can be very hard to answer: the what question, the how question, and the who question.

### The What Question

We ask the *what* question of the persecuted church itself. What is their story? What are their strengths and weaknesses? What are their needs? It's difficult, however, to build a profile of the needs of Christians, for example, in southern Sudan. Many of them live out in the bush and cannot be contacted. Official statistics, especially from agencies like the United Nations, can barely be trusted, since they rely on government cooperation for their findings. Also local Christians give conflicting answers as to their primary need. Some say, "Focus on teaching"; others say, "No, we need physical aid." Discerning the needs of persecuted communities involves a lot of guesswork because, by their very nature, these Christians are often forced "underground" by hostile governments.

### The How Question

Those who seek to assist the persecuted ask the *how* question. How do we meet their needs? How do we intervene? A whole group of cultures are lined up here—missions organizations, church denominations, advocacy groups, even governments. But which tactic of intervention will work? Will slave redemption just fuel scam rackets? Or is it worth the risk anyway? As one missions director told me, "The point is not the redeeming of slaves. This tactic captures the public imagination and allows us to put the persecuted on the map. We do it for the publicity value."

Even when the tactics have been deployed, how do you measure success? If you ask the U.S. government to pressure the Sudanese leaders, and nothing appears to happen for a time, does that mean the tactic has failed or simply needs more time?

### The **Who** Question

Donors and supporters ask the *who* question. They look at the various helping organizations and ask, "Who will use my money wisely?" The responsible donor wants to distinguish those merely making a noise from those really making a difference, but the donor rarely has the time and expertise to investigate personally. Even going to southern Sudan would not be that helpful, since you see only what your particular hosts allow you to see. So it becomes a matter of trust: Can I rely on this organization to be as effective as they claim to be? How can I make sure I do not support organizations that will do more harm than good?

The next three chapters will take these questions in turn. But it is vital to stress that the whole tactical issue is not a small matter. We have already seen in this book that the deployment of the wrong tactic can harm, not help, the persecuted. And there is something even more disturbing here too—it can happen that some agencies, in their desire to raise income and profile, *use* the persecuted rather than *serve* them. This is a largely unconscious process, and it's a consequence of the sharp rise in the number of agencies that got involved in assisting the persecuted in the 1990s.

## Something's Not Right Here

My concern in this area crystallized in a something's-not-right-here feeling, as I sat in the U.S. Senate Foreign Relations Committee room in 2001. On the surface I should have been very happy. A good friend of mine, Bob Fu, was receiving an award from an excellent human rights organization. They were presenting religious liberty awards to a series of people representing oppressed groups in China, a diverse array including underground Catholics, Protestants, Uygurs, and Falun Gong. The award speeches were interrupted by the arrival of political luminaries, including Senator Jesse Helms and Congressman Chris Smith, who broke in to sing the praises of the organizing body and call for a tougher stance to force China to treat its religious believers better.

What was it that was bothering me? It wasn't the excessive backslapping. Sure, everyone presented themselves as virtual Solzhenitsyns, committed to speaking even just "one word of truth" to "outweigh the whole world." This was Washington, D.C.—not a town for shrinking violets but for mutual self-congratulation in the interests of career advancement. I was used to it.

What was bothering me was this: everyone was saying how important speaking the truth is, but few were actually speaking it. To be blunt, they were exaggerating the truth and politicizing it.

For example Bob Fu, a Beijing underground house-church leader until he fled in 1996, was introduced by someone who told us the difference in China between the state-controlled church, the Three Self Patriotic Movement (TSPM), and the house churches. It was said of the former, "To register, you have to go along with government doctrine. For example, you can't preach on the second coming; you can't evangelize under eighteens."

This was untrue. True maybe twenty years ago. Absolutely untrue now. I had just come back from a three-week China trip and must have heard the second coming doctrine preached five times in TSPM services and witnessed (unofficially, mark you) Sunday schools for children in at least three of these churches. The TSPM is neither the monster of its detractors nor the haven of liberty of its defenders. Badly compromised at the top, there are nevertheless many fine pastors and Christians worshiping within its walls.

Jessie Helms, then the chairman of the Senate Foreign Relations Committee, shuffled to the mike to read a prepared statement that began, "There is no religious freedom in China today; there is only religious persecution." Also untrue! Great progress has been made in the past twenty years in China. The Cultural Revolution, when all religious expression was outlawed, is long gone. A measure of tolerance has been introduced, not enough, of course, but some. Four weeks previously, I had sat in an illegal house church in Xian, central China, watching fifty young people burst their lungs singing hymns. "Are you not afraid the police will come?" a friend of mine asked.

The young people replied, "Oh, they don't bother us. It's only if we received thousands of dollars from abroad or were in a network of house churches or were teaching something eccentric, then we would have to be careful."

Millions of Christians in China within the TSPM and the house churches are, for all intents and purposes, left largely unmolested to practice their faith. There isn't religious freedom in its fullest sense. There are still unacceptably high levels of harassment and even torture of some house-church leaders. But the situation is complex. The generalization has no place in a country as complex and vast as China.

Then came the political spin. Helms warned that China must not receive the Olympic Games because of their record on religious persecution. Catholic Christian activist Joseph Kung told us never to buy anything with a "made in China" label, as it supports prison labor.

All I heard, from people who should have known better, was a bunch of exaggerations and extrapolations from some extreme incidents. While one understands the need to drive a campaign on emotive material, the danger is that those mounting the campaign cannot tell the difference between an extreme case of persecution and a more typical one. Worse, they didn't seem to *want* to know the difference.

I asked Bob Fu, "How long have you been here in D.C.?"

He replied, "Oh, about a day and a half, just kicking my heels."

I said, "You mean, no one from this organization has debriefed you?"

He shook his head a little sadly, "No, they just wanted to hand me the award."

This experience has been multiplied in advocacy contexts a hundred times. I am weary of looking into the eyes of the persecuted believer being honored and seeing the question, *Why doesn't anyone take an interest in my story?* I don't want to paint this with too broad a brush, but there is a lack of professionalism among many advocates that prevents their understanding the true nature and extent of persecution. They want sound bites from their sources and nothing more. They have no interest in the details.

The upshot is, if those who are doing advocacy are unaware of the real complexity of persecution, then how are they going to know whether their tactics in reducing persecution are appropriate and effective? Advocacy is in danger of becoming the sounding of shrill noises in defense of the persecuted that draws applause from—you've guessed it—other advocacy groups. But the end user, persecuted Christians, are being left out of the equation primarily because they do not happen to be—in this case—within D.C.'s "Beltway bubble."

There is a cost in influence to the kind of extreme statements peddled in that Senate Room. The Chinese government can easily dismiss the criticisms as exaggerations (which they are) and invite others over to see the reality. They can target individuals who have swallowed an extreme version of events and cause visitors to perform a spectacular about-face when shown a more tolerant picture, thus gaining a coup for government propaganda, which is also full of distortion and denial.

Dr. Carol Lee Hamrin, for twenty-five years a senior China specialist at the U.S. State Department, warns, "When you demonize, or counter-demonize, for example, by saying that the TSPM is just a government tool, you are going to lose because you are trying to win a propaganda battle with the Chinese Communist Party, and if there is one thing the CCP is really good at, it's propaganda!" Also, she adds, the confrontation tactic may be completely counterproductive. She tells this parable:

> You have an army and you take the troops up a hill to engage the king who is sitting atop a huge cliff bristling with guns. They are shouting taunts from the top. The air is thick with insults. It looks

like war is inevitable. But this is an incomplete scenario. You discover that some friends have been sneaking in the back way to the
fortress, where it is not so heavily guarded. They have discovered
that the king of robbers is more like the wizard of Oz. He's weak.
Similarly in China, the CCP is not this all-powerful force. It's weak
in many areas, all smoke and mirrors. But remember: *the main asset
of the king is the confrontation on the cliff—it keeps him in power.* Consequently, what does that mean for strategy? Should we assault the
cliff, and unite all the people up top behind this King? Or should
we withdraw, and let the fort fall by itself?[3]

Hamrin maintains that a quiet engagement dialogue with China
can spring more Christians out of jail than a public name-and-shame
campaign. Others might say that reflects the cautious softly-softly
approach of the State Department, but the point simply is that
sometimes the most effective tactic in assisting the persecuted may
be a counterintuitive and unspectacular one. There is a place for
the spectacular tactic, but not everything that benefits the suffering
church requires a media shock-and-awe campaign.

Wise intervention, then, is where those who intervene are fully
aware of the range of tactics at their disposal and as informed as
they possibly can be of the full story of the persecuted themselves.
In the next chapter we will discuss the respective uses and value
of each of the main tactics, but for the moment, here are, in my
view, the four most common ways we fail the persecuted when
we try to intervene. Effective intervention relies on the reversal
of each of these failures.

### Overheated Publicity

We fail the persecuted through overheated publicity. It is understandable. We want to help the persecuted, but the Western church
doesn't seem to care. To get the attention and support of the average Christian, we profile the most extreme cases. We use graphic
pictures of torture; we highlight the plight of martyrs; we tell the
saddest stories, anything to shake the average Christian out of his
or her self-absorbed torpor and remember that the persecuted are
actually living on the same planet.

Of course, there is nothing wrong with this in itself, but two dangers are ever present that can end up harming the persecuted. One is the danger of extrapolation, when an extreme case is represented as the norm. The other is the danger of exaggeration, when the stories of need are stoked up to raise more support. Both dangers are deadly, because all effective intervention rests on truth telling, and these are distortions of the truth that bring only trouble.

Take the second of these issues: exaggeration. In early October of 2001, I was sitting in a hotel lobby in Amhedabad, India. Two events occurred to disturb my equilibrium. One was the arrival of the cricketer, Sachin Tendulkar, a diminutive batsman of supreme skill who cannot go anywhere in India without being mobbed. After that, a friend came rushing up to me with a fax sheet, asking, "Have you heard the news?" He was literally palpitating with excitement. I assumed the worst, fearing that Muslim or Hindu extremists had gone on the rampage against Christians somewhere again. But as I grabbed the paper, I read a headline that immediately puzzled me. It was an article headlined: "300 Million Dalit 'Untouchables' on the Verge of Conversion to Christianity."[4]

The lead paragraph ran: "According to Gospel for Asia, there is a great probability of a revival that could begin on November 4, 2001. Three hundred million Dalits (low-caste 'untouchables') are on the verge of turning to the Christian faith."

This was puzzling because I had just come from Delhi after talks with Christian leaders there. I knew of the rally, but no one had said anything about three hundred million Dalits on the move to conversion. Indeed, one of my main contacts, Dr. John Dayal, the vice-chairman of the All India Christian Council, had been invited to speak at the rally and told me simply, "There is a civil servant called Ram Raj, who has called on a million Dalits to come and take part in a mass conversion ceremony from Hinduism to Buddhism. Probably less than one hundred thousand will come. It's essentially an anticaste rally, and Christians have been invited to show solidarity. It's a good initiative."

That was it! But what a different story was being put forward in the article. First, it was claimed that three hundred million Dalits were soon to convert to Christianity, putting an intolerable strain on the resources of the Indian church. The conversions would start on the date of the rally, and the article quoted a spokesperson from Gospel for Asia who said they fully expected to see at least a third of the three hundred million Dalits come to Christ in the next few years. Second, it was clear that certain ministries were using the potential influx of Christian converts as a fund-raising tool to print Bibles, buy radio time, and raise up "ten thousand more native missionaries."

A few weeks later, I was back in Delhi. I found out that Ram Raj, the organizer, was furious at some of the Christians. Claims had been made by certain Indian Christians in America that Ram Raj had been "led to the Lord" and given permission to give out tracts and Bibles at the rally. One group said they had set up a tent to counsel all the new converts. Ram Raj wrote a stiff letter to two of the culprits: "Please do not encash [cash in] while putting my name on the website, emails and elsewhere which is miscommunicating my philosophy and my beliefs."[5] He stressed that contrary to the publicity on various ministry websites, no one had received permission to give out any books on the day of the ceremony.

I spoke to John Dayal again, who shook his head sadly: "The political significance of the rally has been overshadowed by some Christians exaggerating the spiritual significance of the event." Of greater concern was that the exaggeration of "three hundred million Hindus" about to defect to Christianity had come to the attention of Hindu extremists, who were pressuring the government to cancel the rally and threatening violence against those who dared attend. But there never was any mass conversion to Christianity among the Dalits planned for that day, nor had Christian leaders received permission to evangelize or distribute literature. The exaggerations were spiraling out of control as the Internet carried the rumors at ten times the speed of truth.

Some Christian leaders flew to Delhi to witness the beginning of the great revival. Dayal, a shrewd Christian with a Ph.D. in sociology, predicted to a T what would happen: "Less than one hundred thousand will come; a few Christians will give greetings, the government will disrupt the flow of people to the venue, and that will be that. But my issue is this: because a missionary miracle won't occur, Christians are going to be disappointed. Instead, they are missing the massive symbolic significance of this—it is the first public protest that Hinduism has failed as a system."

And so it played out exactly as he said.[6] Yet those who hyped the event filled their coffers, and, in Dayal's words, "gave fuel to the extremists and set back years the Christian dialogue with Dalit leaders." The church was hurt by the hype. The persecuted had been used rather than served.

Certainly this situation demonstrated the importance not only of truth telling but of language. In an Internet age, there is no private language. You cannot use your website to call on your supporters in North Carolina to "smash the darkness of Hinduism in prayer" and not expect Hindu extremists to latch on to it and make life worse for Christians in India. It may not be possible to construct nonoffending language in the area of religion, but discernment is surely needed to know the difference between stating the truth as an act of witness or as an act of insensitivity.

Above all, let the claims be true. I remember being confronted by a high ranking official in China who showed me a clipping from a famous American evangelist who claimed that the Bibles in China were printed without the book of Revelation, "because you can't talk about the second coming there." The claim was utter nonsense. All the Bibles have all sixty-six books. But I felt ashamed as he said to me, "You are supposed to be people of the truth, and you know this is a lie. How can you expect us to treat your people better when your leaders goad us with lies and untruths?" Mind you, this was an interesting lesson in truth telling from a Communist Party official who had lied to me countless times. Yet it would have strengthened my position if this evangelist had got his nose out of ideology and into the realm of fact. I could have helped the church more if he had stuck to the truth. The facts are that when it comes to persecution, we do not need to exaggerate. The truth is bad enough!

### Tactical Polarization

We fail the persecuted through tactical polarization. This is when those who employ one tactic to assist the persecuted engage in denigrating those who employ another tactic, instead of acknowledging the value of an array of tactical approaches. Those who use name-and-shame publicity tactics dismiss those who use behind-the-scenes dialogue, and vice versa. Those who print Bibles in China dismiss those who smuggle them. A former archbishop of Canterbury, Robert Runcie, sniffily labeled Bible smugglers on a trip to China as "evangelicals with a sore conscience." The insult delighted his Chinese hosts, but Runcie was unaware that the number of Chinese Christians was far larger than his official hosts had told him, requiring legal *and* illegal delivery to meet Bible demand. His remarks only assisted the government denial of the true size of the house-church millions, and, as a prominent house-church leader Moses Xie told me at the time, "No one is going to bring Bibles to Christians they are told do not exist." A further failure to assist the persecuted here is the shocking misdirection of energy. Energy that should go into assisting the persecuted gets dissipated in an unseemly round of squabbling and criticizing.

Of course, a robust debate should always take place about the effectiveness of particular tactics. One must ask which tactics are working and which are not. Some organizations get attached to certain tactics and may not like the implication that their work is not as useful as it once was, any more than the man with the "Repent or Die" placard around his neck will hardly appreciate being told that his evangelistic method may no longer be the best way to express the love of God for fallen sinners. Also good Christians are always going to disagree sincerely as to which tactic works best and when it works best—all the more need to bring greater civility and less polarization into the inevitable debate.

I have heard some Christian organizations say, "In all our tactics, we steer clear of politics." But tactics are by their very nature political. One ministry I worked closely with smuggled Bibles extensively into China, yet they still claimed they did not involve themselves in politics. By "politics," they meant going to a congress or a parliament and becoming a lobby group or asking for government assistance. But totalitarian states make no distinction between church and state; the act of smuggling anything to an underground movement that is organized outside their control constitutes an intensely political act, however nonpolitical the mission might consider it to be. Like it or not, helping the persecuted is a political business!

It is in the more overtly political realm that, not surprisingly, much of the tactical polarization occurs. In late 2002 Robert Seiple, the first-ever U.S. Ambassador-at-large for International Religious Freedom, took aim at a congressionally funded committee, the U.S. Commission on International Religious Freedom (USCIRF), for preferring to "curse the darkness" instead of "lighting a candle."[7] He was referring to their penchant for issuing biting press releases against persecuting governments. Seiple thought the tactic counterproductive, saying, "I have never been comfortable with the 'punishing' approach . . . while it may appeal to our public machismo at home, it rarely moves the ball forward abroad." This touched off a firestorm in the pages of *Christianity Today*, resulting in a debate between Michael Horowitz and T. Jeremy Gunn. The titles of the two positions say it all. Horowitz: "Cry Freedom: Forget 'Quiet Diplomacy'—It Doesn't Work"; Gunn: "Full of Sound and Fury: Polemics at Home and Abroad Does Not Prevent Religious Persecution."[8]

The high profile of the debate, however, was a positive sign that the issue of helping the persecuted was on the public agenda like never before, at least in the United States. This was due to two primary factors in the mid- to late 1990s. The first was the creation of the International Day of Prayer for the Persecuted Church (IDOP), begun in 1996 with five thousand participating churches. At its peak in the late 1990s, more than one hundred thousand churches were participating, with more than 70 percent of American churches involved—an astonishing rise and one of the most significant grassroots movements in recent years.

The second evidence that the persecuted were on the public agenda was the passage of the U.S. International Religious Freedom Act (IRFA) in November 1998.[9] Christian organizations and individuals put their differences aside—at the last gasp—and cooperated sufficiently to ensure passage of the bill that few thought had a chance of passing, least of all the Clinton administration who opposed it.

In fact, tactical polarization nearly wrecked the bill's passage. It began life as the Wolf-Specter Bill, or more correctly the Freedom from Religious Persecution Act, which passed the House in May 1997 but had little chance of passing the Senate and becoming law. Some characterized this bill as Michael Horowitz's brainchild, and there was no doubt he was instrumental in pulling together a varied coalition of partners such as the National Association of Evangelicals, Tibetan Buddhists, and Jewish lobbyists. These groups came together in the mid-1990s to pressure Congress to review U.S. trading policy with China. But Horowitz was a bruising political operator whose hardball politics made him enemies as well as friends. Also, he was comparatively new to the religious liberty world, and many who had worked longer in the area felt his bill lacked the nuance required to be workable in practice, being especially wary of the call for automatic sanctions against regimes that tortured Christians.

Some of this group, led by John Hanford (who later became the second Ambassador-at-large for Religious Freedom), began drafting an alternative bill that would have a better chance of passing the Senate. It was known as Nickles-Lieberman, but it was never even presented to the Senate, as infighting between the "new" and "old" groups threatened to create a total impasse. The drama of the bill's eventual passage has been written up in a masterful chapter by Allen Hertzke in his book *Freeing God's Children*. He saw that the disagreements were primarily over tactics first and personalities second:

> Advocates of Wolf-Specter made contact with Hanford, but could not come to a meeting of the minds, or even a modus operandi. There was simply too fundamental a divide: Wolf-Specter partisans demanded tough public measures; Hanford and his allies sought change through quiet diplomacy. As the lobby campaign heated up, the sides were increasingly personified by Horowitz and Hanford, who became bitter adversaries. . . . To backers of Wolf-Specter, Hanford seemed obstructionist, objecting to any bill with teeth. To opponents of Wolf-Specter, Horowitz acted as if he would ramrod the bill through Congress without the normal give and take.[10]

The dueling bills both looked doomed, and when Nickles-Lieberman was removed from the Senate docket on July 22, 1998, it seemed as if all chance of passing legislation had disappeared. In the end Hanford and some associates rapidly drafted a compromise bill, and over the summer some key opponents of the idea of a religious liberty law shifted sides. At the last minute Hanford and Horowitz buried the hatchet, and the newly unveiled International Religious Freedom Act flew through both Houses of Congress in October 1998 and was signed into law in November—barely three months after nearly everyone thought it was dead.

The act created four mechanisms to tackle religious persecution abroad. Within the State Department, an office of Ambassador-at-large for Religious Liberty Abroad was created, and the department was charged to produce an annual report on the status of religious freedom in each country in the world except the United States. The act also created an independent Commission on International Religious Freedom (USCIRF), designed to represent interests in Congress and hold the State Department's feet to the fire if it lagged in enthusiasm for the cause. Finally, the act required the administration to compile a list of "countries of particular concern," where religious rights are being grossly violated, and the president is enjoined to act decisively.

Since 1998 relations between the USCIRF and the State Department have been predictably poor, with name-calling and catcalling being the order of the day. Within this political firefight, it is questionable whether the persecuted church has benefited. This is all the more ironic because, as persecution scholar Paul Marshall observes, "To the Seiples and Hanfords [the first and second Ambassadors-at-large ] who always call for the quiet diplomacy tactic, I say, 'You wouldn't even have got your jobs if people like Michael Horowitz and Nina Shea hadn't screamed and yelled publicly.'"[11]

Clearly, there is a need for the various cultures of assistance to "grow up," stop denigrating each other's efforts, and get on with their own. As Hertzke writes, "Without Wolf-Specter, there would have been no Nickles-Liberman."[12] The heartening prospect is that if it happened once, it can happen again . . . even in Washington, D.C.

*Propaganda Parroting*

Propaganda parroting occurs when visitors to persecuted countries are content to parrot the propaganda that is fed to them rather than look beneath the surface and see the darker truth. In my experience it is often clergy and church leaders who exhibit an allergy to this "darker truth" of persecution. Often they end up as unwitting apologists for government methods that actually increase persecution.

Religious VIPs are important in the whole persecution "game." The pope, the archbishop of Canterbury, Dr. Billy Graham, and many others can use their positions of power to speak out on behalf of their persecuted brethren who cannot speak for themselves. More crucially, an audience with the *persecutor* is often granted to foreign religious VIPs who can use their access to the ruling elite denied to the indigenous Christians. Yet these VIPs often come with their own (usually denominational) agendas, and it is these agendas that can result in a refusal to face the darker truths of persecution. Often, this amounts to a colossal naïveté that hurts the persecuted.

I remember traveling with a delegation of clergy (who shall remain nameless) to a city in southern China in the late 1980s. We were visiting China's largest official seminary, where more than two hundred Christians from minority tribes were receiving their theological education. At first, we were impressed, being shown around by the smiling president. He took us to a warehouse and showed us palettes of Scriptures printed on the TSPM's Bible press in Nanjing. They were in minority languages. Three features made me uneasy. First, he said that fifty thousand had been printed as a result of a donation from a Western missions organization. A quick calculation revealed that practically all fifty thousand were sitting right there. Second, he introduced us to the person in charge of distribution, his daughter. Third, when asked why they were not distributed, he shook his head and said sadly, "The minority tribes can't afford them." Immediately, there was a clamor from the VIP clergy to pay for some of these Bibles to be distributed. "What a miracle we are here just in time!" said one.

But they should have smelled a rat. Would a Western organization that was so keen on minority tribes that it funded the printing of fifty thousand Bibles be unaware that the tribes could not afford to buy them? I expressed my skepticism and was immediately dropped from the delegation on account of my being "an ungrateful presence in the face of generous hosts."

One phone call to Hong Kong was all it took to get the story straight. The donating organization had indeed paid extra to the TSPM for the free distribution of the Bibles. They were furious that the Bibles were sitting in Kunming and became fully aware that the seminary president and his daughter were profiteering by attempting to sell them off. A news agency, News Network International, highlighted the case, but no church denominations would get involved.

A few years later, this man overreached himself. His entire faculty resigned, sick of the corruption, and the seminary was closed down for a time. I visited him again last year. Basically he's not a wicked man, just a sad one who couldn't turn down the winning lottery ticket when it was proffered him. Perhaps the system was to blame, but no one blew the whistle when it mattered because these visiting clergy were out to create links with TSPM seminaries for their denominations. Their agenda resulted in a "see-no-evil" attitude that failed to address the corruption and cronyism at the seminary. One lecturer told me privately, "Here, these clerics had a perfect opportunity to help us ensure that these Bibles got to the Lisu and other groups, but they were just wined and dined into a complete lack of suspicion, and these poor Christians continue to be without the Word of God. Thanks for nothing."

This naïveté—if that is the right word for such a deliberate stance—is often thought by evangelicals to be the exclusive preserve of liberal clergy. Snorted a TSPM insider in Nanjing, "There's no fool like a World Council of Churches fool." But evangelical leaders are by no means immune, despite having better connections to the grassroots, underground communities.

When the evangelical archbishop of Canterbury, George Carey, visited China in 1994, he rebuked Bible smugglers as "troublemakers." On his return to the United Kingdom, the press informed him that he had made these remarks on the five hundredth anniversary of the birth of William Tyndale, the man who had to smuggle his translated version of the Bible into England. Carey had never received a proper briefing on the entire trip. He was tired and unable to listen to those in his entourage who could have given him a broader perspective than the official line he was getting from his hosts. But why did Carey parrot the official propaganda in his exiting press conference? He must have known he had heard only one side of the Bible-shortage story. Why not parry the question with the simple, "I don't know enough about China to answer that!" Instead, he assumed that what his hosts had told him was the whole truth, stirred up a needless controversy, and returned home to Britain looking foolish in the eyes of the press because he had failed to realize that China in 1994 had a situation similar to England in 1494.

The root issue is, whom do you trust to tell you the truth when you make a visit to a country where the government is oppressing Christians? Western Christian VIPs exhibit commendable levels of suspicion when dealing with government officials but almost none when dealing with officials of government-controlled churches, especially if these officials are wearing a clerical collar. Yet the two groups are often the same. One is the master, the other the servant. The upshot often is that visiting VIPs accept as true the official version of events and fail in their duty to speak out on behalf of the truly persecuted, whose existence the officials may utterly deny or whose problems they may rationalize away.

For example, in China, Western church leaders frequently visited Bishop Ding Guangxun, longtime leader of the TSPM. Ding's job was to tell visitors that the idea that there were millions worshiping in house churches independently of the TSPM was absurd, and if you want to help the church of China, then deal openly and *exclusively* with TSPM-nominated channels. The word for this is propaganda. Let Ding say it, and Ding is by no means a purely negative individual. But if his propaganda is swallowed, then the visiting religious leaders end up assisting government persecution of house-church Christians. They have been manipulated into a tacit (sometimes specific) denial of the true size, nature, and needs of the Chinese church, and they have been made participants in a strategy designed to starve the independent churches of outside aid. After all, why assist a group of Christians that do not exist? But they will see that they do exist if they commit to examining the darker data. Few do, to the detriment of the persecuted. The game has usurped the cause.

### A Focus on the Urgent Rather Than the Strategic

We fail the persecuted by letting the urgent crowd out the strategic. Yes, we must intervene. The Christian who is getting his teeth spread around a Pakistani jail needs our decisive intervention to secure his release now! Not next week. Not next year. Now! The church firebombed twice in the last week in Ambon, Indonesia, needs our aid instantly before it happens again. The Christian family who fled extremists burning their village in northern Nigeria needs immediate help lest they rot, forgotten in the depressing circumstances of a refugee camp.

There is a danger, however, that too much of the "intervention energy" goes into securing short-term, high-profile releases and fixes, which all too often come at the expense of longer-term strategies that deal not with the symptoms but with the deep causes of persecution. The inevitable rules of fund-raising may be responsible, though they can hardly be blamed. Everyone would be touched to support a call to build a house for a martyr's widow, but fewer are likely to reach into their pocket to assist a fifty-year plan to create Christian primary schools in Indian villages.

Yet if revolutions are launched as children are raised in an atmosphere of hate, Hindu extremists in India are well on their way. They hatched a plan in the late 1990s to send five hundred thousand teachers into the interior of India. Each teacher would arrive in a village of normally between fifty and two hundred people and offer to give the children a free education. The parents would leap at the chance, being unable to afford to send their children to school. But the children would be taught the *Hindutva* ideology and especially some poisonous myths that Christians want to take over their country. As Dayal says, "They are raising up the next generation of the Hindu Taliban." The numbers are staggering. Twenty million children will pass through these schools in the next fifty years, while, according to Christian educationalist Dr. Gabriel Gonsalves, "It is almost impossible to find a Christian teacher to go to a village and work in obscurity for fifteen years, dedicating their lives to the influencing of maybe just twenty children in the ways of truth, love, and justice."

If extremists have fifty-year plans to bring about persecution, where are the Christian fifty-year plans to combat it? There is a failure to realize that persecution, like mighty rivers, flows from seemingly insignificant streams, and it is far easier to dry up a tiny spring than damn up a river. As we have seen, before persecution becomes a campaign bringing extreme suffering, it starts out as myths in books, dehumanizing jokes in clubs, false theories and facts going uncontested, and scapegoating the victim rather than the victimizer. It takes a strategic mind to see that this is where persecution is most effectively stopped, before the culture is held for ransom by extremists.

For all their tactical disagreements, Horowitz and Seiple both reveal a keen strategic intelligence in this department. Seiple states unequivocally, "The biggest threat to the successful intervention of Christians in today's world is a superficial faith."[13] Deeply upset by Christian killing Christian in Rwanda, the worst genocide of modern times, Seiple knew that the biggest problem causing religious persecution and preventing its reduction was that too few Christians took their faith seriously enough to know their faith "at its richest and deepest, and know enough about your neighbor's faith to show it respect."[14] He went to the spiritual heart of persecution. Clearly, the best and deepest way to combat persecution is to make mature disciples of Christ. This is the work of the church, and it is struggling in its most basic task! Our job then is to help with this perennial priority.

Horowitz also sought solutions at the religio-cultural level. He divined that modern liberalism gives you status only if you are a victim. If you are not a victim, you do not count. To help push the International Religious Freedom Act along, Horowitz began by altering public perceptions: "We shifted [Christians] from victimizers to victim, and the legislation had to pass because no one can walk away from the victim classes and get away with it today."[15] What remains to be done, according to Horowitz, is to get Christians to wake up to their own heritage and break what he terms the "whispering caricature" in the secular culture, which holds that Christianity is bad for the individual and for the nation. In language remarkable from the mouth of an Orthodox Jew, he says, "Christians have been completely frightened by the bigots who just say *you gave us the crusades, so don't interfere any more or you'll just cause more wars,* and instead they need to remember that it was Christians that abolished slavery, gave us human rights, the ideals of democracy, and so on—discover your history and recover your sense of pride and then you will stand up for the persecuted and build better nations that set people free. It won't happen until Christians reconnect with their own history and stop going around the world apologizing to everyone."[16]

Of course, not all strategies to assist the persecuted have to do with cultural engineering. A common problem with having concern for the urgent is that it can overshadow a proper understanding of the larger needs of the persecuted. In 2003 an English Christian magazine called *Enough* published shocking pictures of Chinese Christian prisoners being tortured by police. The title of the piece was "Torture: The Reality for China's Christians."[17] For me the problem was not the savage nature of the shock tactic; it was the fact that the needs of China's Christians were presented primarily in terms of stopping torture when greater needs were going unmentioned. This bothered me because, shortly before, it had been my privilege to spend a weekend with ten top house-church leaders in China. What I heard changed my life, and it became clear that stopping torture—however important—was not uppermost in the minds of these Chinese leaders.

These ten were amazing. I knew the leader who had founded the ministry in 1987. He saw 200 converted in the first year. When I visited him in 1991, there were 30,000 in the movement. Now, there are 350,000 members, with people coming to know Jesus at the rate of—get this—875 a day!

You would think that with growth like that, these leaders would be leaping and dancing. And when they told me about the growth,

I shouted, "Hallelujah!" They smiled, then promptly burst into tears. "What am I missing?" I asked. "You are missing the reason we are gathered here this weekend—*to ask God why he brings people to himself far faster than we can disciple them.*"

If this sounds ungrateful, then consider their challenges. Last year, more than ten thousand of their membership left to join a vicious cult called *Lightning from the East*. Said the leader, "We can only ask new converts to disciple new converts, and it results in so much bad teaching, we are beginning to fear that the gains of the revival could be undone."

Another one of them said, "This revival looks statistically incredible, but it is spiritually vulnerable. Millions of Chinese Christians are just one unanswered prayer away from moving on to another religion."

The ten were studying the history of revival. I had brought them a syllabus from my old professor, and as we went through all the revivals two points became clear. *First, revivals don't last very long.* They are temporary phenomena. "We may not enjoy this growth very much longer," said one of the group, "because the revival killer is coming—consumerism."

In the words of Li Tianen, a famous Shanghai pastor, "Consumerism makes you think you don't have to suffer to follow Jesus. It makes you think you can have lots of things, and Christ as well. In reality, you just end up with lots of things, and most of the time you don't even realize Christ has gone." China is experiencing rampant capitalism. Everyone wants to get rich quick, and many are.

*Second, revivals do not necessarily have a long-term impact.* Some revivals disappear without a trace. Think of the Welsh revival of 1904. What has Wales got to show for that but mostly empty churches today? These men were all concerned. "We must make sure this revival changes China."

"Help us," they said. "This is the Chinese church's most urgent need—for the Western church to enable us to turn new believers into mature believers, so that this revival will change Chinese society."

So we must state this with great sensitivity—their most urgent need is not to stop torture; it is to help them make disciples!

Said one of the leaders, "Westerners seem to see China's Christians either as an entirely persecuted church—which it isn't—or as an entirely free church—which it isn't either. Torture happens but not to most of us. Make a hue and cry about torture by all means, but don't be distracted from realizing what the Chinese church really is and needs—we are a *revival church*, and we need your assistance with the blessing and burdens that revival brings." He added, "Remember, it's your revival too. You prayed for it as much as we did, and we will come to you with the blessing as China opens up more in the future."[18]

The persecuted church deserves our best effort. Surely we are bound to help the entire persecuted community, not just a few hundred within it. We must be smart and strategic in our interventions. We still may fail, but it must be out of a desire to listen and serve the persecuted first. Our ministries and our own interests must run a distant second to that aim.

What can we do? What are our options? How can we be confident that our aid will benefit the church? We must consider the range of tactics available and come to grips with the tricky business of discerning what works best and when!

# 10    What Works When?

## Seven Tactics
## of Intervention Assessed

When, in the March 2003 issue of *Christianity Today*, two religious rights advocates differed sharply on how best to help the persecuted, the whole question of what tactic works best and when was, paradoxically, well aired yet also ignored.

Michael Horowitz called for strong public denunciations of oppressive regimes backed up by punitive sanctions. He wrote, "First is a lesson I know as a Jew—that silence never works with tyrants." Those who stay silent, he argued, "must bear the moral burden of, and responsibility for, the victimized believers who suffer and die on their watch." As an example of this robust approach working, he cited the passage of the U.S. Jackson-Vanik amendment, which banned trade with the Soviet Union for refusing to allow Jewish dissidents to emigrate. The USSR backed down, proving that tyrants are "often a lot more fragile and vulnerable than they appear."[1]

T. Jeremy Gunn called for a quieter, nonconfrontational dialogue, citing the universal principle that "foreign governments (similar to most human beings) do not usually respond positively to denunciations and pressure."[2] After all, he asks, is Cuba a more democratic, tolerant state today for all the decades of sanctions and denunciation? In contrast, he tells of the experience of a panel of experts in Kazakhstan analyzing new religious laws, which were set to be more restrictive. The quiet, considered debate, and a low-key presentation by an American diplomat ensured that the tougher laws were set aside without the ruckus of a bruising public spat.

But why were both men asked to denigrate the validity of each other's tactic—a task Jeremy Gunn, commendably, did not rise to? A more sensible question would have been, since both tactics work, which works best and when? When does naming and shaming work, and when is it counterproductive? When does quiet diplomacy work, and when is it inadequate? Surely both tactics should be put at the disposal of the persecuted. Our job is to discover when one or the other is needed, or when both are needed at the same time!

This chapter assesses seven forms of tactical intervention. There are probably more forms, and some of them blur together. No one has all the answers to effectiveness, least of all me. There is also not enough space available in this discussion for a comprehensive treatment of each method. The purpose here is to provoke a sense that more tactics are available than some believe and that all of them can work in certain circumstances. I will try particularly to present the perspective of the persecuted Christians I have met on my travels who rarely get the privilege of testifying in front of a Washington, D.C., committee. Controversy over the correct tactic will always persist. No one can sweep that away. But one does hope for more mutual respect. After all, if those who work for the persecuted cannot tolerate each other's views, our credibility is destroyed before we have started.

## Tactic 1: The Role of Prayer/Intercession

Ask the persecuted, "How can we help you?" and you will invariably find that their first answer is "Pray for us!" Usually their second answer is "Pray for us!" And their third answer is "Pray for us!" There is absolutely no question that when it comes to tactical assistance, it is prayer that the persecuted crave more than anything else from their less persecuted brothers and sisters.

It's simple to see why. The persecuted realize the value of prayer because they are more experienced in it. Situations of utter helplessness are occasions when all one can do is pray. If a Christian in America or Europe is fired because of his or her faith, there are many avenues available to seek redress, including filing a grievance, phoning a lawyer, claiming compensation, or even looking for other work. But the severely persecuted person is usually just sitting in a jail, and the only action available is to pray.

Moses Xie, a man who spent more than twenty years in jail in China for his faith, shared with me that when asking visitors to pray for him he was really after three distinct outcomes: "First, I want them to experience the blessing of prayer for themselves. They will go to God on my behalf, but they will receive a great blessing from being in the presence of God. I have noticed that Western Christians don't seem to pray that much. Second, I know that as they pray, their burden for the persecuted will increase, and as their burden grows, so their commitment to assisting us in all sorts of other ways will increase also. Prayer alone makes them *be the body*. Third, I want them to release more of God's power into our situation through intercession, since I know that God has bound himself not to act until we ask."

Not every persecuted Christian, of course, espouses this understanding of intercessory prayer, sometimes called "dominion theology," which teaches that God cannot act unless invited, taking literally the principle in James 4:2: "You do not have, because you do not ask." Yet most believe that we must ask for specific outcomes from God. It is not enough to simply pray, "Thy will be done." This misses God's incredible invitation of prayer, actually to request the form His will should take in any given situation. Thus Jesus asks specifically in Gethsemane, "Take this cup from me." But Jesus's request does not force God to act, for the Father's will is better, and Jesus ends by realizing that it will be better to drink the cup, and is strengthened accordingly. He stresses this when He adds: "Yet not what I want but what you want" (Matt. 26:39). The important point is that Jesus asked for something specific first and then saw more clearly the outline of the will of God. If He had failed to ask, He would not have seen how necessary it was to go to the cross, nor received the strength to endure it.

Brother Andrew, a faithful servant of the persecuted who, when he is not visiting the persecuted, is usually encouraging prayer for them, once wrote a book on this very point. Called *And God Changed His Mind*, Andrew called the "Thy will be done" prayer method "fatalism" and a failure to influence God's "open" mind. His book contains an astonishing claim of the power of intercessory prayer on behalf of the persecuted and is worth reproducing here:

> Back in 1983 our organization, Open Doors, called for seven years of prayer for the Soviet Union. We were convinced that the evil conspiracy that had brought untold misery and torment to the Body of Christ worldwide was headquartered in one place: Moscow. Millions had died as a result of genocide in Communist nations, and hundreds of thousands were in prison for their faith. We decided to take the offensive against Satan by attacking his strongholds. Many Christians around the world joined us. We prayed particularly that the barriers that have kept God's Word out of Eastern Europe and Russia would be removed and that Christian prisoners would be set free.
>
> Within a year we began to see results. We heard for the first time about an obscure man named Gorbachev. We began to hear the words *glasnost* and *perestroika* instead of the usual Communist rhetoric. The winds of change we prayed for began to blow, and there was no holding them back. Finally, just under six years from the time we first began praying, the walls between East and West began to crumble. The Berlin Wall—a worldwide symbol of Communist oppression—came tumbling down. Prison doors began to open. Eastern Europe rose up against the powers that had held them in bondage.
>
> In 1989, after more than thirty years of smuggling Bibles behind the Iron Curtain, I challenged the Russians openly to allow our organization to distribute a million Russian-language Bibles to Soviet churches. Incredibly, they said yes. And at this moment [he was writing in 1990] still less than seven years after we began praying, we are able to report to our prayer partners the glorious news that *not a*

*single Christian leader remains in prison or concentration camp in the Soviet Union for his faith.* That, my friend, is what happens when we pray.[3]

Of course, it can never be proved that prayer caused all this. It is believed by faith. Canons of logic and science remain too crude to uncover cause and effect in the spiritual realm. But for the Christian who believes that prayer does move the Hand that moves the world, this must be the most exciting way to engage with the persecuted.

This may explain the amazing rise of the prayer movement, IDOP, first organized by the Religious Liberty Commission of the World Evangelical Fellowship in 1996 with a few hundred churches in the United States. Now at least a fifth of American Christians in mid-November each year remember the persecuted in prayer.[4] The impact is significant and illustrates Moses Xie's point that prayer can be the starter for other persecution initiatives. For one thing, the movement has proved to be a remarkable ecumenical catalyst, bringing liberals and evangelicals together and creating potent alternatives to partisan bickering. For another, as Allen Hertske discovers, the IDOP concept was expanded in 2001 in Midland, Texas, to be a community-wide event with massive media impact. No fewer than forty congregations held special services, reaching into the home of the future president of the United States and creating a momentum that assisted the passage of the Sudan Peace Act.[5] Prayer movements clearly lead to power coalitions.

An obvious objection arises from the faithful prayer partner, though, especially one who may have asked long and hard for a persecutor to be saved or a church to be spared, and yet who has seen the fire of tribulation only flare higher. The more they pray, the more persecution seems to intensify. Dr. Abdul Menes Noor, a Presbyterian pastor in Cairo, takes this on by asking, "Were the early believers disappointed because God did not answer their prayers for James positively?" Peter was released from prison, but James was martyred. Menes answers, "I do not think so. Their Acts 4 prayer shows that their main petition was for boldness and miracle performing to witness to Jesus's power. This petition is always given. We pray for all the persecuted Christians. When some of them are tortured, or slain by the sword, or shot by bullets, we know that the blood of the martyrs is the seed of the church. We also know that their crowning has come when they die."[6]

The greatest challenge of all, then, in intercession is to see in faith the sovereign God extending His kingdom through every reversal and sorrow. The greatest thrill is to see it happening.

But what is an intercessor? "An intercessor," says William Willis, "is a man who prays and weeps in the secret place of prayer until God stoops down and dries his tears."[7] Willis was a Welshman who came and spoke at the Love China Conference in 1975 in Manila. It was organized by Brother David, who went on to fame as "God's Smuggler to China." Brother David (alias Doug Sutphen) was astonished to learn that William Willis was kneeling in his hotel bathroom for *seven hours a day*, asking God for China. At the end of the conference, Willis asked Doug if he would take him to a point where they could look into mainland China, which at that point was utterly closed. Doug recalls, "I took him up to Lo Wu, in Hong Kong, and we gazed into paddy fields stretching beyond the barbed wire. Brother Willis put his arm around me and said, 'Young man, this is what the Lord told me. Soon China will open up, and when it does, it will remain open for the Lord.'"

Doug was stunned. "This was October 1975. We had hardly heard a thing from China in fifteen years. All we knew was that bodies had floated down the Pearl River from the chaos of the Cultural Revolution. But a few months later, the Chinese Premier Zhou Enlai, was dead. A year later Mao Zedong was dead. Two years later Deng Xiaoping was 'resurrected.' And China was open."[8]

I used to visit that same lookout point in Lo Wu all through the eighties and nineties. There are no paddy fields now. Instead, you will see gleaming skyscrapers, factories, and apartment buildings and hear the urban roar of the world-class city of Shenzhen, the first gateway to China. I would stand there remembering what Doug had told me about William Willis, who had long departed this life. I looked at the city and wondered, *Who built this? Who made Shenzhen possible? Was it the work of Deng Xiaoping and his four modernizations policy, opening China up to Western markets for the first time in 1978 after thirty years of isolation? Or was it a seventy-five-year-old man, Brother Willis, who built this city by putting his elbows on the rim of a toilet in Hong Kong and interceding in prayer for seven hours a day with tears and groans?*

I believe it was Brother Willis! I believe the opening of China was a spiritual miracle long before it became an economic miracle. Intercession forces us to ask, "Who is really running the world?" It is God, and that is why the most contradictory revolution of the twentieth century—a Communist Party embracing capitalism—became the means of a door being flung open to the gospel, where the world's largest revival could be fueled and served.

But this kind of intercession is costly. As Willis told the Love China delegates:

> There is a price to be paid. . . . May I remind you of the words King David uttered 3,000 or more years ago. Do you know what he said? *Shall I offer unto the Lord that which hath cost me nothing?* What does your praying cost you? . . . When Jesus saw Jerusalem He wept over it. God is looking for people who will weep over this city and every city in these islands. What's your answer?[9]

## Tactic 2: The Role of Truth Telling/Publicity

It is probably a fair generalization to say that while it is not always helpful to speak out on behalf of a persecuted *individual,* it is always helpful to speak out on behalf of the persecuted *church.*

It is the individual case that requires great sensitivity. In 1998 I received ten thousand dollars to establish a public database of Christians in jail for their faith in China. At the time there were scores in jail, and an authoritative list would be a vital way to arm visiting VIPs with some hard evidence to cut through the official stonewalling of, "We do not have any believers in jail here."

To my surprise, however, 99 percent of the Christians and their families did not wish any publicity and would not give their consent to have their details published. This was a surprise to me because the persecuted church in the former USSR had embraced the tactic very enthusiastically, and Open Doors and other agencies kept a current and very public file of more than three hundred Christian prisoners. But nothing comparable could be made to work for China.

Chinese Christian leaders all gave the same reasons: "We do not wish to get out of jail. It is a way we identify with Christ and spread the gospel where it is desperately needed." Indeed, one of them, an evangelist from Shenyang, went so far as to say, "To be jailed is to be rewarded. Don't take our reward away." The other reason they gave was more pragmatic. It had not escaped their notice that those evangelists who had received international publicity during their detention were unable to resume their ministry after their release, since they were shadowed so closely by government spies. So they said, "We don't want a fuss made so that when we come out, we can pick up where we left off."

This is not to say that the publicity tactic is always counterproductive in China. The international outcry over the arrest of the founder of the Born Again house-church movement, Xu Yongze, in 1997 was vital in securing for him a lighter three-year sentence. At one point the authorities were considering jailing him for being a cult leader—which could have brought a twenty-year sentence or even the death penalty. The damage to China's international reputation caused by the negative publicity forced them to think again. In the end, he was convicted for leading an underground house-church movement.

And there are exceptions to the rule. The pastor of an unofficial house church in Guangchou, Samuel Lamb, is a dedicated self-publicist, welcoming every visitor with his story in smudgy little mimeographed books, with the details of recent persecution incidents all outlined. He has been visited by VIPs such as Billy Graham and astronaut Jim Irwin, but his prized possession is a pen from the Ronald Reagan White House, where a watching brief was kept on his welfare.

China veteran Tony Lambert insists on four key rules when publicizing individual cases of persecution:

1. Permission must be gained from the person concerned or, more usually, their immediate family. It must be their call.
2. The tactic should be talked through with local church leaders and approved. They are in the best position to know if publicity will help or hinder the testimony in their area.

3. It is used as a tactic of last resort, after other methods have failed. This is because of publicity's power to compromise the ability of the person to return to their ministry as before.
4. The publicity must not contain any "intelligence gifts" to the authorities.

Publicity does work. In June of 1999 three Uzbek Christians in the town of Nukus had been found guilty of drug possession and given long sentences. One of them, a twenty-two-year-old pastor of the Full Gospel Church, Rashid Turibayev, was sentenced to fifteen years hard labor; the other two were given ten years. It was one of the worst miscarriages of justice in religious liberty cases of the 1990s and reflected an aggressive government campaign to stamp out unregistered religious activity. In an old, tired ploy, police swooped down on the men's homes and—amazingly—came out carrying bags of drugs! The ploy enabled Uzbek authorities to press serious criminal charges.

For five months the three lay in jail while various legal options were tried. An appeal was scheduled for mid-July. One of the three was handicapped, and one other was refused medicine to treat tuberculosis. Their families were destitute, barely able to afford to send one 26-pound food package into the prison each month, knowing the best would be gobbled up by greedy guards. On the day of the appeal, the three appeared in court, thin and tired. The appeal was turned down, and they turned away, shoulders slumped. It was time to take their case to the world.

Then two Christian journalists began to publish the story, and advocacy agencies also began to use the information to ask tough questions of the Uzbek government. In a matter of weeks, Uzbekistan was becoming known as a "persecution state." Shocked government officials were taken aback at the power of publicity, and on August 19—five weeks after the appeal—the three were released quietly by presidential decree. When local lawyer Gary Kasparov went to look at Pastor Turibayev's case file after his release, he discovered that all the papers relating to the alleged drug discovery in his home had been removed.[10]

Publicity works!

But one must not assume that just because publicity is used, private representation and other tactics must stop. In the case of Bob and Heidi Fu, Beijing house-church leaders arrested in 1996, both publicity and quiet diplomacy helped secure their release. When Bob Fu was arrested, he recalls, "I was badly treated until one day the attitude of my captors completely changed." He later traced it to the day after his case was published in the pages of Hong Kong's leading English language newspaper, the *South China Morning Post*. The publicity gained him better treatment, but a later suppression of publicity also allowed his case to proceed at a diplomatic level in Hong Kong uncomplicated by public posturing and shaming. Thus he and Heidi proceeded from Hong Kong to the United States as religious refugees in 1997, just hours before the handover of the territory back to mainland China.

Enough has been said in the previous chapter about the dangers of overblown publicity, which usually creates more harm than good. In general, however, there is not enough truth telling about the persecuted. More truth tellers are needed. It is no coincidence that IDOP campaigns and other conferences perpetually recycle such slogans as, "Be a voice for the voiceless" and "Shatter the silence," clear indicators that leaders still feel that the story and needs of the persecuted remain untold and unheard.

In the Western world, it is hard to get the story of the persecuted into the public domain because of three particular diseases. The first is what Paul Marshall calls "secular myopia," where the secular mind, which controls the media, refuses to see religion as an important causal factor in anything.

A second disease that keeps the persecuted out of the public eye is what an academic friend of mine calls "the documentary deficiency," where the stories of persecution all too often come from sources that, for security reasons, cannot be named. There is a mentality, especially in the academic and legal realm, that if persecution does not come with documentary evidence, then it doesn't exist. But this, though wise in certain contexts, penalizes the persecuted unfairly. It is not their fault that their suffering does not come with a paper trail, and even if they have documents, such as membership rolls, they would be foolish to publish them with a government intent on stamping them out.

The third disease is the stifling climate of political correctness, which refuses to see Christians as anything but imperialist persecutors of those in other religions. Particular institutions have come under fire for giving in to this culture, and none more heavily than the World Council of Churches (WCC). Their failure to speak out on behalf of the persecuted in Eastern Europe is well documented,[11] but even the fall of the Berlin Wall has not changed their apparent commitment to reserving all their efforts for supporting fashionable left-wing and extreme feminist causes. The late Diane Knippers, president of the Institute on Religion and Democracy, took the gloves off in a speech to the WCC Assembly in Harare in December 1998: "There are glaring omissions in the political and social agenda of the ecumenical movement, and one of the major omissions is its failure to stand up for the persecuted church."[12] She criticized particularly WCC officials going to Khartoum, hobnobbing with Islamic leaders, and never even mentioning the Christians of the south of Sudan against whom these leaders were waging a severe persecution.

But perhaps the greatest reason the truth is not told about the persecuted is that leaders who could speak the truth are too scared. To tell the truth on behalf of the persecuted is to be pitched into a bitter battle. The truth teller will be vilified, misunderstood, and shunned. It is a hard price to pay, as George Carey, the former archbishop of Canterbury, found out in March of 2004. Carey delivered a hard-hitting yet erudite speech at Rome's Gregorian University on the topic "Christianity and Islam—Collision or Convergence?"[13] The speech was lengthy, positive in tone, generous toward Islam, and upbeat about the prospects for interreligious peace.

Very few who did not hear the speech read it through, and two statements (perhaps poorly phrased) in the speech were taken out of context. They became headlines, and Carey was lambasted. One statement called on moderate Muslim leaders to condemn suicide bombers more forcefully, adding, "Sadly, apart from a few courageous examples, very few Muslim leaders condemn, clearly and unconditionally, the evil of suicide bombers who kill innocent people." The other statement was, "It is sad to relate that no great invention has come for many hundreds of years from Muslim countries."

One of Dr. Carey's Islamic dialogue partners, Dr. Zaki Badawi, on the BBC's *World at One* program, tore into him for making these statements yet blithely admitted that he had not read the speech. A Channel 4 documentary in the United Kingdom featured some prominent Muslims accusing Muslim leaders of bleating "Islamophobia" as a deliberate tactic to stifle all criticism of Islam,[14] and this may explain why few interacted substantively with Carey's comments. Carey remained unrepentant, however, and maintains to this day that interreligious dialogue was benefited by his blunt speech.

## Tactic 3: The Role of Private Representation

Private representation is when individuals in a private capacity seek to assist the persecuted by making representation—usually quietly—to the persecuting government or authority. While some may hold powerful offices of state, they are seeking in their private representation to use the power of friendship as a lever, though the threat of further action may be implied.

I became aware of the importance of private representation through the work of an American Catholic businessman who made it a priority to use his extensive contacts among China's officials to ask for the release of Chinese Christian prisoners. Though it is hard to say for sure, his quiet efforts over dinner tables, meetings in offices, and using his skills of friendship, cajoling, even threatening or shaming on occasions, ended in the release of scores of prisoners, arguably far more than through public pressure.

The key ingredient here was trust. The Chinese officials trusted this man. He refrained from embarrassing China publicly, so he could not be dismissed as "anti-China." He had standing as a businessman who was benefiting China economically. His information was rarely inaccurate; indeed, he was able to surprise a number of officials into an awareness that persecution was a bigger problem than they knew. Through experience he also developed an ability to go to the right person to get things done, avoiding the climbers, the braggers, and the downright incompetent. Above all, he knew how to communicate in a Chinese culture, knowing when to be aggressive and when to go slowly, and how to present solutions that were both effective and face-saving.

This tactic suffers from underestimation because of its low profile. While I was interviewing a Christian lawyer in London recently, he told me that forty years earlier, he had befriended his college neighbor, a shy Muslim boy with few social skills. The friendship had lapsed until one day the Christian received a letter from his former friend. He had become an important figure in the judiciary of his Middle Eastern state and was writing to get advice on how to deal with a case where Christians were being attacked by Muslim extremists. The two were able to correspond, and the judge wrote back to say, "This case has worked out to the satisfaction of the parties concerned—an outcome I would not have thought possible a few weeks ago. I turned to you because you know the law and seem to be a Christian that does not bash Muslims. Indeed, you were the only person at university that showed me sincere friendship, and I put that down to your faith in part. Your advice has given me a positive perspective on Christianity I simply would not have got over here, trapped as we are with the stereotypes that the media and the extremists feed us with. Thank you." Clearly the friendship influenced the ruling of the case, but that will never be written up as part of the story.

Private conversations between political leaders of different faiths or of no faith may have a huge impact on the outcome of cases too. In his presidential memoirs, *Keeping Faith*, Jimmy Carter tells of a confidential conversation with China's supreme leader Deng Xiaoping in January of 1979. Carter, a devout Christian, suggested "that he should permit the unrestricted distribution of Bibles and let people have freedom of worship." Carter then states, "He promised to look into it." And he adds in parentheses: "Later, he acted favorably on both these suggestions."[15] Carter was careful not to claim that it was mainly due to his suggestions, but it is true that within the next five years the TSPM reopened at a significant pace, and Bibles began to be printed, albeit in hopelessly small quantities. But it was a start, and who is to say that the greatest changes do not begin as the result of face-to-face interactions with leaders who respect each other.

But it doesn't have to be a dialogue between the great leaders; the ordinary Christian can play a huge role as well. The most obvious tactic here is letter writing. Two letters are typically written: a letter of encouragement to the victim and a letter of protest to the persecutor. When Pastor Hamid Pourmand of Iran was facing the death penalty on charges of apostasy, the judge at the Islamic court said, "I don't know who you are, but apparently the rest of the world does. You must be an important person, because many people from the government have called me, saying to cancel your case." That was because the Iranian government and their embassies throughout the world had been bombarded with thousands of letters on Hamid's behalf. The judge did remove the charges of apostasy on May 28, 2005, though Pastor Hamid is still in jail serving a sentence for converting from Islam to Christianity. The great value of a letter-writing campaign is that it brings the eyes of the world into dark places, preventing deeds of oppression that can succeed only in the dark. Very often the more letters that are sent on behalf of a Christian prisoner, the better he or she is treated.

More crucially, letters of encouragement provide the strength to endure. I knew a Columbian prisoner who used to lie on his pile of letters from Christians. He said, "I could not read their messages, but as I lay on them I felt the love of Christ flow into me from all parts of the world, and I knew I was not alone. I was able to go on." A young Mexican Christian, Sister Marta, exiled from her home after refusing to participate in pagan rituals, told an Open Doors visitor, "When I become afraid or sad, I take [the letters] and look at them. Now I know I am not alone." All too often something as simple as a letter makes all the difference. You don't have to be a senator to exercise power on behalf of a Christian prisoner.

## Tactic 4: The Role of Legal Intervention

Legal intervention involves using the force of law to assist the persecuted. It can include lodging appeals, filing briefs in court, passing laws such as the International Religious Freedom Act, and, in drastic cases, military intervention authorized by international law. Admittedly, legal maneuvering is so often tied up with political pressure it is hard to see where one leaves off and the other begins.

Often this tactic is dismissed as a waste of effort. In countries where Christians are severely persecuted, the rule of law is paid scant regard. Judges are bought or intimidated, and justice is whatever the ruling party or leaders say it is. But even in cases where the rule of law is ignored, there can be three useful effects of taking the legal route.

First is the *ammunition effect*. Taking an official to court for overreaching his or her brief or lodging an appeal against the result of a show trial may be a legal waste of time in the country itself, but it provides critical ammunition for the exertion of political pressure from outside the country. Whenever one goes to a person in power in the West and says, "This person is being persecuted; help him," the usual answer is, "I don't believe you; show me the proof." If there is a legal trail documenting the persecution, then the pressure to intervene is much greater. It is an unfortunate feature of the cynical world in which we live that no story is believed until a legal document is produced. But to make a legal fuss in a persecution case, while it may not help get the prisoner out of jail instantly, may well help the person's case as his or her international profile becomes known.

Second is the *embarrassment effect*. While there are countries that care nothing about international opinion, such as Zimbabwe, Eritrea, and Burma, most states do try to present a positive image abroad. Even a country as totalitarian as China changed its legal system in the 1990s to criminalize house-church activity, so that its apologists could argue abroad that "no one is in jail for *religious* reasons in China today," because the act had been made a criminal offense.

Why bother to use this tactic? Because there is only one international political discourse left, and that is the language of human rights. Of course, these countries are out to exploit and subvert the rules of discourse, but the international commitment to the rule of law renders them vulnerable to the bad publicity that a botched trial or an effective appeal could bring. Often there are specific periods when legal pressure bears more fruit than at other times. When a host of Eastern European states were queuing up to join the EU in 2004, some Christians mounted legal challenges resulting in the dismantling of a raft of discriminatory legislation that had been designed to protect the state churches. Suddenly in Hungary, for example, it was more important to enjoy the common market of the EU than protect the institutional privileges of the Reformed Church. Turkey will be an important battleground also in this respect, as it lines up hopefully for EU membership in the next decade.

However, many countries with persecuted Christians have laws that are just fine, it's just that no one remembers them. In India, for example, Open Doors teaches pastors how to file legal appeals after persecution incidents. Called "First Information Reports," pastors were entirely unaware of their rights under existing laws. Extremists were intimidating them in ways that the laws forbade, and police were obliged to protect them. As journalist Vishal Aurora says, "Our judiciary needs strengthening, and the police need to be depoliticized, and so Christian lawyers are necessarily in the forefront of stopping persecution."[16]

Thirdly, there is an *empowering effect* when Christians stand up for their rights, much as Paul did when he used his Roman citizenship to demand his audience with Caesar's court in Rome. Not all pastors are convinced of this, however. Many Christian leaders in India believe that persecution should simply be accepted, without making a fuss. As C. B. Samuel told me, "These pastors say to me, 'We'll take the beating and share the gospel; if we raise a stink, we lose our opportunity to share the gospel.'"[17] Sometimes persecution should be embraced with all one's heart, and sometimes it should be fought against with all one's might. It takes wisdom to know the difference.

The long-term aspect of the legal intervention tactic should not be overlooked. Christian lawyers, for example, should be aware that the elites of emerging nations are on the lookout for new systems of ethics and are open as never before to seminars on how a greater understanding and application of the rule of law could bring social stability to a nation. The story of how the rule of law builds a great nation is a Christian story! Would it surprise anyone to know that Christian input on this very topic is in hot demand from China today?

Legal competence allied to street-wise savvy is needed here also. I remember one international ministry based in America that conducted much trumpeted legal interventions on behalf of underage Christian prostitutes in Bombay. They forced the police to take action, and the girls were removed. But they failed to go to the court where the brothel keepers were being arraigned. The keepers gave false names, gained bail, and were back on the street just in time to round up the girls, who had been cast adrift by the judge, who said, "Go back to your own village." The ministry never noticed because they were too busy developing the photos from the night's raid and writing up their press releases. Said Anson Thomas, an old hand at this game, "They should have known to go to the court and make sure the brothel keepers gave their real names. That's the only way to prevent them from posting bail and to keep them in jail long enough to get the girls away from their clutches."

## Tactic 5: The Role of Illegal Intervention

Illegal intervention is when the form of assistance to the persecuted involves methods that contravene the laws or wishes of the government of the land. Everyone understands the need for these methods ever since Peter declared to the Sanhedrin, "We must obey God rather than men!" (Acts 5:29 NIV). There are some aspects of the Christian faith that must be practiced no matter what political or ecclesiastical authorities may say. No one can forbid a Christian to pray or worship or read Scripture or share his or her faith. If the state forbids any of these, disobedience to the state becomes the inevitable result of obedience to God.

Controversy in this area centers on when, rather than if, this tactic is appropriate. For example, some people who advocated smuggling Bibles to China all through the seventies and eighties now say the tactic is unnecessary given that since 1987, a joint initiative between the China Christian Council and the United Bible Societies created the Amity printing press, a state-of-the-art Bible press capable of printing millions of Bibles per year and sold through official churches.

The person who made the most spectacular turnaround on this issue was Doug Sutphen. As the leader of Open Doors Asia in 1981, Doug mounted Project Pearl, a cloak-and-dagger operation that would not look out of place on the pages of a bestselling novel. A million Bibles were packed into a tennis court–sized barge and towed under cover of darkness from Hong Kong to the coast of mainland China, narrowly avoiding detection by a Chinese destroyer. The barge was sunk near a shallow sloping beach, and its cargo floated to the surface in watertight packs of thirty thousand Bibles each. Then two Zodiac boats hooked the packages and carried them to the water's edge, where more than a thousand Chinese Christians were waiting with lorries to spirit the Bibles away to house churches throughout the country.

The whole event was unique in scale in the history of Bible smuggling and touched off a storm of protest that spilled onto the pages of *Time* magazine. The Chinese government said it was "imperialistic" and lodged a strong protest with the United States. According to Doug, the Reagan White House issued a crisp reply to this effect: "Print the Bible for your people then, and this will not need to happen." Rumors were spread that most of the Bibles were burned, which was untrue, and even some missions that applauded the intention thought the project too ambitious in scale. Time Magazine estimated that 80 percent of the Bibles were delivered successfully.

A decade later, Sutphen left Open Doors to found a new mission called East Gates Ministries International, and with the help of Ned Graham, son of Dr. Billy Graham, was able to harness the fund-raising capacity of the Grahams and their ecumenical contacts to place an order for a million Bibles with Amity Press in 1992, completed in three years. This order broke the mold because it was claimed that the Bibles would be distributed to the underground house churches, thus overcoming the biggest criticism of Amity Press to date, that the Bibles could be bought only by the minority of Christians who worshiped in the state-controlled Three Self churches. Doug grandly declared at the time: "The era of Bible smuggling is over"—a huge coup for the Three Self propagandists, since he was the author of the bestselling *God's Smuggler to China.* Not surprisingly, howls of protest greeted him again. He was accused of selling out to the official church, abandoning the house churches, and misrepresenting the Bible need of China's Christians.

Over a meal in Hong Kong in 1996, a chastened Doug told me, "I only meant Bible smuggling at that time was over *for me,* not for everyone." However, his life does illustrate something vital about the illegal intervention tactic—that the illegal often provokes the legal. Doug Sutphen recalls meeting Han Wenzao in 1996, then the chairman of the China Christian Council and the head of Amity Press. Han admitted to him: "Project Pearl meant we had to build Amity Press. It put so much pressure on us we could not go on with small printings." Han also said he would never make that declaration public. Insiders know what they cannot admit, that an illegal tactic often results in a legal concession.

The pattern is often easier to see in history. When Englishman William Tyndale decided to translate the Bible from Latin into English and use the new invention of the printing press to reproduce it, he had to flee the country. In 1524, while only twenty-nine, he settled in Cologne, and by 1526 he was ready to smuggle six thousand copies of the Bible in English into Britain. The whole British naval fleet was put on alert, and boats were stopped and searched. Yet tens and then hundreds of the Bibles got through.

The bishop of London tried another tack. He sought to buy the entire print run through an intermediary. His intention was to burn them all. Tyndale got wind of it and approved the sale, saying, "Oh, he will burn them. Well, I am the gladder, for I shall get the money from these books, and the whole world shall cry out upon the burning of God's word." And so it was. The bishop burned them, and Tyndale used the money to improve the translation and print more—at the church's expense.

Tyndale's work formed 85 percent of the King James Bible. "The noise of the new Bible echoed throughout the country," said Tyndale. It was pocket sized, easy to conceal, and thus went everywhere. The theological heavyweights of the church railed against it. Thomas More scorned it as "putting the fire of Scripture into the language of plow boys." Tyndale was captured by assassins and then strangled and burned in August 1536 for heresy. His last words were, "Lord, open the King of England's eyes."

This prayer was answered, and the English reformation was fueled by a spate of translations. The Coverdale Bible (translated from a German Bible) in 1535 was the first legal Bible. In 1537 the Matthew's Bible was published, an amalgam of the Tyndale and Coverdale Bibles; then in 1539 came the Great Bible, placed in every church. Three different Bibles were published in six years. There were so many that King James had to authorize a special standard version in 1611.

And so Tyndale's illegal intervention turned out to be for the legal benefit of everyone who holds an English Bible in his or her hands today.

Given all this history, the question still needs to be asked: is Bible smuggling an appropriate tactic to meet Bible demand in China today? The answer depends on how large you consider the Chinese church to be. If you believe the Three Self leaders, the Protestant church in China is no larger than fifteen to twenty million. If you believe those who have contact with house-church leaders, you will receive estimates that the total is anywhere between sixty and eighty million and possibly higher. Clearly, those who accept the higher estimates as true know that the Bible need of China is far greater than the single legal initiative of Amity Press can meet. The press is limited to processing orders only from TSPM churches, and these orders, rather suspiciously, rarely exceed 3.5 million a year, when the capacity of the press is six million per year. Although the press has printed more than forty million Bibles since its inception, ministries like Open Doors continue to insist that there are still shortages of Scripture among the churches of the rural revival.[18] The needs of the Chinese church run at such a high level that they remain beyond the capacity of any single initiative to address. The era of Bible smuggling is not quite over!

Of course, the principle must not be forgotten that one serves the suffering church the way it wishes to be served. If tomorrow, Chinese house-church leaders calculate that the disadvantages of handling illegal Bibles, with all the security risks involved, outweigh the advantages of receiving them, then the tactic must be stopped. The local church should always be allowed to make the call! Unfortunately, this simple principle has sometimes been ignored. I remember one ministry asking Open Doors if they could use Open Doors's network to distribute smuggled Bibles. "Why did you take so many in if you cannot distribute them?" this mission was asked. Back came the less than adequate reply, "We had a big fund-raising drive last year and promised to take in a million Bibles." This goal had been fixed without adequate consultation with the local church.

Often Bible smuggling defines the discussion on illegal intervention, but there are many other strategies involved here, such as leaking documents, sneaking leaders who are about to be arrested out of the country, or providing Bible teachers for underground seminaries. In Middle Eastern countries, such as Egypt, it is unfortunately sometimes necessary to smuggle Muslim converts out of the country to stop their families from killing them.

Where the powerful in a country hate Christ, most of the assistance that is given to the church will have to be given in defiance of law. Illegal intervention is necessary when no legal options exist to serve the church.

## Tactic 6: The Role of Political Pressure

Political pressure is when people in the government of one country use the power of their office to influence the religious policy of another government that may be severely persecuting Christians. The pressure can be used on individuals within government or actually against government policy itself. Though President George W. Bush is not admired by all Christians, on a February 2002 visit to China he shared his faith with Chinese political leaders and called on China to end the persecution of religious believers. This is pressure. It is not U.S. government policy to share one's Christian faith with other leaders. On the other hand, it is the declared policy of the U.S. government to press other nations to improve their religious liberty record, especially in the wake of 9/11.

There are two primary arenas here.

### Individual to Individual

Political pressure can be used when an individual in one state uses his or her political muscle to assist in the case of a persecuted individual in another state. Positive examples abound here. When visiting Egypt, I interviewed a young man who had been tortured by the police in 1991, when he and three other friends were rounded up and jailed for being Muslim converts and running a church for Muslim-background believers. One of his pastors, Dr. Abdul Menes Noor, called his friends in Washington, and Senator Richard Lugar was particularly persistent in calling up key personnel in the Egyptian government and asking for the four men to be released. Another useful exchange came between James Baker III, the secretary of state at the time, and Egyptian President Hosni Mubarak. "Why do you care about that garbage?" snarled Mubarak, referring to the four men. "Because they are my brothers," answered Baker. The four were released after a few months, significantly due to the political heat applied by American Christian politicians.

A restriction to this kind of intervention is that it tends to work only in prisoner cases. It is much harder to influence the government of Egypt to grant Muslim converts to Christianity full religious freedom. No one has succeeded there so far. Also the intervention only works with those state leaders who have a vested interest in maintaining good relations with the pressuring power. Egypt most certainly wishes to keep on the right side of the United Sates. But senators and representatives have been calling the Eritrean government for over a year now, and their pleadings have not altered one whit the mistreatment of the hundreds of Christians in jail at this time.

Individual politicians can also attempt to influence the persecuting culture for the better, and since political change happens mostly at a glacial pace, it would be impossible to label particular speeches and exchanges as successful or unsuccessful.

When President Bush visited China in 2002, he met with students from Tsinghua University. In a speech carried live to the Chinese nation, Bush told the audience in a very nonthreatening and winsome manner how the adoption of the Christian faith had helped him live a better life. He ended with these words: "Faith points to a moral law beyond man's law, and calls us to duties higher than material gain. Freedom of religion is not something to be feared; it's to be welcomed, because faith gives us a moral core and teaches us to hold ourselves to high standards, to love and serve others, and to live responsible lives."[19]

Afterward the students were extremely positive, and the speech did strengthen the hand of that faction within the Chinese government that was pressing for a more liberal policy toward the house churches. There is very little to show for it at this stage, but it was definitely received positively at the time. Bush helped defuse the view that Christianity was always dangerous and subversive, and although that doesn't spring a Christian from jail or result in a new law, it still represents a seed dropped into fertile soil.

### State to State

One state can exert pressure on another to improve its religious rights record. State pressure on the whole is an extremely blunt instrument. Even the might of the United States, making drastic interventions in Afghanistan, found that they could replace the regime but not improve the religious tolerance record, as the U.S.-backed regime set about producing a constitution that worsened conditions for Christians. "We were better off under the Taliban," said an underground believer in Kabul. The chaos of present-day Iraq also proves the impossibility of mighty armies to build new cultures of tolerance.

It is in the milder versions of this tactic where most of the debate occurs. After six years, has the International Religious Freedom Act made much difference? I asked this question of five committed religious liberty advocates working on Capitol Hill, who all wish to remain nameless. They cited three improvements. First, the State Department is beginning to get the message that religion actually matters in foreign policy. The State Department has long ignored religion as a factor at all and certainly has not kicked up a fuss about religious abuses. While no one would say that this has changed significantly, State Department officials at least have to produce a report once a year on the religious liberty situation and are required by law to monitor religious liberty in every foreign country.

Second, the amount of accurate information on religious liberty has increased. This is mainly due to the publication of the International Religious Freedom report, published every September. This has necessitated the gathering of more reliable information, with each embassy required to produce reports each year.

Finally, the U.S. Committee for International Religious Freedom (USCIRF) has kept the issue on the political agenda by sounding some shrill notes. They ensure that religious liberty does not disappear without a trace as a policy consideration in government.

Of course, the act has changed little throughout the world, but then it has not existed for long. Six years is barely a day in politics. As Paul Marshall warns: "When you pass a law, all you have is a law. You need to build a culture of concern that makes the law work. That takes longer, and that critical core has not yet been built up, but that is not the law's fault."[20]

It's Michael Horowitz who seems most aware of this, as he seeks to keep religious liberty in the public eye by pursuing what he calls "a Wilberforce agenda," bringing diverse groups together to push for positive social change. The key to political influence is to build coalitions. Despite what some secular commentators claim, evangelical Christians by themselves have no power to control the legislative agenda. They need to join forces. The International Religious Freedom Act was a case in point, making use of a previous coalition of feminists concerned about China's antiwomen policies, labor unions angry at China's use of prisoner labor, as well as evangelical Christians incensed about the treatment of Chinese Christians. So he has expanded the coalition to push other acts through, such as the Sudan Peace Act, which brought the Black American churches onboard, and the North Korea Freedom Bill, which has galvanized the Korean community. Slowly but surely, new communities are learning how to exercise influence in the defense of religious liberty.

Oddly enough, however, Christians tend to overestimate the value of political pressure more than any other. Carol Lee Hamrin noticed the irony of this: "I find this a strange paradox—that religious rights pundits seem to want their government to solve all religious problems abroad, but at home, to keep clear and let the churches solve them."[21] It's true. Some Christians reduce helping the persecuted to political advocacy. You want to get that person out of jail? Write to your member of Parliament! You want to make life better for the Christians in Pakistan? Pressure the President! It's understandable that evangelicals, so long estranged from the centers of political power, should overestimate their reach. But Hamrin has some valuable advice here:

> After twenty-five years of working in the State Department, I think it would have been better if NGOs [nongovernmental organizations] and churches had engaged more, and the U.S. government less so. You see, Chinese people are cynical about politics. Anyone from government is automatically distrusted. If you represent the U.S. government, they will say, "Well, the U.S. is our rival and wants to keep us second rate." Better to build the links directly with the leaders and keep clear of the agenda-laden realm of politics altogether. Then the state can be freed to do what it does best—keep the door open so the more effective groups can step through.[22]

Like it or not, the state's power is primarily negative. It is there to restrain evil. But it is the church that is on the earth to reveal Christ, who alone can make us triumph over evil. This major key of theology should receive its due place as we work for the persecuted.

## Tactic 7: The Role of Positive Engagement

Positive engagement refers to Christians contributing to building up the society where the persecution is taking place. This can include conducting relief work, building and running orphanages or schools, teaching English in state universities, setting up investment projects, and even running profitable businesses, all in the hope that the benefits of the engagement eventually will result in better treatment for the persecuted.

You always walk a tightrope with this tactic because you have to deal first and foremost with the persecutor. Say you form a travel agency to send tours to Burma. You might say that you are opening Burma up to the outside world, and in so doing the persecuted Christians there will be helped because the Burmese government will become more responsive to international opinion. Also you might argue that you are taking Christians in not only for the purpose of tourism but for intercession. Nevertheless, in the short term, it is only the elite oppressors who will benefit, as they receive the payoffs to allow the agency to operate in their country. Also what if other businesses don't follow your lead and pull the Burmese economy into the global marketplace? Indeed, what about the symbolism of your engagement? Do your dealings with a military dictatorship constitute a tacit approval of their suppression of the legitimately elected pro-democracy leader, Aung San Suu Kyi?

A concrete example would be Amity Bible Press in China, built at a cost of more than seven million dollars to the United Bible Societies in 1987 (the biggest project in their history). They still provide the technical expertise to run the presses and supply the Bible paper free to their partner, the China Christian Council. This joint venture was always designed to be a business, with the press taking orders to print Scriptures and religious books for other countries. But it was also designed to help alleviate the vast shortage of Bibles among China's Christian population. With more than forty million Chinese Bibles printed and largely distributed to date, the value of the project is obvious. But it still has its critics who fear that the press's use as a propaganda tool in the hands of the official church has resulted in a successful suppression of the needs of the house churches. Also, the rush to be positive should not make anyone too sanguine about the unjust conditions that allow the press to flourish at all—conditions in which the government grants to its own state-controlled church the monopoly to print, produce, and sell Bibles. That's a sweet deal for the government but a bitter pill for many Christians. As Hans Peterson asked in a hard-hitting article, "Why Can't All Christian Bookshops Sell Bibles?" There are fifty private Christian bookshops in China at the moment, but they have the dubious distinction of being "the only Christian bookstores in the world that are forbidden to stock Bibles."[23] We would not stand for this in any Western country.

So positive engagement always involves a tradeoff. There are clear benefits and clear drawbacks. The benefits start with the creation of trust, and with trust, comes influence. If Christians work hard and show commitment to improving the life of a society, its leaders are grateful, and over time their suspicion may be assuaged. Building and staffing schools, hospitals, and orphanages are especially useful.

Another benefit is that positive engagement shatters the caricature of Christianity as a negative, imperialistic religion—an image critics use to drive the persecution of Christians. In addition, certain types of business can result in a liberalization of society that indirectly lessens the pressure on the persecuted. I have a friend in Beijing who set up a company selling software in the firm belief that in making the Internet more freely available in China, he will lessen the ability of the Chinese government to control its population and will assist house churches in accessing material safely. He tutors five young house-church leaders to do their sermon preparation on the World Wide Web. They are particularly fond of a website with Spurgeon's complete sermons and access a range of material that otherwise would have to be smuggled in.

A final benefit of this tactic is that, if enough positive engagement occurs, it can nudge the country out into the international orbit and make it more aware of human rights standards and more vulnerable to foreign pressure, which can be exercised in the defense of the persecuted.

But there are drawbacks too. First, many positive engagement projects suffer from the "Trojan horse" charge. In Islamic countries, Christian-run hospitals are often accused by extremists of "buying converts," even though there is no intention of doing so. Often the ethics can be complex. If you sign up to teach English in China at a state-run university, should you keep completely quiet about your faith if asked? If so, what is the point of being a *Christian* teacher of English in China? On the other hand, if you witness, however discreetly, are you breaking your contract, which was purely to teach English?

A second drawback, as we have seen, is that engagement very often comes with a propaganda price tag. Commentator Jonathan Chao talked about this with the official Chinese church. He said, "It's children's playground stuff. They say, 'You can't be my friend if you stay friends with him, because he doesn't like me and I don't like him.'" Thus the price of working legally in China is often to criticize publicly colleagues or ministries that refuse to work with the TSPM. Often the process is so subtle that the positive engagers unconsciously parrot TSPM propaganda. Engagers feel that they have to speak up against the enemies of their hosts to maintain their links and status with the hosts. If they genuinely have to, then when does it become too great a price to pay?

Third, the price of engagement can sometimes result in a blunting of the radical Christian message. Christianity is not just about being nice to your neighbor. It might bring stability to some societies, but it also contains some extremely subversive and dangerous ideas that could be very destabilizing. When some Beijing house-church leaders realized that their faith meant that they should stand up for the rights of exploited workers, they formed a trade union, and immediately the authorities clamped down hard. Two foreign Christian teachers had mentored these house-church leaders and, scared of being slung out of the country, suddenly dropped all contact with them. Their actions have still not been forgotten or forgiven.

When engagers get into bed with the power elite, it is often a temptation to compromise the message to maintain the relationship. The Christian faith puts to flight those who are greedy, corrupt, and violent. Engagers need to be aware that when they release a gospel as incendiary as the Christian one, sparks may fly. If the price of influence is silence—even in private—about persecution, then that is surely too expensive.

Finally, great sensitivity needs to be paid to the local church when engagers conclude agreements with their persecutors. Chinese Christians felt betrayed when Billy Graham, in his desire to foster better relations with his hosts, shook the hand of Bishop Ding and was photographed with him. Ding's failure to repent of his denunciations in the 1950s that assisted in the jailing of Wang Mingdao and others has always tainted him in the eyes of most of China's Christians. Yet Moses spoke to Pharaoh, even if Nehemiah refused to see Sanballat. It's not wrong to interact with persecutors, but it is hard to do so in such a way that it expresses solidarity with the persecuted, rather than seeming like a betrayal of them. To his credit, Graham's entourage worked extremely hard to successfully explain to the house churches why he had to shake Ding's hand, and much good from his trip resulted.

All this is to say that to engage positively with totalitarian societies for the benefit of the persecuted is a hazardous process, requiring skills of perseverance and savvy that most of us don't have. But if the engagers are willing to confront and not just be co-opted, then the persecuted will be in their debt, even if the benefits take years to accrue.

From this brief overview of tactics, I hope it is evident that they all have their uses. Above all, the key factor that binds them together in effectiveness is a trustworthy relationship with the persecuted church itself. This does not mean that the intervention always has to be controlled by them. It is quite common to find the persecuted, because of their marginalized status, to be quite ignorant of the value of international pressure or even of the way power works in their own societies. Tactics of intervention are negotiations within a context of relationship between those who seek to serve the persecuted and those who are persecuted severely. The closer this relationship, the more varied the tactical intervention can be. House-church leaders in China, for example, will no longer feel betrayed if some foreign Christian VIPs shake the hand of their persecutors, since they can trust the VIP to present their views well. The worst thing for us to do is to deal with the persecutor without consultation with the persecuted.

But what if you cannot get involved to such an extent as these tactics require? What if the only resource you can offer is your money? How do you ensure it goes to the right organization, the one that serves the persecuted the best?

# 11 The Donor's Dilemma

The donor's goal is to make sure that his or her contribution goes to the organization that makes the biggest impact, as opposed to the biggest noise. The dilemma is that, in practice, it is almost impossible to discern the difference.

I had a donor friend who illustrated this well. Previous careers as an accountant and PR consultant stood him in good stead to be able to judge a bad outfit from a good one, or so he thought. Burdened for Egyptian believers—mostly Copts—he searched around for a ministry to which he would donate a considerable sum of money. His principle of discernment was a sound one, as he explained: "I was determined to give my money to the ministry that best served the local church and acted according to their wishes."

Yet the more research he conducted, the more confused he became. After hours of downloading lengthy articles off the Internet and calling some friends, he discovered that the ministries he thought he should give his money to had all been chastised by the Coptic Church leadership. His favorite ministry splashed the story of how a Coptic village was razed by Muslim extremists, and the

Coptic leadership had said, "Do not publicly release these details of persecution, because the Egyptian government feels criticized, and they turn on us and make life harder for us." So my friend had to conclude, "All the best ministries fell foul of this rule. They had used the publicity tactic extensively, embarrassing the Egyptian government, and according to the Coptic leaders, this made persecution worse not better."

In the end he donated the money to an ecumenical outfit that never mentioned persecution in their publicity material, but he remained uneasy. Was their silence about the persecution of the Copts an act of strategic positioning, an act of moral cowardice, or an act of simple ignorance? It was five years before he found out it was the latter, and he has been kicking himself ever since.

This discovery was made on a trip to Egypt, during which he was introduced to some distinguished Coptic bishops. Mentioning the outfit he supported, he was amazed to see the bishops all reacting the same way. "Oh, don't give your funds to them. They never stand up for the persecuted. They pretend it doesn't go on. We wish they would go away." Then they gave him a list of ministries he would be better off supporting, and they were the very ones that the Coptic leaders had criticized. He said, "I'm confused. These are the ministries you condemn. How can you ask me to support them?"

One very gracious bishop took him quietly aside. After a long sigh, this is the gist of what he said: "Let me tell you how it is for Christians here in Egypt. We are a vulnerable minority in a Muslim-run country. Despite Christianity having started here, the culture believes that Christianity is a foreign religion and that all Christians are pro-America, pro-Israel, and anti-Islam. We are on trial *every day*. And every day we have to make the same defense speech: 'No, we love our country, we do not support everything America does, and we are appalled like everyone else at the way Israel treats its Palestinian population.' So when our foreign brothers and sisters criticize our government for persecuting us, we have to criticize them back, because we live here and do not wish to be seen to be siding with those who are against our leaders—that is interpreted as disloyal. But we need *you* to speak out, because the persecution must be exposed and pressure must be applied. So here's the game we must play together: *you protect us by criticizing the government, and we protect ourselves by criticizing you!* Welcome to the Middle East!"

That's the donor's dilemma in a nutshell. My friend did his level best to be a discerning donor but failed because the crucial information was not available in published sources. The Internet—wonderful resource though it is—failed to provide him with enough material to make the best decision. He concluded, "I learned that I had to trust organizations to know how best to help the persecuted. I would have to leave the particular tactics to them, but I was still left with this issue, *on what basis do I give my trust?*"

He came up with a system called the *Three Beyonds*. He determined only to support ministries who were, as far as he could tell, beyond grandstanding, beyond celebrities, and beyond manipulation.

To evaluate the "beyond grandstanding," he was careful to look at whether a ministry had a program to deal with the causes of persecution, or whether they were just going for high publicity and short-term fixes. He was particularly annoyed at one ministry that took a television crew to southern Sudan to film their buying back slaves. When the program aired, it caused a great outcry. But the whole trip was essentially a publicity stunt. The organization itself did not redeem many slaves. Other organizations, though less boastful, had programs that were more substantial.

He chose ministries that were "beyond celebrities," because he refused to support ministries that relied on the popular appeal of celebrities to reach a mass audience. He felt that celebrity-dependent strategies usually did not build a committed core of supporters but were big splashes for quick money. He preferred to give his money to organizations that worked slowly at educating and informing their supporters through church networks.

He refused to be manipulated by extreme images or stories of torture. He chose ministries that were "beyond manipulation." He was suspicious of ministries that used extreme cases in their publicity. He wanted to support ministries that profiled *typical* suffering, as opposed to *extreme* suffering, on the belief that if you were going to serve the persecuted, you should help the majority that suffer and not just the extreme tip that were suffering terribly.

Fair enough, but these categories are hardly foolproof to deliver us from the donor's dilemma. After all, some tactics that have huge publicity mileage can also be equally effective. The endorsement of some celebrities, like Dr. Billy Graham for example, who are trusted by some audiences, can show that the ministry is full of integrity. Also, as we have seen in the previous chapters, there is nothing intrinsically wrong with the use of extreme stories to highlight greater need. Nor is it wrong to make those who are being tortured in jail an absolute priority, even if their release does not in any way deal with the causes of persecution that put them there.

Probably there are no foolproof tests, but a combination of essential ones will surely increase the chances of supporting the best organization. I'm convinced that the best donor of an organization who seeks to help the severely persecuted is a person who is burdened for, informed about, and a witness to the suffering church. The key element is to have a relationship with the persecuted themselves and the organization that serves them. Only in the context of a relationship can trust develop. This all boils down to the following tests.

## The Encounter Test

*Does this ministry give me the opportunity to encounter the persecuted for myself?*

There is a very critical and overlooked principle in all service: *the best way to make a difference to others is to first let them make a difference to you!* The *others* in this case are the severely persecuted. Does the organization give you the chance to go and meet and serve these needy Christians? Will you gain an experience of the persecuted, or is the ministry interested only in your money? The best ministries should covet *you*, not just your money. Your time, your prayers, your words, and your energy are all even more important resources than your money. So ask of a ministry or organization: is it inter-

ested in who I am and anxious to take me into relationship with
the severely persecuted?

Find out if the ministry gives you opportunities to go to the field,
where you can pray, deliver Scriptures, or express encouragement.
The fact is that these trips are often life changing. Three things usually happen. First, you are challenged and changed by the faith of
the persecuted. Second, you gain a unique insight into the work of
the particular ministry and are able to judge its effectiveness in a
way you would not otherwise be able to do. Third, you are informed
about the issues; you have a context within which to deal with the
controversies that arise. So donor commitment is deepened, and
donor confusion is dispelled.

Take the last of these. Over many years Open Doors has encouraged its supporters to become Bible couriers to the churches
behind the Iron and Bamboo curtains. The trips often include a
meeting with persecuted believers. After such a trip, when the
"Bible smuggling is counterproductive!" cry is raised, those who
have been Bible couriers to, for example, China, are unfazed and
not tempted to change their allegiance. As one British Bible courier
explained, "We sat down with a house-church leader and asked
him many questions about the Bible need. He said it was still
great, and he warned us that those who were not in touch with
the house churches would periodically condemn Bible couriers
because they did not know the size of the need. I heard it from
his lips. So when I got back and a controversy broke out about
these 'troublemaking Bible smugglers,' I said to myself, *It is just as
my persecuted brother said, and I know the truth because I have heard
it from his lips.*"

But by far the most important point is this: a good ministry
knows that the Christians of the persecuted churches first want
their *message* to be heard, and only second, for their *needs* to be
met. I overhead an exchange in a seminar recently where the
question was asked, "Why does God allow a part of His church to
be so persecuted?" Back came the answer, "So that the rest of us
might remember what true Christianity looks like!"

The story of the persecuted church is more than a testimony.
It is a story of the whole scope of God's action that those of us,

especially in the West, must receive if we wish to live balanced Christian lives ourselves. Otherwise we will forget that we should be in trouble, that we should suffer, and end up embracing paler forms of Christianity that just promise us a thinly disguised material self-fulfillment.

I remember once taking a Chinese pastor to a Christian bookshop in Los Angeles. His reaction forced me to reexamine the way Christianity was being taught to me. I thought he would be overwhelmed by the variety of Bibles, reading aids, books, and multimedia material on display. He was, but not in the way I expected. He stopped in the middle of the store, turned to me, and said, "It must be very hard to be a Christian here."

"Why do you say that?" I asked.

"Because how are you going to keep your faith simple with all this available?"

We walked around the store as he told me what he meant. He picked five books off the shelf. All had similar titles like "The Christian's Secret of a Happy Life." He leafed through them and said, "Each book seems to say there's a secret to living a happy life in Jesus. But their secrets are all different. They all say there is one secret, but each has a different secret? That's confusing."

"Well, that's just marketing," I explained, a little defensively.

But he went on. "Does that mean I have to buy all five books to really know Christ? That makes me anxious. What other secrets might I not be aware of? I have to buy more books. And soon I would have more books than I could read, and I would not be happy but guilty that I had spent money on all these books that I had no time to read."

He put the books down on the floor and said quietly, "In China I prayed for God to bring me books. He did, but only at the rate of about four per year. So I read those books thoroughly. I copied out passages. I made summaries for teachers. I learned whole chunks by heart. These books really formed me. The point I'm trying to make is that if you have too many books, it's difficult to read one properly. I'm not saying it's impossible, just hard. And this variety actually makes faith more complicated than it really is."

It's true, but so difficult to see when we are constantly seduced by the latest, the best, the newest, even within the Christian culture. Persecution pares life down to its essentials and keeps the practice of the faith simple. My friend went back to China to keep the basic routines that have given him life. As he put it, "Every day, make sure you pray, witness to others, and above all, praise God."

He taught me a daily habit he learned in prison. "Every morning when you wake up, don't get up, just stay in bed and for ten minutes thank God for anything that comes into your mind. It might be for the wallpaper; it might be for friends; it might just be for life. Anything. Once you get going you discover that the world is full of grace, God's grace. With that attitude you are ready to live the day for God—because you are overwhelmed at how generous God is to you, to everyone."

It's so simple, and yet isn't there something in us that finds the simplest activities so hard to keep up? Maybe that is why we pack our lives with an infinite variety of routines and habits. Anything but just continually doing what is simple. I learned from that persecuted brother that day a critical truth about the Christian life—that one must fight daily to keep the faith simple. It was a transforming encounter, and I had never even traveled to his persecuted environment.

As a Vietnamese evangelist once said, "Christianity is the only religion that never believes in graduating anyone—we are to stay at the first grade all the time, grateful to Jesus, repentant for our sins, expectant for his coming. Don't graduate, or you'll leave the basics behind."

So donors, support the ministry that guarantees an encounter—no matter how indirect—with the persecuted! Encounters happen at all levels. Not everyone can make a trip, but we can listen to the voice and thoughts of the persecuted in meetings or tapes, or read them in magazines and books. Pick the ministry that is committed to bringing to you the challenge of the persecuted. The message should come before the needs.

In my view this is the most important test. I will run through the others more briefly.

## The Prayer Test

*Does the ministry make prayer for the persecuted an absolute priority?*
We've already seen that the number one request for assistance from the persecuted is for prayer. Any good mission should reflect this priority. Do they provide enough prayer information? Do they run prayer trips to the affected country, where intercessors can travel together and pray *in situ* for the situation? Any ministry worth its salt should provide the donor with a continual prayer structure so that the needs of the persecuted can be incorporated into one's daily prayer, and hopefully into the prayer life of one's church. Though I wouldn't make a hard and fast rule of it, I am always interested to know if the organization has a full-time person dedicated to the mobilization of prayer on behalf of the persecuted. Is there a prayer line to get updates? Is it updated regularly? Does the ministry organize prayer chains? Pick the organization that values you because you are first and foremost a praying Christian. That is the greatest support you can render the persecuted. They wish the power of God in their lives. The only way you can release it to them is to go to the throne of God. And of course, the more we pray, the deeper our burden, and the deeper our burden, the greater our commitment. We are in the process of becoming better donors. It's not just about money!

## The Integrity Test

*Does this ministry have a sound accountability structure?*
I've never forgotten a conversation with an extremely rich Christian, who must remain nameless. Suffice it to say that in the year of our conversation, his tithe amounted to twenty-seven million dollars. He wished to support many Christian organizations and commissioned an investigation. He wanted to find those ministries in which the life of the leadership was morally clean, the organization was not used for the promotion of the founder's or leader's family, and the board of the outfit was independent and strong. He ended up making this startling confession: "Barely 5 percent of the ministries we looked at passed all three of the tests!"

I like his criteria. I too am very suspicious of a ministry that seems to exist for the benefit of the founder's family. That makes accountability very hard to ensure, as family loyalty is so apt to take precedence over other loyalties, quite apart from the fact that it makes the organization less meritocratic. And, yes, the leader must exhibit a sound moral character. This is often discerned by an examination of who is listed as recommending the person and the ministry. But it is the realm of finances and the board that I look at most closely.

First, *the finances*. The key consideration here is, how difficult is it to get a full financial statement from the ministry? Any ministry that seeks your money should have full transparency in this regard. Where the statement is hard to obtain, there is often something to hide. I look no further into them. Other questions are: Does the ministry have an internal audit committee? Are they externally audited by a reputable firm of accountants? Are they a member of an ecumenical organization that insists that particular financial standards must be met? For example, if you are living in the United States, and the ministry is part of the National Association of Evangelicals, ask if they are a member of the Evangelical Council for Financial Accountability. Granted, all this digging about does not guarantee that everything is fine. And of course, many persecution ministries cannot give details as to how they spend the money raised in target countries, as that would endanger the persecuted believers there. But these are guidelines, which, in combination with other tests, lead to the careful giving of trust.

Second, *the board*. I want to know if the board has independent powers or can be dissolved at the whim of the president or founder. Also, is the board composed of a good mix of professions, skills, gender, and age groups? Elderly boards stacked with lawyers and accountants usually smack of "rubber stamping." The ministry should be making an attempt to have a board that has a diverse membership and is useful in holding the ministry to account on the donor's behalf. The board is your advocate. Make sure you trust it! Make sure you know what you have a right to ask for.

Naturally, there is a lot more to accountability than this. I think it is usually a bad sign if the ministry is extremely litigious, for example, or the leader craves publicity. These are just a few ways to check whether the organization has the competence, not just the intention, to spend money well.

## The Cooperation Test

*Does this ministry work in tandem with other ministries and create winning coalitions for action?*

No ministry should ever fight persecution alone. The phenomenon is too large and the numbers of the persecuted too great for any single mission or organization to take on itself. Persecution is combated most effectively when various ministries and churches form *movements* together. As we have seen, the U.S. International Religious Freedom Act of 1998 was passed because churches and missions joined together with trade unionists, liberal Jewish groups, and even radical feminists. Certainly, when assisting the persecuted takes us into the realm of politics, we have to create broad coalitions to bring about change. The key here is not to reject a ministry just because its leaders appear on the same platform as those with very different beliefs or outlooks.

But how does one tell how well a ministry works with others? There are some signs. Does this ministry bad-mouth other ministries? It's usually not a good sign if a ministry criticizes other missions. One may legitimately defend particular tactics that come under attack, but if the defense attacks the veracity and effectiveness of other ministries, this should be a warning sign. Attacking other ministries does not serve the persecuted, because it sows division and disunity, and the persecuted deserve our unity. I look to see if the mission I am going to support is a working member of, for example, the Lausanne Committee for World Evangelization, where the members pool their knowledge. It is reassuring when a mission tells you what it is good at and where others may be better. Not all ministries have the same focus. Those that have extensive programs in the churches where persecution is most severe will rarely engage in political advocacy, since that will get them labeled as "antigovernment" and compromise their ability to work in the target countries. So some ministries specialize in advocacy, and others in program. Each needs the other, because each does a work that is incomplete by itself.

I also look carefully at the language used by the mission in question. Is it polarizing? Does it bait governments? One wishes to see ministries not just reaching out to their own sub-ghetto of supporters but ensuring that their language is responsible in an era when boastful or denigrating comments make things harder for the persecuted churches.

## The Strategic Test

*Do the tactics of this mission address the long-term causes of persecution?*
We have already mentioned this, but it is worth reiterating. Is there an awareness of *typical* persecution as opposed to *extreme* persecution, and do the tactics of the ministry really get at the long-term causes of persecution? This is not to reject ministries that build homes for the widows of slain pastors or expend resources in freeing Christian prisoners. In practice, most ministries do all that. The question is, *in addition*, are they working to change the very conditions that resulted in the pastor being slain or the Christian evangelist being jailed? Is there evidence of long-term thinking in their plans? Does their program have a youth focus, seeking to minister to a new generation? Is enough attention being payed to education, Bible teaching, and pastoral mentoring—unspectacular but essential long-term tactics that combat the hate in societies that drives the persecution of Christians?

An evaluation such as this requires a critical attitude on the part of the donor. I was just talking with an Indian Christian who advises development agencies, and I asked him what he would say to any donor. This is what he said: "I would ask them not just to be moved, but to be critical. Put a gap between hearing the terrible story and writing the check. And don't get wowed by numbers."

He told of a recent experience when three donors had come to southern India to support orphanages, and three local ministry representatives had made a pitch for their funds. One said, "I have fifty boys in my care, and I need five thousand dollars." Another said, "I have five hundred boys in my care, and I need three thousand dollars." The third said, "I have five thousand orphans, and I need more than twenty-five thousand dollars." The third got the funds. My Indian friend was furious. He said, "If they had asked critical questions, like how many adults are befriending the children? The fact was, with the outfit that has five thousand kids, the children are left alone in huge impersonal orphanages. The mission with fifty boys employed ten couples who essentially adopted five boys each—far more important in forming their minds and hearts, but the donors never looked beneath the figures." They didn't consider strategy.

Each donor will vary in how they assess effective strategy. I tend to support programs that are people-based rather than technology-based. I am more interested in supporting five Bible teachers to China than a Christian television broadcast for example, but that reflects my own subjective experiences. I also prefer agencies that deal with the underground churches, not just official state churches. Each donor, depending on his or her experience, will have a feel for strategies that are truly fruitful.

Finally, ask yourself, Is this ministry really seeking to reproduce itself, or to serve the church? I toy with the idea of calling this the "modesty test." I've just been mediating in a conflict between some donors and the representatives of a very charismatic Western preacher who is raising millions to build a seminary in an Asian country where persecution is occasionally extreme. One donor perceptively asked, "When will your seminary be handed over to the local church and you will not be needed anymore?" This utterly flummoxed the evangelist. Quite frankly, the project was a way of extending his own ministry, and not, in the first instance, of serving the local church.

Ultimately, the donor should seek to support the mission with the greatest knowledge of and the longest-term focus for the persecuted church.

## The Complexity Test

*Does this ministry exhibit an awareness of the complexities as well as the challenges of the persecuted churches?*

The principle is simple: the outfit that knows the most about the persecuted church is likely to find the best ways to serve the persecuted. The key here is to watch out for exaggerated information or to see if the ministry gives overall briefing information. They should know their facts for one thing. I was amazed to find a rather large ministry raising funds for the assistance of "forty million evangelical Christians under fire from Muslim extremists in Indonesia." This should raise alarm bells for any donor. A quick glance at *Operation World* shows how wide of the mark these claims are.[1] The total number of evangelical Christians in Indonesia is reported to be 8.5 million, and the total number of Christians from all denominations is between 12 and 24.4 million. I happen to know the figure was plucked from a sermon of a hot-headed preacher who was giving a "prophecy" of what was going to happen in the country by 2020.

As we have stressed again and again in this book, understanding and assisting the persecuted is a tough, complex business. Yet missions should seek as much as possible to inform donors about the complete context of the persecution, and not just provide a profile of its extreme tip. While the desire to use emotive stories in appeals is understandable, I am always reassured when there are links on the website of the ministry so donors can get themselves more fully informed. The best policy is when the ministry itself provides easily accessible briefing material, either in person to major donors or generally to its supporters.

## The Experience Test

*Does this mission have a good track record in serving the persecuted?*

It's always worth looking into the history of a ministry, because the donor needs to know if it has the expertise and experience to do what it claims to do. How long have they been at it? What is their track record? What is their reputation? Do they keep their key leaders over time, or do many leave, preventing continuity? Have they built up a level of expertise that others draw on? Again, I don't wish to press this too far. Sometimes new tactics are needed, and often a new outfit will arise to fill the need where more established ones fail. But it is wise to ensure that the ministry that is soliciting funds has the capacity and the experience to complete the task they promise to carry out with your money.

## The Controversy Test

*Does this mission get into trouble as they serve the persecuted?*

The fact is, helping the persecuted is often going to offend quite a number of people, especially if the persecuted form an *underground* community. If you render assistance to China's house churches, then the leaders of the official state church are going to condemn you because you are not working with them. The government will also criticize you because they have to defend the lie that there are no underground Christians. Helping the persecuted always involves a fight, and effective ministries should have battle scars.

It's very important for a donor not to shy away from ministries with tactics that generate controversy. As Gen. Raymond Millar, formerly the head of research for Open Doors International, used to quip, "If you shoot into a bush and the bush shoots back, then you know you are shooting into the right bush!" Rather, be worried about those ministries that no one bothers to criticize, which could be an indication that their ministry is so irrelevant or so small scale or compromised, it escapes all notice.

The behavior of a ministry, when criticized, is also very revealing for the donor. Is the ministry belligerent, overly defensive, or self-assured and measured in its responses? Does it denigrate the validity of other ministries, especially those that may use rival tactics? I used to be very saddened by the spokespersons of a well-known ministry who bought Bibles from the official Amity printing press in China. Then they criticized those who took Bibles in surreptitiously as "stupid troublemakers who want to do their deeds in the dark." There is no need for this kind of rhetoric. Let the actions speak for themselves. It is hazardous to assume that your contacts always have the whole truth about how best to engage with the church in a country, especially if the church is large and diverse.

## A Great Donor

Eight tests, then. Of course, they do not guarantee that the donor will never regret his or her generosity. As we have stressed, it is about trust. The donor gives that trust carefully and responsibly before God, and if the funds are misused, then there is a real and terrible sense that God's judgment will fall on the heads of the receiving ministry.

There is such a thing as a great donor. Great donors do not necessarily provide great wads of money. Their greatness lies in their commitment to the persecuted. The challenge is to find a ministry that allows the donor to be a witness *to* persecution, a burdened prayer warrior *for* the persecuted, and well informed *about* the persecuted. These features take them beyond the realm of dilemma into knowledge. Once you have a relationship with the persecuted and those who serve them, you will know whom to support.

The question is, Will you be a great donor or just a good one? As a Chinese evangelist put it: "Don't give to *forget* the body of Christ; give to *be* the body of Christ!" Some donors just give to stop a nagging conscience about their more persecuted brethren. They give to forget. Great donors give to *be* the church, to stand with their brothers and sisters, in prayer, love, and support! They follow to the letter the apostle Paul's best advice to donors:

> The way God designed our bodies is a model for understanding our lives together as a church: every part dependent on every other part, the parts we mention and the parts we don't, the parts we see and the parts we don't. If one part hurts, every other part is involved in the hurt, and in the healing. If one part flourishes, every other part enters into the exuberance. You are Christ's body—that's who you are! You must never forget this. Only as you accept your part of that body does your "part" mean anything.
>
> 1 Corinthians 12:24–27 Message

Great donors want to "mean something" in the body of Christ. They accept their part and play their part!

I cannot stress enough the essential principle that underpins being an effective donor—*the best way to make a difference to the persecuted is to let them make a difference to you!* But how? How can we create a transforming encounter with the persecuted? It's easier than you think, but it's always more profound than you imagine.

*Part Five*

# What Can We Learn from the Persecuted?

# 12   Faith Model

*Am I Walking the Way
of the Cross?*

In the early 1990s a friend and I invited a group of well-known Western Christian leaders to visit China. I won't say what denomination they were from, or even what country, because I want to spare their blushes. But they were a "gang of four." All had books to their name and preached regularly to thousands.

At first, they were excited about the idea, but then they wrote a letter setting down two conditions for their visit. First, we must arrange for at least one of each of their books to be translated into Chinese, "so that adequate follow-up can occur." Second, we must ensure that they would speak only to groups numbering more than two thousand, "so that we can justify to our churches that we are spending our time well."

Frankly we were horrified. They had got it backwards. We replied in a letter: "The object of taking you into China was not so that you could minister to the Chinese church, but so that the Chinese church could minister to you." They assumed that because they were teachers they were going to teach. Actually, we wanted them to learn.

None of these men had seen revival as their Chinese counterparts had. None was running cell-structure churches with memberships in the tens of thousands. None had been thrown in jail for his faith. None of them was facing the headaches of discipling thousands of converts per week. What did they really think they could teach the Chinese Christians?

To be fair, the four were embarrassed and apologized for their attitude. Then the situation suddenly tightened in China again and it was impossible to take them in. But their initial attitude is sadly typical of many Western Christians regarding the persecuted church—we think of them solely in terms of needing our help rather than the help they can be to us! We minister to them, through prayer, giving, courier work, and so forth, but we rarely let them minister to us. The truth is, we just don't know how.

There are at least three ways that our faith can be transformed by an encounter with a community of persecuted Christians—through a *faith model*, a *faith warning*, and a *faith boost*. Each forces us to ask a particular question of our own walk with God:

*Faith model*—Am I walking the way of the cross?

*Faith warning*—Am I in enough trouble for Jesus?

*Faith boost*—Is my God big enough?

Let's start with the first of these.

In the east wall of Salisbury Cathedral is a five-lancet stained-glass window. Dedicated to Prisoners of Conscience, it appears to the eye as a subdued jumble of jagged blues, indigos, and purples. There seems little organization to it, even after much study. Disembodied heads can just be made out, a cup here with dripping blood, an anchor there, a wisp of yellow, but the story eludes the eye.

I gazed for an hour until an usher came up to me and whispered, "You have to come and see it in the early morning when the sun is shining. Otherwise you can't make out the story."

Sure enough, I returned the following morning to find a blazing pattern. Where there was once confusion now there was clarity. Yesterday's messy jumble was today's majestic narrative. A twist of yellow blazed with glory in the central lancet, depicting the Father sending the Spirit to the Son on the cross—the prototypical "prisoner of conscience" who brought hope to all others. The cross stood out so clearly I was astonished that I had missed it the previous day.

The testimonies of the persecuted church reveal things about God that we already know. All we need to know is contained in the Bible—the fullest picture of God available to us. But the fact is, our Bible—like the stained glass window at Salisbury—can appear complex and baffling, and we are apt to overlook facets of its truth because the eyes of our experience do not generate enough light to make out some essential patterns.

I think of the persecuted church like a morning sun that reveals what is already there in the Scriptures, truths that we may have missed. They illumine the central features of our faith that are found in the Bible but are so often "hidden in plain sight."

The ultimate challenge of the persecuted church is to teach us things about God that we can incorporate into our daily walk. If all we do is pray for the persecuted, support the persecuted, march for the persecuted, then it's still a question of us helping them. We have not actually allowed the persecuted to change our lives.

But they can! The experiences of the persecuted illumine the beating heart of the Bible, of our faith, of our God in ways we must incorporate into our own Christian lifestyle. As we shall see, their insights are not new—they merely highlight what is already there in our faith. But because of our luxurious circumstances, we may have missed what is really there. In this way the persecuted can be a faith model, providing habits of holiness that we can emulate to grow closer to God.

There are a hundred possible lessons to draw, and future books will surely be written devoted to this theme alone. Here, let me focus on three insights from the persecuted that will help us with specifically Western challenges of living the Christian life.

## The Way of the Cell

In the West each of us is influenced by the information revolution. New technologies driven by the silicon chip have resulted in an explosion of information, which in theory should make us better informed. But we are realizing that while the total amount of information has vastly increased, good information is harder to find. We can't see the truth for the "data smog."

Worse. To search for truth in the information age is incredibly stressful. Voice mail, email, Internet—all were supposed to make our lives easier. Yet they have added hours to our working day. The computers seem to mock us because we can't keep up. We are valued in the marketplace only if we can do five things at once. We almost wish we were a computer.

The persecuted church has an answer—build yourself a cell! At least that's what Wang Mingdao said.

Born at the turn of the century, Wang Mingdao was one of China's most famous church pastors and evangelists and, until his death in 1991, received famous religious VIPs like Billy Graham. Wang was the genuine article. While his official counterpart, Bishop Ding, was mysteriously protected during the Cultural Revolution, Wang spent much of it in solitary confinement. Finally released in 1980, his steadfast faith during twenty-three years of imprisonment inspired millions of Chinese Christians. Said one Shanghai pastor, "Wang Mingdao proved that God existed—no one goes to jail for that long and comes out with their faith still intact if God is not real."

Yet his visitors often found him unattractively trenchant and fierce. He was fond of wagging his finger and saying to his guests, "You do not have revival because you do not walk the hard road." For Wang, revival could only come on those who knew that walking the way of Christ would be hard, requiring courage, determination, and sacrifice.

But what does the hard road look like for the Western Christian, where (thank God) we will not spend twenty years in jail for our faith? In three separate interviews with Wang Mingdao I gained a little inkling into what his answer might be.

The first time I met him he asked me suddenly, "Young man, how do you walk with God?" I listed off a set of disciplines such as Bible study and prayer, to which he mischievously retorted, "Wrong answer. To walk with God you must go at walking pace."

Frankly I had no idea what he was talking about, and I let it go as the ramblings of a slightly senile old man in his late eighties.

The next time I visited, he was sharper from a good night's sleep. I remember looking at him and confessing that I was finding it hard to relate his experience to mine. I said, "I will never be put in jail like you, so how can your faith have any impact on mine?"

He seemed nonplussed, then started asking me a series of questions: "When you go back home, how many books do you have to read this coming month? How many letters do you have to write? How many people do you have to see? How many articles do you have to produce? How many sermons must you preach?"

He kept up the questions, and I answered each time. After about fifteen of these questions, I was beginning to feel panicked at the amount of work ahead. I mopped my brow and looked gloomily at the slice of watermelon on the plate in front of me.

He seemed to sense this, and we sat in silence. I suppose he was just trying to be polite. Suddenly an insight burst into my consciousness with scalding ferocity: *I need to build myself a cell!*

I shared this with Wang Mingdao, and he grew very excited. He explained: "When I was put in jail, I was devastated. I was sixty years old, at the peak of my powers. I was a well-known evangelist and wished to hold crusades all over China. I was an author. I wanted to write more books. I was a preacher. I wanted to study my Bible and write more sermons. But instead of serving God in all these ways, I found myself sitting alone in a dark cell. I could not use the time to write more books. They deprived me of pen and paper. I could not study my Bible and produce more sermons. They had taken it away. I had no one even to witness to, as the jailer for years just pushed my meals through a hatch. Everything that had given me meaning as a Christian worker had been taken away from me. And I had nothing to do."

He stopped, and his eyes moistened again. "Nothing to do except get to know God. And for twenty years that was the greatest relationship I have ever known. But the cell was the means."

His parting advice was, "I was pushed into a cell, but you will have to push yourself into one. You have no time to know God. You need to build yourself a cell so you can do for yourself what persecution did for me—simplify your life and know God."

The third time we met was not long before his death. I referred back to our first talk and asked, "Why did you say, *to walk with God you must go at walking pace*? Surely God can walk, run, go at any pace He likes. Why would God choose to walk and ask us to walk?"

His answer haunts me still: "Because He loves His garden!"

Wang Mingdao never explained, but I think I got his drift. Eden is where God comes walking, looking to speak with Adam and Eve. The whole world is a fellowship garden. And the aim of human life was and still is to walk in this wonderful garden with this wonderful God! If we work, as we must, but do not walk, as we might, we lose the meaning and joy of life, and no amount of religious freedom will compensate.

In that exchange with Wang Mingdao is one of the keys to the faith of the suffering church: God does things slowly. He works with the heart. We are too quick. We have so much to do—so much in fact we never really commune with God as he intended when he created Eden, the perfect fellowship garden. For Wang Mingdao, persecution, or the cell in which he found himself, was the place where he returned to "walking pace," slowing down, stilling himself enough to commune properly with God. Revival can come only to those who make room for God.

The Japanese missiologist Kosuke Koyama talks of the "three mile an hour God" of the Bible, leading the Israelites out into the desert for a forty-year walk at three miles an hour so they would learn "that man does not live on bread alone but on every word that comes from the mouth of the LORD" (Deut. 8:3 NIV). Three miles an hour—the pace at which we walk. Forty years—to learn a twenty-word truth. It's hardly a productivity rate we would be satisfied with, but then, if a great truth is properly learned, maybe we have to redefine spiritual productivity. There seem to be lessons we can only learn at three miles an hour. God is more interested in how deep the truth goes than in how much we know.

For those who want God to be more real, perhaps a slice of the answer is to slow our lives down to a spiritual walking pace—imposed on the persecuted by circumstances—so that we can know God instead of merely serving Him. It may take a cell if we follow Wang Mingdao's advice, but then, if he is right, the cell becomes a garden.

But how? Here's another hint from the experience of the persecuted church. I once knew a Chinese evangelist to whom a mission had given five thousand Bibles to distribute. They were dismayed to discover that after two years, very few of the Bibles had been distributed. They began to wonder if he was selling them off on the black market. I was called in to mediate, and in a tense meeting, this was the reason the evangelist gave for not distributing the Bibles at a faster rate: *"I have discovered that it is dangerous to learn truth at a rate faster then we can practice it."*

This man began his ministry in the 1980s, when Bibles were extremely scarce. Traveling around revival provinces, he found that each week roughly a hundred people would profess faith. Being an itinerant preacher, he could not linger to disciple them. He had to keep moving on because the police were tracking him. His dilemma was, "I have no Bibles to give to these new converts, but I must leave them something so they can keep on growing into God."

He devised a unique method of "self-discipleship." Out of a hundred converts, he picked five people at random and said, "You are each going to lead a weekly group of twenty people." He went down to a stream and picked out five smooth stones. On each stone, he chiseled a verse of Scripture. He gave each a stone and said, "Each week, give a different member the stone. Let them live with this verse on the stone, think about it, pray about it, take it into the fields as they farm, put it next to the rice bowl as they eat, put it under their pillow as they sleep, all the time asking God to speak through these words. Then next week, when you all come together, you are to listen to what God has told them about the verse on this stone. As long as the person holds the stone, they cannot be interrupted. After they release it, you may extend the discussion to the others.

After everyone has spent a week with the stone-verse, swap the stone with another group, and do the same again."

He promised to return in six months, though in reality it was often a couple of years. He frankly expected many of the converts to have fallen away but was astonished to discover that nearly everyone was going on in the faith. He felt he had stumbled onto a vital truth about discipleship, and that is why he was explaining to these mission representatives that he did not give a Bible to the new converts at first but required them for a time to use the five-stones method.

He said, "I don't want them to encounter too much truth too fast. Otherwise, they will get into the bad habit of never using what they know. A verse a week is the right pace. It slows them down to believe at the heart's pace. It is dangerous to learn truth faster than we can practice it."

Is this a way to go at walking pace, to build a cell, where the Word can deeply dwell? The great German theologian Dietrich Bonhoeffer disciplined himself never to meditate on more than one verse a week. He said that if you read too fast, you believe too little. This meditation did not substitute for Bible reading, of course, but he felt that Bible meditation was just as important, and the canvas needs to be kept small if "walking pace with God" is to be achieved.

That is one way of building a cell. Persecution is the ultimate stimulus to simplify life, so that space for grace is created. Without this stimulus, we must build our own cell, and our whole existence depends on it. We were created first for fellowship and only secondarily for service. How sad it is that so many of us work *in* the garden *for* the Creator but never walk *through* the garden *with* the Creator! This invitation to walk with God in His garden, say the persecuted, is one we must pay any price to accept.

## The Way of the Knot

A second great revolution we are living through is the scientific revolution—the belief that we can control our destiny by understanding and harnessing the forces in our world via the careful methods of scientific study. The achievements are immense. Breakthroughs in medicine have given us life expectancies of eighty-five and up. Engineering inventions have given us homes that would be the envy of an ancient Solomon. And, indeed, the so-called managerial revolution is part of this, which teaches us methods to control the use of time so that we can achieve our goals. The bottom line is control. Though the optimism may have disappeared in more recent times, the faith has not. We are the ones in control of the future. If there are problems, our human ingenuity will eventually solve them.

The ultimate example of this is our reliance on statistics. Most discussions begin today with the phrase, "Latest studies show . . ." We cannot even take a moral stand today without waiting for scientific studies to back us up. Science is the new lingua franca. If you want to get something done in today's society, you must couch your proposal in the objective, factual language of analysis. If we want to hear what the universe is about, it is not to the theologian or philosopher we turn, but to the nuclear physicist, the biochemist, the geneticist. They are the new high priests of our world.

Of course Christians are not totally infected, but since these revolutions are the air we breathe, we may imbibe more than we know. Against this view the persecuted church reminds us that we are not in control of the future. Indeed, we have to accept that there is much about our world and our lives that will remain mysterious, including our own life's purpose. We can symbolize this mystery with the complex pattern of the Celtic knot (see diagram). The mystery can be baffling yet is bounded by God's circle of protection.

The country that impacted me most in all my travels was North Korea, the original hermit kingdom and last Stalinist stronghold. On my first visit I was met by a guide who stepped forward and said, "Welcome to heaven! You are now in the earthly paradise of Kim Il Sung. Come and see our paradise."

I was whisked off to the opera. During the performance, there was an occasional translation in English projected at the side of the stage. It became clear that the opera was about the great deeds of Kim Il Sung. It also became clear that the opera had been written by Kim Il Sung. Imagine my surprise when I saw one of the chorus lines: "Kim Il Sung gives eternal life to the Korean people for a thousand years." Okay, setting aside the dubious theology that makes eternal life last only for a thousand years, I thought, *What is such a religious concept doing in the mouth of such a materialistic Communist?* As I was mulling this over, the opera ended with great fanfare, and suddenly a smiling face at least fifty feet high (of Kim Il Sung) was projected onto the back of the stage. Everyone jumped up from their seats and cheered wildly with their hands above their heads. I thought, *Oh my, I've arrived on the pages of Orwell's* 1984.

North Korea is the most Communist society in the world and also the most religious. The new gods are Kim Il Sung and his son, Kim Jong Il. They are said to have supernatural powers, and the whole society is a vast coercive network to force continual worship of these "deities." The worship is not subtle. You can see bands of schoolchildren laying offerings at the feet of huge golden statues of these figures at the center of every town. Everyone is taught to revere them. Refuse and the penalty is to rot in a carbon-copy camp of Auschwitz.

One day I was taken to an art gallery and shown a painting. It was called "Rout of the SS *General Sherman.*" It depicted a ship on fire, and Koreans with red trousers slaughtering those on board. My guide explained, "This is when the ancestors of Kim Il Sung, our Great Leader, beat back the big-nosed Yankee imperialists who were coming to invade our land."

I remember being quite depressed during this visit. All traces of the church and God seemed to have been scoured from the land.

There was a hatred of everything Christian, and I felt so sorry for the twenty-two million people of the country, cocooned from birth to death in this atheistic nightmare. I wondered, *How on earth God could establish His kingdom in such a place?*

A week later I was passing through Manila and picked up a book on the history of the Bible Societies. I was flicking through the pages when my eye caught the phrase, "SS *General Sherman*," and I began to read the story of R. J. Thomas. As I read, my question was answered.

R. J. Thomas was a missionary to China in the middle of the nineteenth century. He had a heart for Korea, but Korea was a hermit kingdom even back then. No foreigners were allowed in. So he went to China instead and bided his time. In 1865 the opportunity he had been waiting a lifetime for came along. An American ship, the SS *General Sherman*, was going to steam up the Taedong River to the capital, Pyong Yang, in hopes of luring the Koreans into trade. Thomas bought a berth on the ship, hoping to meet some scholars in Pyong Yang who spoke Chinese, and took as many Chinese Scriptures with him as he could carry on board.

The trip was ill-fated. In a port on the way to the capital, some of the *General Sherman*'s crew killed three Korean men in a barroom brawl. When they reached Pyong Yang, the rumors had grown to such an extent that it was impossible to berth. The people of Pyong Yang were convinced the foreigners had come for their children to make soup from their eyeballs. There was nothing to do but to turn around and head down the river.

But they got stuck on a sandbank. Seeing them stranded, the Korean defense lashed a series of small ships together, set them on fire, and they drifted to surround the *General Sherman*, which then caught fire. Everyone on board had to leap into the river. As they waded to shore, they pulled out their swords but were all clubbed to death by the waiting Koreans.

Thomas also waded to shore. Before he could speak, a club swung with murderous force dashed his brains into the water, but his killer noticed he had not emerged with a cutlass, but was brandishing books. He wondered if he had killed a good man and picked up a couple of the sodden books.

Drying them off, he separated the leaves and saw that they were nicely printed. He could not read but decided to paper the outside of his house with the pages, as was the custom at the time. Imagine his astonishment when he returned from the fields a few weeks later to find a clutch of long-nailed scholars earnestly reading his walls. One of these scholars became a Christian by reading a Gospel portion plastered onto the wall. A generation later his nephew assisted in the first translation of the New Testament into Korean.

Yet Thomas never lived to see the fruit of his labor. In fact, as the club swung toward his brow, he may well have thought the trip had been a tragic mistake. He died, his life's purpose unfulfilled, his potential unrealized. For anyone aware of Thomas's death, his life was a mystery for years afterward.

But his life was not in vain. The meaning of life does not consist in what we make of it, but in what God makes of it. When we yield our lives to Christ, He makes us living stones, part of an eternal kingdom constructed on the cornerstone of Christ Jesus Himself (1 Pet. 2:4–10). Success is not about achievement, then, or what we make of ourselves. It's about placement, or what God makes of us.

So instead of obsessing about what our life's purpose is—as so many do today in the Western church, while seeking to control the future—we take the lesson from the persecuted church that it is okay to die quite unaware of our life's meaning. We can rest in trust that God, in His mercy, has made us a "living stone."

This is how God builds the kingdom. And what is remarkable is that it is ordinary people that, through the grace of God, bring great changes. The sheer dramatic effrontery of it takes my breath away. It's perfectly captured in these wonderful verses in Psalm 118: "The stone rejected by the builders has now become the cornerstone. This is the LORD's doing, and it is marvelous to see" (vv. 22–23 NLT). God takes the rejected things of the earth and builds His eternal kingdom from them.

That is why we say the persecuted Christians walk the way of the knot. A Celtic knot has no discernible beginning or end but is a complex pattern of tightly drawn spirals and curves symbolizing the mysteriousness of creation and of God. Yet the knot is always bounded by a circular border, showing that God encircles this seeming chaos with His protection and love. Your life's purpose may remain a mystery to you, as may the events of your world, but that's okay. God is in control. We are relieved of the responsibility of understanding everything and the need to change it.

## The Way of the Nails

A third great revolution we are living through in the West is the therapeutic revolution. It is quite simply the idea that your life's significance is measured in terms of how well you fulfill your potential.

Like the others, it's not a bad revolution per se. At its best, it teaches people that they are full of unique gifts and must grasp every opportunity to develop those gifts to their maximum extent and live a rewarding life. Everyone defines the reward differently. For some it is to make money. For others it is to be good mothers or fathers. For others it is to develop themselves artistically, accessing their "shadow side" in the quest for wholeness.

But at its worst, pursuing the reward results in chronic self-absorption, and we relate to others in utilitarian terms, cultivating relationships with those who can help us toward our goals and discarding those who cannot. Needless to say, the extent of civic participation has plummeted the more the therapeutic revolution has prospered.[1]

Western culture is full of ways to get to this goal of full potential. Men's and women's movements all claim to help us tap into the latent potential of our masculine or feminine side. Equal education for all is a major political priority. Self-help literature dominates the bookstores, and for those who can afford them, therapists can provide expert input for breaking down that unconscious block to success. Everyone must at least have a planner, with elaborate goal-setting forms and customized calendars so that each day we grow into the kind of person we want to be.

But is the purpose of life to fulfill our potential? The experiences of the persecuted flatly contradict this. For one thing, most persecuted Christians are deprived of the *opportunity* to fulfill their potential. As one pastor in Russia told me, "We live in a world where the beasts and antichrists appear to be winning." The persecuted church is full of would-be scholars who remain illiterate, would-be musicians never allowed to pick up an instrument, great political visionaries never allowed to lead and command. They do not get the chance to fulfill their potential. Of what significance are their lives then? Are we to describe these mute Miltons and silent Pavarottis in tragic terms? Or is there another way to understand purpose in life?

The Russian pastor is right, and his comments illustrate the fact that the persecuted see their world and their lives through apocalyptic lenses. Their world is that of the book of Revelation—of antichrists who set themselves up as God, of false prophets who beguile entire societies into worshiping these antichrists, of beasts that put the faithful under great pressure, even to the point of death. Miss that about the persecuted and you miss everything.

But the staggering thing is, that's our world too! *Apocalyptic literature does not merely describe the world as it will end, but the world as it is now!* I will always remember overhearing this dialogue between an American pastor and a Chinese house-church pastor.

> American pastor (AP): What book of the Bible is most precious to you?
>
> Chinese pastor (CP): Well, probably the book of Revelation because . . .
>
> AP: Because your suffering makes you long for the end of the world, and you are strengthened by the vision of how it will end, with Christ's victory?
>
> CP: That too, but we don't just take Revelation to be a description of the way the world will end; we see it also as a description of the way the world is now.
>
> AP: I'm not understanding you. Surely Revelation is a book that tells us how the world will end.
>
> CP: And I am telling you that it is also a description of the way the world is now. Suffering has made this clear to us in China.

Clearly prosperity has hidden this from you in America. You see, we had a Caesar here in China, called Mao, and he, like the Caesar of the early church period, demanded what was not only his but God's. As in Revelation, he used a beast to coerce us (Communism) and a false prophet to beguile us (false bishops). When we resisted this idolatry with the "testimony of the Lamb," we were slaughtered and jailed. In this way, we saw that Revelation is a description of the spiritual war that always goes on in any society, including yours.

AP: But it's not going on in America today. You say we have that hidden from us. What do you mean?

CP: Well, this conflict is obvious to us in China. You could not miss that Mao was setting himself up as an idol and demanding worship. So the veil was removed, and we saw the world as it really is—a place where idols are demanding our worship. But this is not obvious to you in America because it is more subtle.

AP: Maybe it is not happening at all. We are a Christian country, and we have a Christian president.

CP: I tell you, there are Caesars or idols in your society just as much as in ours, and even in your churches. And there are false prophets telling you that the idolatry is biblical, and beasts coercing you. For example, your Caesar may not be a person but an idea. In our fellowship we have a clever young man who lived with an American family for a year while studying. The couple was generous, but he noticed something about them—they were always exhausted. Both worked incredibly hard, though they had plenty of money. They had three cars, two homes, expensive country club memberships and, as far as he could tell, gave only the minimum to the Lord's work. They never asked him a single question about the Chinese church, and when he left, they gave him an envelope with twenty dollars in it. He told us, "I felt so sorry for them. They thought they were free, but they were slaves. They were dropping from exhaustion because they had to live up to something called the American

Dream. But they never knew that the pursuit of that life had stolen their hearts from Christ."

Do you see what I mean? Persecution is a way of forcing us to bow down to God, but those who do not have the light of persecution don't even see that they are bowing down. That's why you need to listen to the persecuted church. We can give you an insight that will enable you also to see the world through "apocalyptic eyes" and thereby become one of the persecuted yourselves, which is your true destiny. We are the people who are called to resist the idols.

AP: Hmm, if what you say is true, then consumerism could be a more effective killer of the faith than Communism.

CP: You are right, and this is what we are afraid of here. Consumerism clutters up life so much that we fail to see the world as it is—full of idols trying to steal our worship from God. We can help you, and you must pray for us also.

So there is much in our world that conspires to deprive us of the opportunity to fulfill our potential—we might die young, we might not get access to education, and so on. It is obvious that the purpose of life cannot be fulfilling our potential. That opportunity is a privilege extended only to a few. It is not a right enjoyed by all. We will all get the opportunity to fulfill our potential as human beings, but most will have to wait for the "new heavens and the new earth." That is one reason the persecuted look forward so much to the second coming of Jesus Christ.

So what is the purpose of life now, in this world of beasts, lies, death, and oppression? Here again the experiences of the persecuted point us unmistakably to a vital biblical principle: *God builds his kingdom not on our achievements, but on our sacrifices.* It is not the fulfilled life that God takes but the yielded life. The purpose of life is to lose it for God. He told us so in as many words: "Those who want to save their life will lose it, and those who lose their life for my sake . . . will save it" (Mark 8:35).

I once heard Henri Nouwen in a sermon put it this way: "In the kingdom, you can only heal if you have first been wounded; you can only lead if you have first been a servant, and the way we are wounded to heal, humbled to serve, is when we allow nails to be driven through ourselves, so that we die, and God's resurrection power is unleashed through us." That's why the way of dying to self is the way of power—we have to be dead first to be the recipients of resurrection power.

The prayer Jesus said before He went to the cross was, "Father, . . . let this cup pass from me; yet not what I want but what you want" (Matt. 26:39). I like to think when He said, "not what I want," that was the first nail. In a very real sense, Jesus nailed Himself to the cross. Once He had given up His will, His sacrifice was inevitable, and our salvation assured.

And so this pattern—in a less heroic form—is repeated in us. We also must walk the way of the cross so God can use us and we can be what He intended us to be. That is the message of the persecuted church in a nutshell—you have to die to do the will of God and be used by God!

Again, how does this happen? I remember interviewing a former Muslim extremist in Egypt. He had been a member of the Islamic Brotherhood and thought nothing of it if he was told that to rape a Christian girl was an act of virtue. He had converted to Christ in his early twenties and led a church for Muslim converts. This is illegal in Egypt, and the fellowship was betrayed to the police. Soon this young man found himself in prison. He was tortured. An electric cattle prod was pushed into his mouth. He was whipped and hung from the ceiling with his hands tied behind his back. But all this paled into insignificance compared to what other prisoners called "the experience." He was pushed into a stone box, a cube about five feet square. No light. No latrine. And he was left there for a month, food being passed through a grate every few days. Most prisoners went mad as a result of "the experience"—but not him.

He found Christ there, and the words he used to describe his experience are still the most brilliant description of the process of how persecution actually delivers more of God:

> In great suffering you discover a different Jesus than you do in normal life. Normally we are able to hide from ourselves who we really are and

what we are really like. The ego is well defended. But pain changes all that. Pain and suffering bring up to the surface all the weak points of your personality. You are too weak to mount the usual defenses, and you just have to gaze at what you are really like. I was a wreck in that cell. I was reduced to tears all the time. Crying, weeping, sobbing, wailing in the never-changing utter darkness. I came face-to-face with how awful I really was. I saw all the horrible things I had done, all the horrible things I was. I kept seeing myself again and again in the crowd shouting, "Crucify him!" But just as I was about to collapse into complete despair and self-loathing—and probably die—an incredible realization burst into the cell like an exploding star. It was this: *Jesus loved me even right then, as I sat in my own filth, weak, helpless and broken, empty and sinful. Even in that state, He loved me, and Christ rushed in and filled me, and the filling was so great because I was so empty.*

"The filling was so great because I was so empty." There is the great untold secret of the persecuted church—the most liberating place we can live as Christians is when we fully accept our weaknesses and let Christ in. This is where the filling comes from, and the joy, and the blessing, and all because we have been emptied by the suffering.

Persecution's role is to empty us . . . to be filled.

Normally we do not embrace weakness. Often we might even think that God is fortunate to have us on His side. Persecution is a way God creates emptiness in our hearts. But that emptiness—which seems so hard to bear—is the prelude to liberation. Only empty hearts are filled with Jesus. This is so biblical it is bizarre that we missed it in the first place. It's the Beatitudes. Who gets filled? The poor. Who gets filled? The sorrowful. Who gets filled? The persecuted.

Welcome persecution because it will bring Jesus close. It will break our hearts too, but then our hearts are made to be broken—broken to be mended by Jesus. What an invitation! This is what we are alive for.

This somber note is not the place to finish, because not only do persecuted Christians model dying for God, they model great joy in God. It is a thrilling paradox that the two run side by side. That's why they talk of "sweet persecution."

In the mid-seventies the KGB in Moscow picked up an underground Baptist leader whom they suspected of printing illegal Scriptures on a homemade press. They beat and tortured him to find out the whereabouts of the press. But he uttered not a word.

In desperation they brought in his sixteen-year-old son. They said, "We will beat him to death in front of you unless you tell us where it is." Immediately the man began to waver. This was too much. How could he watch his precious son die?

The blows began to descend. Crunch of bone and scream of agony—these were the sounds that went straight to his soul, and he was just about to cry out, "Stop, I'll tell you; save my son," when suddenly his boy cried out in the midst of his pain, "Dad, don't give up. I can see Jesus coming for me, *and He's beautiful!*"

With those words, the son died.

In the midst of a beating, there is beauty. Every persecuted Christian will tell a similar story that as they suffer for Christ, they see more of the beauty of Christ and are filled with an inexpressible joy.

So as we die, we live. As we suffer, we rejoice.

No wonder we need the faith model of the persecuted to make those paradoxes clear. But if we dare to follow their lead, we will find them to be gloriously true!

Underneath these stories, however, is a challenge to the Western Christian particularly—you need to be *in trouble* to live out these wonderful truths.

What trouble should we be in?

# 13 Faith Warning

*Am I in Enough Trouble
for Jesus?*

The biblical scholar William Barclay famously described a New Testament Christian as having three remarkable characteristics: "One, they were absurdly happy; two, they were filled with an irrational love for everyone; and three, they were always in trouble!"

Persecuted Christians are constantly in trouble. As a Palestinian pastor put it, "If you speak truth to power, power always reacts." An encounter with the persecuted reveals the incendiary nature of this gospel we follow, and if our witness does not provoke some sort of explosive reaction, we have to check whether our gospel powder is damp or dry. We should be in trouble for Jesus! If we aren't, something is wrong. This is what is meant by a faith warning.

Of course, it is the gospel that gets us into trouble not ourselves. We live in a world of idols, and if we refuse to worship those idols, the idols—ironically—always hit back. Here is a good definition of an idol: something that becomes more important to you than God is. Like it or not, we live in an arena of conflict, though some of us prefer to keep our eyes "wide shut" to this fact. We have to fight, because every day we receive a thousand messages asking us to be more self-centered and to love Christ less, asking us to put the idol first and Christ second.

Persecuted Christians are not tempted into the illusion that the world is actually a friendly place that does not mind our identifying with Christ. The world for them is unmasked in its hostility to Christ.

Once when visiting Czechoslovakia in the 1980s, I delivered a Bible to an elderly pastor. He had not seen a Bible in years. He smelled it, kissed it with trembling lips, cradled it, and then with great reverence, opened it. Then he turned to me and said, "Let me tell you of my wounds." And he poured out his trials for God, which included seven beatings by the secret police and the awful seduction of his daughter by a government agent who then fooled her into betraying him. Then he turned to me, his eyes boring into my soul, and asked, "What wounds have you for the Master?" I was embarrassed to have so few to share.

Not that the wounds of a Western Christian will match—for want of a better term—the *gore* of the persecuted ones. Our wounds in most cases may be more psychological than physical, our persecutions more to do with discouragement, disappointment, and discrimination than with beatings and betrayals. But wounds they are nevertheless, and no less faith shaking to our world than to theirs.

Perhaps the key to the faith warning is to realize that it can be our *culture* that is hostile to Christ, at root idolatrous and leading us away from Christ, even though the rhetoric may be quite Christian. It was a young artist in Shanghai that brought this home to me.

Her name was Ping An, and she was a Chinese landscape painter. In the course of her training at a very prestigious academy, she became a Christian. A traditional Chinese landscape painting depicts sheer mountains rising into mist-covered summits, streams falling spectacularly into wide, shimmering lakes. Any human figure in such a painting is always tiny, reflecting a belief that humans are insignificant relative to the glories of nature.

But Ping An was reading Genesis 1, and her eyes widened when suddenly she realized how radically different the Christian view of creation was to the one she depicted on her traditional canvases. She recalls, "What amazed me was that the story of creation culminates with the creation of Adam and Eve, not the mountains, seas, or heavens. We Chinese find mountains and rivers a lot more impressive than human beings. But God turns that upside down and values a fragile life more than a mighty rock."

The next day she sat in the classroom and drew a landscape in its traditional form, then placed two figures at the center, drawing them much larger than usual. It was a break with tradition to say the least.

She returned from her lunch and was told, "The governors have asked to see you." She made her way to a room where six stone-faced men sat in a row. To the right of them hung her new painting. "What is the meaning of this?" they asked.

Ping An tried to explain, but a very distinguished professor interrupted her. He said patiently, as if to a child, "Look, if I thrust a branch into you, blood flows out and you die. But if I poke a branch into a mountain, the mountain makes it into a tree. How then can you possibly say we humans are more significant than mountains? They go on forever. We are here for a fleeting moment. That's why we paint human figures so small."

"No, we are not insignificant," she flashed back, and to the astonishment of the committee, she quoted the words of Jesus in Luke 21:33: *"'Heaven and earth will pass away, but my words will not pass away.'* Don't *you* see, it's God's words that make things significant. He doesn't talk to the mountains. He talks to *us*. He has made the mountains *for* us! Isn't it incredible?"

The governors did not agree. She was expelled from the school, barred from any further artistic training, and now ekes out a living as a teacher, doing portraiture in her spare time. But it was her traditional Chinese culture that was at odds with her new Christian convictions. Her clash had little to do with the fact that she lived in a Communist country where the worship of God was severely restricted.

In the same way, we all have to awaken to the same clash of values in our own culture. I returned to Pasadena, California, to write up the story of Ping An, when a friend came to me with an interesting reflection. Three years ago his sister was going out to the mission field and needed support. He needed a car, and being a lawyer in a well-known Wilshire Boulevard firm, he felt it needed to make the "right statement." He bought a $65,000 Mercedes, gave $5,000 to his sister, and the following year traded up his Mercedes for a faster coupe version. Support for his sister did not diminish. Faithfully he gave her $5,000 a year.

Three years later he worked out some math. Without thinking, he had traded in to get a new Mercedes every year and invested a further $45,000 in a four-wheel drive Ford Explorer, making a total expenditure of $175,000. "Financially speaking," he said, "I never felt it, but when I visited my sister in India and realized what she could have done with a third of that money, I felt ashamed. The truth was, I didn't need the sporty Mercedes coupe—I just wanted to look successful and blend in with the partners, nor did I really need the Explorer. I was so busy with work I used it on only two weekends."

What shattered him, however, was that he had spent so much money on himself and had never been challenged once that such expenditure was selfish. At church his friends drooled over his car. He never heard preaching that challenged him to think about it. His Christian friends were so busy buying similar cars and extra homes near Lake Arrowhead that when he shared his first pangs of concern, they looked uncomprehendingly at him.

He said, *"I suddenly realized that to live in a way that offended no one in California actually offended God."* He sold his Mercedes, got rid of his Explorer, and now drives a Volvo. The $72,000 he saved went to his sister, who used it to start four rescue houses for child prostitutes in Calcutta. More than four hundred kids now have been saved from the streets and are being educated at this lawyer's "minor" expense.

But the story does not end there. His Volvo became an object of scorn in the firm's parking lot. A senior partner, assuming his investments had failed, even offered him a loan to buy a Porsche.

Finally, convicted that his fourteen-hour work days were not good for his young children, my friend began leaving the office at six. He has been told, "You will never become a partner because you are not in the office enough."

He was another Ping An—in trouble for his faith. He realized how really radical Jesus's values are and how they critiqued the very culture that he used to breathe in so unthinkingly. The questions of the persecuted church are simple: Are you in trouble for Jesus? Where are your wounds? If you don't have any, maybe you've forgotten you're in a fight at all.

## The Radical Life

Brother Andrew puts it this way: "Persecution is because of the radical life, not the other way round. Why are we not having persecution? Because we are dodging it. There are many Bible verses like 2 Timothy 3:12, 'All who want to live a godly life in Christ will be persecuted.' We go around that because we don't like that verse, and we interpret it so that it becomes meaningless. Or we apply it only to the time of the apostle Paul. If we are radical in our Christian walk, we will be persecuted."[1]

To this, an objection could be made: "Look, I live in a Christian culture. It will never persecute me for being a Christian. And I'm in the suburbs where life is well regulated and easy."

What on earth is "trouble" going to look like in that environment? Here we have to remember the subtlety of the devil, who is always seeking to subvert our worship. Religious people are no less prone to idolatry than their secular counterparts. Jesus himself spent most of his time arguing to a group of believers that the God they thought they worshiped, they were in fact alienating. So it can get very subtle. I want to say that the pressure of the world, the flesh, and the devil comes from so many sources that we can safely say that every Christian will experience it, no matter if their culture is formally hostile to Christianity or fundamentally formed by it.

I remember a couple in the United States who refused to participate in their neighborhood Christmas celebration. The husband was an accountant and figured he spent more than $2,000 on Christmas lights and decorations each year to doll up his house with the most extravagant designs of reindeer, snowmen, and Santas. Everyone along the street did the same to ensure that their neighborhood won a coveted prize for their decorations.

But one day in November this couple was having a Bible study, and they asked themselves the question, "Did Jesus really come so that we could spend two thousand dollars on turning our house into a neon fairyland?" The answer was no, and they decided not to spend the money on the lights, giving the money instead to a foundation in Thailand that rescued young ethnic women from sex slavery.

As a result they became social pariahs in their neighborhood, because the coveted prize went to another suburb. The wife remembers, "I used to dive behind the sofa whenever anyone came to the door, as they were invariably neighbors complaining about our meanness." They were even accused in the local paper of being "modern-day Scrooges, refusing to enter into the Christmas spirit." This was in a suburb of San Francisco where Christmas was supposedly being celebrated.

This rather amusing story illustrates a serious point. Whatever culture we are in, we are always being subtly coerced into spending our money, or time, on what is not of Christ. Persecution afflicts us all if we stand up for Christ. The world, the flesh, and the devil will never reach an accommodation with Christ. Like it or not, we are caught up in cosmic warfare. The gospel has landed us in it. We will all be scarred by the battle. We will all experience persecution. The difference is only one of degree and type.

A further reaction to this faith warning might run like this: "I've racked my brain and I really cannot see any evidence of persecution in my life. Sure, I have experienced suffering but not for Christ's sake. I've got a great job. Everyone knows I'm a Christian, and I've never experienced an ounce of discrimination on the basis of it. My family are all Christians and have never harmed me. What does this mean? Does it mean that I'm not a serious Christian?" By no means.

There are two replies to this condition. One is, be thankful. It may well be that God has led this person into a pleasant land and given him or her favor in the eyes of everyone. But remember, it probably will not last!

The second reply is, be careful. Remember why the apostle Paul was in such trouble. It's not simply because he was a Christian. He was in trouble specifically because he was a *preaching* Christian! It was his habit to go into the synagogues and argue for the gospel that caused the persecuting reaction. So we always have to ask ourselves, "Are we actually confronting the powers-that-be in the name of Jesus?"

In Hong Kong I knew an older expatriate Christian couple that was very wealthy, but from their vast mansion on the peak, they could not rid themselves of a nagging feeling that their Christian lives were getting stale. They mentioned to a priest how uncomfortable they were with feeling "too comfortable," and he replied, "Come with me."

At three o'clock in the morning, they found themselves roaring about the streets of Hong Kong in a VW camper, breaking the speed limit and speeding away from armed men. The priest had linked them to a ministry that picked up stray teenage girls who had run away from their homes. The couple was astonished to learn that fifty-five girls a night fled their homes in the city of Hong Kong. The girls were reported missing, and the ministry, which had an arrangement with the police, attempted to find them. But another group of people were listening in to the police bands—Hong Kong's triads, criminal gangs who also trawled the streets looking for the runaway girls to force into prostitution. If they found a girl before the police or this ministry, and the girl was attractive, she was shipped off to Japan as a sex slave, never to see her parents again.

This couple, who until then had seen Hong Kong as purely a place to make money, now found themselves involved in a deadly war to find the stray girls before the gangs did. Sometimes they arrived at the same time as the gangs, and they experienced "persecution." Once they were shot at. Another time a gang member threatened them with a knife. Said the wife, "I just never knew there were these dramas on the street, because my life was all about insulating myself from these human needs. Money does that. It enables you to block out the needs of the world, and soon you forget there are others in need, and you just focus on your own needs."

*Sometimes the battle comes to us. Sometimes we have to find the battle.* We have to look at our life and ensure that we are witnessing for Christ. Then the trouble will surely come.

## Know Your Fight

Persecuted Christians know they are in a fight. Every day they struggle. Not being conscious of a daily struggle may be a sure sign that one is losing the battle of life. The ancient psalmist looked at the rich elite of Israel and said, "They have no struggles" (Ps. 73:4 NIV). They should have struggles if they wish to please God. But so many Christians in the world today seem surprised at the language of struggle.

### Continuing in a Struggle

What struggles do the persecuted awaken us to? There is, first of all, *the struggle we are always in.* Everyone who visits persecuted communities comes away with a renewed appreciation of the spiritual battle we are always engaged in. We have to battle our *reluctant hearts,* which are mired in sin and do not want to face God. Why must we always force ourselves to pray? Our hearts are reluctant.

We have to battle a *blinding world,* which dazzles and distracts, trying to disorient us from our true nature and purpose, which is to glorify God.

We also have to battle a *lying devil,* who is forever feeding us lies such as "You are no good" and "God doesn't care about you," trying to ruin the effects of Christ's redemption in our lives.

The great Victorian preacher Charles Spurgeon once said, "The devil does not waste his time flogging a dead horse." He meant that if you are not conscious of fighting a daily battle against your flesh, the world, and the devil, then that means only one thing—you have already lost the battle! It's time to rejoin! A great American preacher, William Sloane Coffin, also quipped, "Jesus knew that *love your enemies* didn't mean *don't make any!*"

*Awakened to a Struggle*

There is also *the struggle we must awaken to.* Said a persecuted Christian in Palestine, "When you become a real Christian, you get reawakened to the fact that the whole world lies in the hands of the evil one, and this reflects in your own culture." She said, "What your culture worships, you have to struggle against."

In her case, it was a worship of extremist terrorists who risked everything to kill Israelis. In standing out against that, she struggled to communicate to her neighbors who thought she was being "unpatriotic."

We have to face up to the same question—what is our culture worshiping? Is it, as Francis Schaeffer once said, "the god of personal peace and affluence," so that we don't mind what goes on in the world as long as our space and prosperity are not affected?

One prayer group in South Central Los Angeles became convicted that a whole generation of their youth was worshiping guns, and that mainstream society—through Hollywood filmmaking—was promoting this. They began to campaign against it, speaking in churches and writing articles for their local paper. They even induced a local supermarket to exchange bags of groceries for guns if gang members handed in their weapons. One night as they gathered to pray, the house where they were meeting was sprayed by bullets in a drive-by shooting. From the car a young man shouted, "My God is my gun!" He said more than he knew, and this group continues to square up to persecution—especially as they are starting to be successful.

*Creating a Struggle*

Finally, there is *the struggle we must create.* Brother Andrew tells the story of meeting Assemblies of God pastor Haik of Iran, who said to him in 1993, "Andrew, when they kill me, it will be for speaking, not for being silent." Pastor Haik was murdered in 1994 for speaking out about the treatment of Christian evangelist and friend Mehdi Dibaj, who was sentenced to death for apostasy. If Haik had stayed silent, he would still be alive. By speaking out, he entered an arena of conflict that cost him everything. But he would have it no other way.

The fact is that we can avoid struggle if we want. Each of us has to make a choice to speak up, to defy the powers that be, and to bring a struggle into being. Otherwise it is a rollover victory for the enemy. Just two days ago in Edinburgh, I was sitting in Princess Street Gardens, a beautiful park right in the center of the city. I watched as a young woman sat down, took out a tin whistle, placed her cap in front of her, and began playing for money. It took all of three minutes for two men to start harassing her. I moved closer, discreetly, to hear the exchange. They could see she was homeless and attractive, and they were pressing her to have sex with them for a lot more money than her music would garner.

In this situation, I intervened (perhaps because there have been too many occasions when I have walked on by) and asked the men to leave, only to receive a torrent of abuse. I talked to the young woman and offered to take her to a Salvation Army hostel off the Royal Mile. She came along with me. The men followed, shouting obscenities. As we went into the hostel, they said to me, "We'll find out where you live!" I took the long way home that night and have not slept so soundly since. But the fight is always there, in front of our noses. The fact is, we usually walk on by.

Persecuted Christians are always in a fight. They struggle all the time—against their own sins, against idolatries in their own societies, and against the orchestration of the evil one who is out to take our worship away from God. Yet these struggles should also mark our lives and churches; surely the devil does not live exclusively in China or Colombia. The apostle Paul has to upbraid the Corinthian believers because, while they are rich, wise, and honored, he is poor, beaten, and persecuted (1 Cor. 4:8–13). Such peace and honor is not meant for this world but for the next. This world is the place of struggle. What's your struggle? What's mine?

The persecuted force us to ask. Everyone ought to have a struggle!

A final objection here is when the Christian might say, "Well, what amount of trouble is *enough*?" If he or she is enjoying a peaceful life, the danger is to go out and do something that provokes trouble that is not of Christ. I remember a pastor of a charismatic church in Hong Kong arguing very forcefully that persecution comes from evangelism, saying, "If we are not being persecuted, it's because we are not evangelizing forcefully enough." He added, "That's the secret of the Chinese revival—they talk of Christ everywhere; they are pushy, aggressive, and strong; and it gets them into trouble, but the trouble is what brings the blessing, the revival."

I argued back with him. "Look, I'm going back to the UK. It's a postmodern world. If I share about Christ on a train, the fellow traveler usually says, 'Hey, that's great for you. I'm a Buddhist, and into biofeedback.' It becomes quite a friendly exchange a lot of the time. I can't say that I'm not persecuted because I'm not evangelizing. And look at Billy Graham—a prophet with honor rather than without it for his evangelistic prowess."

The pastor would not have it. "If you get onto that train in the UK and start passing out tracts to enough people and really pressing for decisions, you'll be persecuted. You'll see."

Ironically enough, I was traveling in a UK train exactly a month after our discussion, and it was a Muslim who was passing out tracts and witnessing—no, bullying—people into conversation. He focused on me with aggression. He trashed my faith, saying, "Christ didn't die on the cross. Your four Gospels are frauds." He was frankly obnoxious. In the end I said to him, with a touch of asperity, "Look, would you please leave me alone? I'm quite content in my faith and have no wish to keep speaking with someone as close-minded and insulting as you."

But I saw him lean back in the chair, a little smile playing on his features. Was he thinking, "Ah, persecuted for Allah's sake"? Because if so, how wrong he would be! He was just being obnoxious. And that might have been me also if I had taken that Hong Kong pastor's advice. It is too easy to create a reaction by being aggressive.

The Scriptures tell us not to bring unnecessary trouble on ourselves but to live quiet lives. To a young church experiencing the "fiery ordeal" of persecution, Peter says, "accept all authority" (1 Pet. 2:13) and "show respect for everyone" (v. 17). Trouble will find us because we are "aliens and strangers" in a world of human beings who prefer to live for their own aggrandizement and dreams rather than for God Himself. If we are not feeling some conflict, we are surely not fighting.

So here is our faith warning from the suffering church: make sure you are in trouble for Jesus, because if the idols that surround you are leaving you alone, chances are that's because you are worshiping them and not walking the way of the cross.

But this does not just apply to the individual. It applies corporately too. Churches ought to be in trouble.

I was discussing this point with a friend of mine who happens to be—for want of a better term—a megachurch pastor. "Ron," he was sharing excitedly, "we are just growing and growing. I never dreamed I'd see so many people lapping up the gospel. We're up to six thousand in only eight years."

"That's wonderful," I replied, "but do you face much opposition as a result of that growth?"

"Oh, no," came the confident reply, "you see, we really concentrate on having a presence in the local community. We run moms' toddlers' groups, soup kitchens, a hostel for the homeless, literacy skills classrooms for underprivileged kids, and so on. The local people wouldn't ever turn on us, because we do so much good. And even the local government calls us up when they have problem families needing housed." He concluded triumphantly, "We're connected into the community in a way that many churches in the past failed to be. Everyone speaks well of us."

While I was delighted to see this church really impacting the community, there was something odd in his attitude. He seemed to think that persecution could never happen when a church was doing good. But what about Christian hospitals firebombed in the Middle East, or Christian-run orphanages attacked in India? Graham Staines in India did nothing but good running a hospital for leprosy sufferers. My pastor friend had missed something. As so many persecuted Christians say, "Persecution is never about us, what we do, or who we are; it's about who we worship—Christ!"

That phrase the pastor used—"Everyone speaks well of us"— comes from Acts 2:46–47, and the context would worry him if he explored it more deeply. "Day by day, as they spent much time together in the temple, they broke bread at home and ate their food with glad and generous hearts, praising God and having the goodwill of all the people. And day by day the Lord added to their number those who were being saved."

If you imagine Acts as a film of the development of the church, freeze the picture at this point, and it is the happiest situation imaginable. It may be the ideal goal for many churches today. Who would not want to be well spoken of in the community? Who would not want to be known for their generosity to each other? Who would not want to be adding numbers daily to their community? It's ideal.

But we have to say, "This is not the ideal for a mature church!" This church in Acts 2 is only a baby church. The picture is only a freeze frame. We have to let the film roll on. It wasn't long after this that Peter and John were arrested and flogged by the Sanhedrin. Not long after that, they had internal church difficulties with the deception of Ananias and Sapphira. Not long after that, Stephen was stoned to death. After that, most of them had to flee from Jerusalem. Persecution, strife, and trouble were on the way—thankfully—because then and only then did they finally take the gospel to the Gentiles.

So it is very important to realize that the placidity that the church enjoys in Acts 2 is due to two factors. First, they are not numerous, just a few thousand, so they are not a threat just yet. But as they grow, they do become a threat to the Jewish community in Jerusalem. Second, they were ignorant of the truly radical nature of their gospel. This gospel is for the whole world. They hadn't really grasped that. Peter and John really only get outside of Jerusalem after the persecution. At this time they are thinking, *We'll keep preaching, and with a couple more miracles the Jews will believe.* Clearly then, everyone speaks well of the church of Acts 2 because they are a small, insignificant bunch that can be safely ignored. When they begin to recognize their radical agenda and their influence, it's as much of a surprise to them as to anyone else.

Once Brother Andrew was introduced to a group of well-known charismatic pastors. They told him they felt their churches were living back in the time of Acts and regaled him with stories of healings and growth. He replied, "Well, yes, I rejoice in all that, but where's your persecution? You cannot be like the church in Acts if you are not also experiencing persecution!"

One does rejoice in the growth of megachurches. They are surely doing something right presenting a gospel that really scratches where the culture itches. Church strategist John Drane talks of a megachurch message: "They appeal most to middle-class professionals who are struggling to manage life, and offer the gospel as the ultimate management tool for life—success." This is not a criticism, but there is a missing ingredient, and that is often the necessity of suffering and the inevitability of persecution if the Christian takes on the powers-that-be. We must gently ask, "What is wrong that all speak well of you?"

In this connection, there is a key word that Christians fear to use because they will be labeled Marxist. It is this word: *structures*! The fact is, evil is embedded in systems of oppression as well as in individual behavior. Fighting the forces of oppression on this structural level brings an entirely new level of conflict. I witnessed a group of Christian lawyers who came over from America to investigate suspicious church burnings throughout Indonesia in 1996 and 1997. They were high powered, well connected, and utterly fearless in their investigation, resulting in the uncovering of the names of two generals in the Indonesian military who had allowed churches to be burned to foment social chaos. Their plan was to let chaos develop until the people demanded a strongman to fix things, and then they would ride in like a ruthless sheriff to the rescue.

Armed with this knowledge, the lawyers returned to Washington, D.C., and placed a report on the desk of a key player. It was ignored. They followed up. Their inquiry was still ignored. Eventually they secured a meeting with the appropriate person. They were warned, "These Generals are signatories of some of our largest arms deals. We will do nothing to jeopardize jobs in our defense industry. And what's more, neither will you." They were suddenly in conflict with a *structure* that was behind the persecution, and it became a much rougher battle. As one of them told me, "We set out to fight persecution in Indonesia; we ended up fighting it in Washington, D.C."

In Latin America it is not enough to say to Christians in guerilla-controlled areas, "Keep praying." The problem is, as a local pastor told me, "Persecution is driven by the drug industry. The guerilla leaders use the farmers to grow the drugs and refine them, and they export them by giving big paybacks to government ministers to look the other way." To fight this, the Christians who refuse to grow poppies must be physically protected from guerilla reprisals and given alternative crops to grow. In other words, a whole new economy must be established to enable the Christians to survive. A new structure has to be built because the old one is the culprit!

So the issue is, What structures of evil do our growing megachurches in the West threaten? Are they really just—as their critics suggest—factories to enable more people to become more middle class? Is the emphasis all on *fitting in*? Has *standing out* become lost under all the talk of abundant living, cluster groups, and career fulfillment? What if, as Ronald Sider claims, a Western middle-class lifestyle is a structural evil? As he memorably said, "We must live more simply, so that the poor might simply live." Where is the confrontation with the evils that result in persecution not only in the West but the confrontation that spreads to cause persecution in other countries also? Let us put it this way—the status quo in any society rarely serves God. Those Christians who realize that Christ calls us to a radical discipleship will threaten the status quo. Those who don't, will not! Get into a church that is a threat to something!

The good news is, this is starting to happen. In 2003 Rick Warren, perhaps the most prominent megachurch pastor in the United States, launched his Peace Plan, which commits his church to tackle the five global giants of evil in the world today: spiritual emptiness, self-serving leadership, poverty, disease, and ignorance or illiteracy. He believes that the church is the institution best equipped to tackle these giants, and they will do so with the "five smooth stones" of planting churches, equipping leaders, assisting the poor, caring for the sick, and educating the next generation. The first letters of these "stones" form the acrostic PEACE.

The significance is clear to see. Warren is moving his church into the arena of fighting the systems and structures of evil; and persecution, if it has not affected the megachurch movement already, will surely come to it now as it takes on these stubborn giants of oppression. Demonic and human forces of vested interest will unite to keep their agenda of ruin on track. Warren is surely right—this is the church's battle, and only the church has the power to win. But we'd better strap on our armor. This is a fight to the death.

The faith warning is, Are we in enough trouble for Jesus? Christianity should always come as a threat to the status quo. If it doesn't, then we need to go back to the drawing board, and ask whether it's Christianity we have really got!

When we enter this fight, the foe can seem overwhelming. How can we tackle oppressions that are centuries old or stop violent men who have their fingers on all the levers of power? It is easy to be intimidated and wonder, *Is the Gospel really enough?*

That's why we must also take a *faith boost* from the persecuted.

# 14   Faith Boost

*Is My God Big Enough?*

Most of us usually encounter the persecuted church by hearing or reading a story of someone who has suffered greatly for God but has been triumphant. Testimonies of triumph travel fast, and missions have served us well to circulate these testimonies. One pastor I knew described the effect of the Open Doors magazine like this: "It felt like I had been living in a closet, and these saints came to me and led me out, saying, 'Actually you live in a mansion, let us show you some of the rooms!'"

He continued, "When I read of men and women who could still praise God after torture or were delivered by mighty acts of power, I would go to my little vicarage study and realize that their God was mine too, and that the 'rooms' they took me to were mine to visit also. I would pray for similar acts of power and strength to occur in my parish."

This is what we mean by a faith boost. It's when Christians reading of these persecuted believers realize that the God who delivered or strengthened the persecuted saint loves them just as much and will help them as much, and so faith is boosted. We are reminded of how big our God is.

It's a very biblical reaction. Think of how much faith in the Bible is deliverance-centered. Psalmists and prophets in the Old Testament looked back to the exodus, that paradigmatic deliverance, where God rescued His people from four hundred years of slavery "by a mighty hand and an outstretched arm" (Deut. 4:34). They were telling themselves, *Our God will do for us what He did for our ancestors.* The same is true for us. Our God will do for us what He has done for the persecuted.

But why do we need to be reminded of this? Perhaps it's because, as comfortable Western Christians, we do not have enough emergencies—situations so hopeless that all we can do is pray. In a house group I attend, each of the members admitted recently that only once or twice a year did any of them need something so desperately from God that they prayed with all their might. Such circumstances were unusual. One couple was moving and asking God to give them their dream house. Another person had a tumor and was praying the tests would show it was benign. Another was in love with someone who did not reciprocate. Such dire needs did not occur that frequently. Over five years as a group we maybe had one crisis every eight months or so.

The persecuted face emergencies every week. They are always crying to God for deliverance, because so often that is all they can do. No wonder they know more about God than we do. It is through their stories, through their testimonies of God's power and love, that our faith can be fortified.

The stories themselves tend to come in two main forms: *deliverance* stories that testify to the rescuing power of God, and *endurance* stories that testify to the faithfulness of God over time.

## Deliverance Stories

At their most robust, deliverance stories make us marvel at the power of God, reminding us that miracles are just as much a part of daily life today as in Bible times. I heard of an evangelist who went to Tibet to evangelize Buddhists. He was caught and actually given a famous sky burial—alive! He was sown into a yak skin and left to die in the baking sun. His Tibetan tormentors—fearful of the spirits—left him alone, not even watching from a distance. It would be a slow and excruciating death.

But death was not his lot. He later told his story to a Henan evangelist. "I think maybe on the second day I began to notice large birds around me. Vultures I think they were. And they began pecking at me. I was so far gone I hoped they would peck my eyes out all the way into my brain and make death come quickly. But after a while, I began to realize that their attempts to eat me had only pecked through the sewing, and it was loosened to such an extent that I was able to emerge out of it like a butterfly from a cocoon."

A man who heard that story said that it turned his life around. A Hong Kong securities dealer, he was about to take his own life after running up gambling debts he had no hope of paying back. His wife left him, taking his child, and then his Mercedes was stolen, all in one week. He went upstairs to his flat and put his head in the oven. As he twisted the knobs to turn the gas on, he suddenly thought of that story, picturing the bird beaks slicing through the sewing. Then he stopped and said to God, "Why don't you save me too?" He fiddled with the knobs for twenty minutes, but nothing happened. The gas had been turned off that afternoon because of an overdue bill. He saw that as God's deliverance and started a new life, confessing his gambling addiction to friends and family. He has not paid his debts yet, but he does have his wife and child back, so impressed were they with his new attitude.

Many are delivered but don't realize it until later, testifying to the disturbing truth that God does not rescue merely His own, or those who pray, but even the worst sinners while still in their sin. In Vietnam I came across a former soldier called Bao. Conscripted by the Khmer Rouge in 1966 when he was only seventeen, he became totally dehumanized by the war. He saw his best friends shot; his girlfriend raped, then strangled. To deal with these traumas, Bao chewed a jungle leaf prized for its narcotic qualities and would lapse into dreams of a perfect world, then waken to the hell of war.

One day his troop ambushed a South Vietnamese patrol, and after a fierce skirmish, only one of the enemy survived. They stood him up to be shot and gave him a last request. The prisoner did not request a cigarette as per the usual custom but asked to be read a portion of a book he had in his top pocket. Bao began to read the words out loud, "And Jesus said . . ." But he got no further. Suddenly the air was full of thunder and the trees around them were shredded with bullets. He dived for cover and just managed to escape the destructive path of the helicopter gunship. In the melee the prisoner escaped.

The next day the soldier asked his troop leader, "What did Jesus say?" The troop leader looked shocked. Bao said, "Look, it must have been something important for that guy to want to hear it before his death." His leader was furious and told him he was reporting him to the political commissar. Bao knew he was in serious trouble. On the march back, he was struck with painful diarrhea, and the troop waited by a tree for him to go a little distance and relieve himself. There was a loud boom, and Bao returned to the tree to find his companions hanging in bits from the foliage. They were all dead. He continued as a soldier for four more years. Every day he wondered *what Jesus said.*

Finally, when he reached Saigon and his side was victorious, he found a Bible on a dead person, re-covered it with brown paper, and read it all the way back to Hanoi. He said, "I finally got to read what Jesus said, and I decided I wanted to die to those words too." But he added, "I was spared by God even when I was in my sins. The diarrhea was what saved me, and that was God. Otherwise I would have been in bits like the rest of my troop. But God wanted to save me, and He spared me to hear what Jesus had to say." What a testimony to the power of God and the power of His Word—to intrigue Bao for four long years with the phrase "and Jesus said . . ."

A preacher friend of mine loved that story. He said, "It reminds me of what preaching really is—speaking words that God takes, sears them into someone's brain, then preserves that life to hear them and understand them. And I see how little I have to do with it. That's what humbles me. I used to think preaching was about how well I spoke. But now I see what God really does through the words that come from my mouth, and that blows my mind."

## Endurance Stories

Yet it has to be said that deliverance stories—though they tend to grab the headlines—are not the norm. A dear old Christian in Beijing used to say to me: "Remember, for every deliverance story you hear, there are ten endurance stories." He was right. The story of the persecuted is primarily one of endurance. It has been since New Testament times. Paul warns that only those who endure with Christ will reign with Him (2 Tim. 2:12). And this is surely right—after all, the things we are "delivered" from come back to take us. The disease that threatened to take our life may have passed, but another will come along and take our life eventually.

God delivers through endurance. If Jesus had been "delivered" from the pain of the cross and miraculously released, we would not be delivered from our sins. He endured so that a deeper, greater deliverance could take place.

I never saw this principle better illustrated than in the story of an old Christian lady in China. A doctor in Beijing, Mabel was well-known for her bright Christian witness. She never married, so she could take care of a sick brother. Her family was wealthy. They lived in a large house in the center of the capital.

All that changed abruptly in 1949. Her large house marked her as one of the landlord class. She was evicted from her house and forced to live in a garden shed with just a stove, two deck chairs, and an old bed. Her Christian convictions meant she was an object of suspicion, and so when the Cultural Revolution broke out, she was stripped of her doctor's post and sent to work shoveling sand in a work gang. But the final indignity was when the Red Guards— teenagers who were given power to direct the revolution—began to visit her, beating her up, parading her in the streets, and forcing her to wear a placard with her so-called crimes written on it.

So thorough were the Red Guards that they erected a large sign outside her house declaring her a pariah because she had distributed "imperialistic literature in praise of anti-Mao factions," which meant that she had given out Bibles in the "mistaken" belief that religion was helpful. For the Red Guards, there was only one "God" allowed, and that was Mao, and only one "Bible" allowed, his Little Red Book.

Mabel descended into hell. Shunned by neighbors, victimized daily by her work gang, and beaten up regularly by the Red Guards, she came back one night into her little shed and said to God, "I've had enough." She reasoned, "I'm in my sixties now, I've lived a good life, and God will not mind me coming to heaven early." So she took a large chopper, held it over her wrists, and issued one last prayer before bringing it down, "Lord, if this is wrong, help me."

She never brought the chopper down. She put it away, sat down, burst into tears, and endured another eight years of the beatings, isolation, and victimization. She said, "Somehow, God gave me the strength to endure, but I never knew how."

Later, many years later, she knew why.

In the late seventies, after Mao died and Deng returned to power, China began to put the excesses of the Cultural Revolution behind it. The hated Red Guards were disbanded; the Little Red Book fell into disuse.

Mabel's house was not restored to her, but she began to receive a stream of visitors. To her astonishment, these visitors were all rather high-ranking members of the Communist Party. Even more astonishingly, they asked her for Bibles.

"Why come to me? Out of all the people in Beijing, why do you come to the house of a seventy-year-old?" she would ask. Each would answer the same: "Well, during the Cultural Revolution, there was a large sign outside your house full of your crimes. One of them was that you had distributed Bibles. I'm here on the chance that you might have some left."

Amazingly that sign, which made her life such a misery, became the means of a new ministry. It kept people away from her during the Cultural Revolution, but afterward, after she had endured, it drew them. Mabel was able to contact a Western mission, which smuggled Bibles to her, and she became the first conduit of Scriptures into China's capital. She became a vital supplier, and a number of high-ranking members of the Communist Party in China today owe their faith to her endurance.

She reflected, "It's been nice to know why. It helps my faith. But it was hard. Every day was hard. I can't say I saw Jesus, or even felt Him close most of the time. I just got the strength to keep going, and that was enough."

### We Don't All Get to See Why!

Not all who endure get to see why. Zhao, a fifty-five-year-old when I met him, couldn't have been more of a contrast to Mabel. His life seemed to have been one of dashed hopes. He hoped to go to university as a young man but failed the examinations. He hoped to have a child, but his wife died in childbirth, taking the child with her. He hoped to make a success of farming in his native Shaanxi, but the river burst its banks and wiped out his crops two years in succession. Three years ago he came to Beijing, penniless at fifty-two years of age, casting himself on the charity of distant relatives. Their charity lasted three months, then they told him to go home to Shaanxi.

But there was nothing to go home to, so he stayed in Beijing, sleeping in a shack in a shantytown at the edge of the city, making ends meet through odd jobs. The jobs were usually hard, backbreaking work—jobs for young men, not for a man in his fifties.

Zhao had been a Christian since he was sixteen. He was literate but had pawned his Bible a long time ago. He prayed ten minutes each morning and asked only for his "daily bread." Most days he got it, but only just. One day he was praying and he saw a vision. He said, "I just saw a flat pan with bread in it, and at once I knew that I was going to be a baker."

Not that he felt much joy in the vision. He smiled and said, "I felt a bit like Jeremiah when he saw visions of pots instead of those great throne visions that Isaiah and Ezekiel were treated to." But he wondered what would come of it.

He did not have long to wait. On his way home from work, he passed an old man selling bread. He cooked it on a flat pan about two feet in diameter, and it was heated with a small brazier. Beijingers are fussy about their bread—it must be fresh and perfect. Zhao visited the old man every day. The man took an interest in him and taught him to bake bread the way he did. After a year or so the old man gave him the brazier and the pan and said, "It's yours. I'm too old to hawk it around the streets now."

So Zhao was a baker, at fifty-four. He got up at four o'clock in the morning to bake his flat loaves, ready for the morning crowds as they cycled to work. Then he would hawk the remaining loaves till dusk, returning to the tin shack where he possessed only a camp bed, a lantern, and a battered case of spare shirts and underwear.

One morning as dawn was breaking, he was flattening out the bread on the pan, and he thought to himself, "My life seems to have gone all wrong, but there must be some work I can do for Jesus."

Thoughtfully, he took a clean stick and drew a cross in the dough. It was unmistakably a Christian cross, and at first he was a bit frightened in case people would report him. Soon he grew bolder and put a cross on every flat loaf. No one asked why, but they did seem to enjoy the bread.

Then one day a woman pushed a sheet of paper into his hand. He saw it was a page torn from some book, and it depicted all sorts of cross designs. Zhao became an artist overnight. He made bread with a cross in the shape of an anchor; then a cross with a thorny crown, then Celtic and Iona crosses. His pièce de résistance was a loaf in the shape of a cercelee cross. Each of the four ends is split, creating two curves that loop back to point at the center stem.

Does anyone say anything? No! Is anyone touched by God? No one knows, least of all Zhao. There is no cozy ending full of triumph to this story, yet there is something strangely triumphant in the way he gets up each morning at four, surveys his pan with a look of intense concentration, and asks God what shape he should bake his bread in that day. He bakes with a solemnity, a dignity, and a slowness of movement reminiscent of priests celebrating a holy sacrament. Who knows? Perhaps he is!

It is on the rock of the stories of Mabel and Zhao, who endure for God in the face of total dehumanization, that the church of Christ grows. They endure. They prove the mettle of God. Years of thwarted ambition or decades of psychological torture cannot triumph. These people testify that God is big enough!

Everyone can identify. These are powerless people, yet God uses them to build mighty kingdoms. And even if they do not feel used, they have the faith to believe that their lives do matter. Each person forms a "living stone" in the kingdom that God builds, and as we know from Scripture, God loves to take the stones no one else will pick up to make His masterpieces.

I like to call this "God's Michelangelo touch." The great Florentine sculptor Michelangelo was not known for his modesty, but to be fair, he had very little to feel modest about. He was the greatest. He felt the need to make this clear to everyone and wondered how he could showcase his supremacy. So he decided he would sculpt a masterpiece that would astonish the artistic world, and he decided to use a piece of marble so flawed, so shallow, so veined, that no other sculptor would touch it. He went to the marble shop and saw a piece of marble that had lain there for fifty years. It was unusable. From this block he carved his fourteen-foot high statue of David. His genius reigned. It's one thing to make a masterpiece from the best marble, but it's a much more dramatic accomplishment to make a supreme masterpiece from the worst of materials.

God is always doing the same, not—like Michelangelo—because He wants to show off, but rather to build His eternal masterpiece out of our lives. But He can only do so if we acknowledge our weakness. Not so He can humiliate us, but so He can use us.

It was another persecuted Christian that brought this home to me so clearly. Her name was Sister Ann. She's long dead. I met her in China way back in the mid-1980s. She was born into quite an educated family and had four brothers who all became doctors. She was not even taught how to read and write. She began to train as a nurse, but her father fell ill, and she had to nurse him. Then her mother fell ill, and she nursed her. That illness lasted twenty years. I never did figure out what the illness was, but during that time Sister Ann hardly ever left the house. No sooner had her mother died than her brother fell ill with consumption. So she nursed him, and so on it went. She was eighty-two years old when her last brother died, and all she had done with her life was to nurse her family members at various locations in her hometown of Shanghai.

As her last brother was dying, she wondered how she would live after he died. She had no savings. The Communists had taken all the wealth of the family. But her brother said to her, "After I'm dead, look under the flagstone in the corner of this room." She found many gold coins there. It was mafia money probably. Her brother had been connected with the criminal underworld. But that was in the distant past and had nothing to do with her. Her future was assured.

So at eighty-two, Sister Ann was suddenly free to do anything she wanted. Trouble was, she was old, illiterate, and beginning to feel ill herself. She was a Christian and approached some house-church leaders, but they had no use for her. She offered to give out tracts, but since she could not read, she might not give the appropriate ones to people. She could not teach the Bible because she had never read it, though it had been read to her many times, and she felt that she knew it quite well. But the leaders were not interested. She was just an old woman. "Just hand over the money," said one, "and we'll make sure it builds the kingdom."

She felt useless.

Suddenly she made a decision. "The one thing I always wanted to do was to travel," she said. "All my life had been spent inside houses by the bedsides of dying relatives. I had never been outside Shanghai." She also thought, *Since I know the gospel so well, I can at least talk about it as I travel.*

So Sister Ann became a traveling evangelist. She used the money to travel by train all over China. No one ever challenged her. She was just a harmless old woman. But she would travel first class, or "soft sleeper" as it was known, and just talk about Jesus to her traveling companions. Many of them were high Party officials who were given the perk of traveling first class. Some were outraged at her attempts to witness to them. But she just said, "Well, what are you going to do about it? Throw an old lady in jail?" Far more of her companions smiled at her and joined her in conversation.

Sister Ann died at age eighty-seven. In the last five years of her life, she must have covered hundreds of thousands of miles. She went to the desert of the far northwest, ending up in Urumqi. She made it by bus to the twelve-thousand-feet-high Himalayan plateau in Tibet, and all the way down to the steamy jungles of the deep south, chattering about the gospel to anyone who would listen. I'd be surprised if in that entire time she slept more than three nights in the same place.

She was too old to work for the house churches, or so the leaders thought. But she was not too old to work for God. Who else would have had the time just to travel on trains for five years? Who else but an old woman would have escaped arrest for witnessing about Christ all the time in public places, which was against the law? Yes, she did a unique work. But she never saw the fruit. She never fretted about the purpose of her life. Persecuted Christians leave the future in God's hands and are content to live with a degree of bafflement, which would appall Western Christians, about what God is up to in their land and in their lives. Yet bafflement is inevitable if God's thoughts are not our thoughts, nor His ways our ways (see Isa. 55:8).

Years later, I met a house-church Christian who was visiting the home of a very high-ranking Communist Party leader. He took a wrong turn in the house and stumbled into a room where the wife of the leader was sitting. To his amazement, he saw she was reading a Bible. They talked, and she said she was a Christian. This was her story: "My husband was traveling to another city one day and was surprised to find in his train compartment an old woman who was coughing badly. They talked a bit, and she told him all about Jesus Christ, and she said to him, 'This is why I'm traveling while I die. I have to spread this news, and this way, everyone comes to my death bed.' My husband was impressed, but he never became a Christian. But I was really taken by that woman's dedication. I thought, 'What is it about Jesus Christ that would compel her to travel all over China even though she was dying?' I found a Bible and was soon saved."

Her husband, despite his professed Communism, was always known to be a friend of Christians and worked hard to prevent the worst excesses of persecution being visited on them in the regions he controlled. But what an amazing way God works! God builds His kingdom, using a broken old lady, traveling the country on mafia money, to reach the powerful in a way that no one else could.

If God can use Sister Ann, He can use any one of us. And He will build His kingdom through us in ways that will make us marvel for all eternity.

Encounter the persecuted. See the great God at work. Grow in faith and boldness. And as a result, enjoy the *faith that endures* to change the world!

# Notes

## Introduction

1. *World Christian Encyclopedia*, 2nd ed., gen. ed., David B. Barrett (New York: Oxford University Press, 2001), 191.

## Chapter 1  The Dying

1. Arabic for "Allah is the greatest."
2. "Muslim Extremist Murders Kurdish Christian," *Compass Direct*, March 14, 2003.
3. Quoted in the BBC World Service series *In God's Name*, at bbcworldservice.com.
4. *World Christian Encyclopedia*, 11.

## Chapter 2  The Creeping

1. See the discussion of this controversy in Victoria Barnett, *For the Soul of the People: Protestant Protest against Hitler* (New York: Oxford University Press, 1992), note pp. 209–11.
2. The figure was obtained from the United Christian Forum for Human Rights.
3. See Mark Tully, *India in Slow Motion* (New Delhi: Penguin Books, 2002), and Ghetan Bhatt, *Hindu Nationalism: Origins, Ideologies, and Modern Myths* (Oxford: Berg, 2001), for more information on the simplification strategy of the Hindu extremists.
4. Interview in *News Today*, January 7, 2003. Quoted in Tim Stafford, "India Undaunted," *Christianity Today*, May 2004, 28–35.
5. See Asha Prema, "Hindu Leader's Arrest in India Leads to Charge of Christian Conspiracy," *Compass Direct*, December 9, 2004.
6. See Alex Buchan, "Secret Circular Encourages Killing and Maiming of Christians," *Compass Direct*, July 2000.

7. With the exception of the Evangelical Fellowship of India, most Christian leaders put the total of Christians in India at "around or over 3 percent," which is roughly thirty million. The EFI puts the total at over 4 percent, Some even put it as high as 5 percent. However, many contend the higher estimates take into account neither the fallback rate of the new converts nor the extensive double and triple counting of converts by evangelical ministries and churches.

## Chapter 3  The Squeezing

1. Interview with the author, November 1994.

## Chapter 4  Legal Definitions

1. Not his real name.
2. Interview with the author, June 1997.
3. Nina Shea, *In the Lion's Den* (Nashville: Broadman and Holman, 1997). David Limbaugh, *Persecution: How Liberals Are Waging War against Christianity* (Washington, D.C.: Regnery, 2003). Paul Marshall with Lela Gilbert, *Their Blood Cries Out* (Dallas: Word Publishing Company, 1997). Marshall's use of contradictory definitions is deliberate. See p. 92 of this book.
4. This qualifier is taken from Article 9—freedom of thought, conscience, and religion—of the European Human Rights Act, 1998.
5. Author's interview with Michael Horowitz, December 2, 2003.
6. World Evangelical Alliance, Geneva Report, 2004, 3; available from www.worldevangelical.org/rlc.
7. Patrick Sookhdeo et al., "The Persecuted Church" (occasional paper 32, produced by issue group 3, Lausanne Committee for World Evangelization, Pattaya, Thailand, September 29–October 5, 2004), 40.
8. Ibid., 11.
9. Marshall, *Their Blood Cries Out*, 248, author's italics.
10. Ibid., 249, author's italics.
11. Kevin Boyle and Juliet Sheen, eds., *Freedom of Religion and Belief* (London: Routledge, 1997), 9.
12. Cited in *Future Church: A Global Analysis of the Christian Community to the year 2010*, Peter Brierley (London: Monarch Books, 1998), 35.
13. Marshall, *Their Blood Cries Out*, 255.
14. Cited in Jenny Watson and Michell Woolf, *The Human Rights Act Toolkit* (London: Legal Action Group, 2003), 178.
15. Boyle and Sheen, *Freedom of Religion and Belief*, 5.

## Chapter 5  Biblical Definitions

1. Quoted in Thomas Schirrmacher, *The Persecution of Christians Concerns Us All* (Bonn: Idea-Dokumentation 15/99 E, 2001), 51.
2. William Barclay, *John*, vol. 1, 3rd. ed. (Edinburgh: Saint Andrew Press, 2001), 51.
3. Quoted in Barclay, *John*, 51–52.
4. Jim Cunningham and Paul Estabrooks, *Standing Strong through the Storm* (Witney, Oxon: Open Doors International, Inc., 2003), 15.

5. *The International Standard Bible Encyclopedia*, s.v. "Persecute; Persecution."

6. Glenn M. Penner, *In the Shadow of the Cross: A Biblical Theology of Persecution and Discipleship* (Bartlesville, OK: Living Sacrifice Books, 2004).

7. Ibid., 151.

8. Sermon 94A, "On the Martyrdom of John the Baptist and on the Persecution Which Christians Have to Endure Even in a Time of Peace," *The Works of Saint Augustine*, vol. 111/4, trans. Edmund Hill (New York: New City Press, 1992), 20.

9. Ibid.

10. My definition is only a suggestion, and I would be remiss to suggest that to read the New Testament and still preserve a more restrictive definition is impossible. In a recent theological dictionary, the word *persecution* is defined as "the violation of anyone's property or physical person because of the victim's identification with a religious group." There are some, however, who still hold out for the extreme meaning.

## Chapter 6  Sources

1. Christopher Catherwood, *Whose Side Is God On? Nationalism and Christianity* (London: SPCK, 2003), 43.

2. Paul Marshall, Roberta Green, and Lela Gilbert, *Islam at the Crossroads* (Grand Rapids, Michigan: Baker Books, 2002), 82.

3. Leszek Kolakowski, *Freedom, Fame, Lying, and Betrayal: Essays on Everyday Life* (London: Penguin Books, 1999), 36–37.

4. Lesslie Newbigin, *Foolishness to the Greeks: The Gospel and Western Culture* (London: SPCK, 1986). See especially chapters 3 and 4, pp. 42–94.

5. Paul Marshall, *God and the Constitution: Christianity and American Politics* (New York: Rowman and Littlefield, 2002), 129.

## Chapter 7  The Persecuted Church—Part One

1. Anthony Browne, "Church of Martyrs," *Spectator*, March 26, 2005, 12–13.

2. The statistics cited, unless otherwise stated, are mainly taken from the 2001 *World Christian Encyclopedia*.

3. It is interesting to see, then, that this rough number of six hundred million corresponds to the number Paul Marshall uses in his book *Their Blood Cries Out* to describe the total number of Christians who are persecuted or suffer "non-trivial restrictions to their faith." Marshall works from two of David Barratt's figures given in 1980, putting 605 million Christians "living under restrictions on religious liberty," and another 225 million Christians "experiencing severe state interference in religion, obstruction, or harassment." This was the source of the oft-cited figure that "currently two hundred to two hundred and fifty million Christians are persecuted for their faith, and a further four hundred million live under non-trivial restrictions on religious liberty." As far as it goes, this is helpful. But there are two quibbles. First, these figures refer to the number of Christians, both practicing and nominal, under restrictive regimes. It is hard to describe a nominal Christian, disinterested in mission, and even disinterested in his or her faith, yet who happens to live in a state that targets the church, as "a persecuted Christian." Second, remember that Marshall restricts the term *persecution* to severe deprivation of one's religious liberties, as per the accepted usage in the

human rights community. I am more comfortable extending the word to all forms of hostility from the world directed to Christians as a result of their identification with Christ. This means that I would argue that every Great Commission Christian either already is or will experience some form of persecution for their faith in their lifetime. So another way to count the global number of the persecuted is to say that nearly 650 million Christians in the world today face persecution for their faith. That picks up on Barratt's 647 million Great Commission Christians, but it is interesting that it is so similar to the other figure so differently derived. The similarity is pure coincidence. Barratt et al. have not offered, perhaps wisely, more recent statistics on the number of Christians living under restrictive regimes. Since persecution is a spiritual phenomenon, the total number of those experiencing persecution at any given moment is impossible to estimate. Some figures are best left to God to calculate. This may explain why currently no suffering church ministry offers an independent estimate of the number of persecuted Christians worldwide.

4. Mind you, this is not to say that power has shifted south with the numbers. The vast majority of the church's wealth and influence is still held by Western Christians. In a world where the average Anglican, for example, is black, African, barely literate, and struggling with famine, war, and AIDS, the church is led by a white, Oxbridge British archbishop who wrestles with the issue of whether to ordain practicing homosexuals to the priesthood. I remember an Anglican luminary speaking at a church in Cambridge and solemnly announcing, "The biggest issue facing the church today is whether to ordain gay priests!" Beside me I heard a fierce whisper, "Of course it isn't. The biggest issue is poverty. It always has been. Why does he assume that the biggest issue in his church is the biggest issue in the world?"

5. Patrick Johnstone and Jason Mandryk, *Operation World: Twenty-first Century Edition* (Carlisle, England: Paternoster, 2001), 5.

6. This is not to say that institutional churches cannot grow. For example, after 1970 the underground Catholic church in China grew from around two million to more than ten million, but simultaneously the Protestant house churches grew from less than a million to more than sixty million.

7. See table 2.2 in Peter Brierley, *Future Church* (London: Monarch Books, 1998), 38.

8. William Dalrymple, *From the Holy Mountain* (Hammersmith, London: Flamingo, HarperCollins Publishers, 1998).

9. "Pakistani Christian Teenager Forced into Hiding," *Compass Direct*, January 23, 2004.

10. They adopted sharia law with the exception that the death penalty for apostasy was not applied.

11. See Open Doors UK Press Release, "Rebuilding Decimated Lives and Churches in Nigeria," July 28, 2005.

12. Quoted in "Christian Leaders in Nigeria Lament Religious Violence," *Compass Direct*, April 5, 2004.

13. There may well be more Christians in jail for their faith in countries like North Korea, but there is so little information that it is impossible even to hazard a number.

14. "Number of Christian Prisoners Doubled," *Compass Direct*, November 2005.

15. Quoted in "Sixty More Evangelical Christians Jailed in Eritrea," *Compass Direct*, January 2005.

## Chapter 8  The Persecuted Church—Part Two

1. Saphir Athyal, ed., *The Church in Asia Today* (Singapore: Asian Lausanne Conference for World Evangelization, 1996), 11.

2. Cited in *Future Church*, 27.

3. Johnstone and Mandryk, *Operation World*, 160.

4. David Aikman, *Jesus in Beijing* (Washington, D.C.: Regnery, 2003), 285.

5. Ibid., 7.

6. George Weigel, *The Cube and the Cathedral* (Loeminster, UK: Gracewing, 2005), 53.

7. "Analysis: The Godless Continent?" BBC Radio 4, broadcast April 21, 2005; transcript available from http://news.bbc.co.uk.

8. Quoted in *Third Way* magazine, March 2005, 5.

9. Mary Ann Glendon, *Rights Talk: The Impoverishment of Political Discourse* (New York: The Free Press, 1991), xi.

10. Charles Colson, *Lies That Go Unchallenged in Popular Culture* (Wheaton, IL: Tyndale, 2005), 165.

11. Taken from Solzhenitsyn's Harvard University commencement ceremony speech, June 8, 1978.

12. See "Security Deteriorating for Russia's Protestant Churches," WEA Religious Liberty News & Analysis, May 6, 2005, by Anneta Vyssotskaia. Published by WEA Religious Liberty Commission. See www.WorldEvangelical.org/rlc.html.

13. Christian Voice Press Release, June 23, 2005.

14. Colson, *Lies That Go Unchallenged*, contents page.

15. Difficult to translate the term accurately. One of the better definitions is "the political notion involving the separation of civil society and religious society, the State exercising no religious power and the churches exercising no political power." From Paul Robert, Le Grand Robert De La Langue Francaise (1992), translated by T. Jeremy Gunn.

16. Quoted in "France Says No to Christianity in EU Constitution," at euobserver.com, September 14, 2003.

17. Quoted in "Unholy Row on God's Place in EU Constitution," *Christian Century*, April 5, 2003.

18. "Secular Fundamentalism," *International Herald Tribune*, December 19, 2003, 8.

19. Quoted in "Anti-Sect Bill Could Hinder Religious Freedom," *Compass Direct*, July 2000.

20. Quoted in "Dialogue with Minority Religious Groups Begins," *Compass Direct*, April 2003.

21. David Limbaugh, *Persecution: How Liberals Are Waging War against Christianity* (Washington, D.C.: Regnery, 2003), ix.

22. Richard Mouw, "A Persecution Complex," posted on www.beliefnet.com, September 15, 2004.

23. Stephen L. Carter, *God's Name in Vain* (New York: Basic Books, 2000).

24. John W. Kennedy, "Corporate Thought Police," *Christianity Today*, January 2004, 26–28.

25. Cited in Limbaugh, *Persecution*, 111.

26. Marshall, *God and the Constitution*, 128.

27. Quoted in "A Case of Faith and College Aid," *Christian Science Monitor*, December 2, 2003.

28. "The Naked Public Square Now—A Symposium," *First Things* #147, November 2004, 13.

29. Carter, *God's Name in Vain*, 4.

30. Interview with the author, December 2004.

## Chapter 9  The Tricky Business of Doing More Good than Harm

1. See, e.g., Declan Walsh, "The Great Slave Scam," *Irish Times*, February 23, 2002.

2. Quoted in Christine J. Gardner, "Slave Redemption," *Christianity Today*, August 1999, 31.

3. A version of this parable can be accessed from a speech by Dr. Hamrin delivered at the 2001 Brandywine Forum, sponsored by the Institute for Global Engagement. See *The Jericho Road: A New Call to Global Engagement* (St. Davids, PA: Institute for Global Engagement and Eastern College, 2001), 124–32.

4. Michael Ireland, Assist News Service, October 2, 2001.

5. Email sent October 27, 2001.

6. See Alex Buchan, "Historic Anti-Caste Rally Repudiates Hinduism as a Political System," *Compass Direct*, November 6, 2001.

7. Robert Seiple, "Speaking Out: The USCIRF Is Only Cursing the Darkness," posted on October 16, 2002, at ChristianityToday.com.

8. *Christianity Today*, March 2003, 46–54.

9. See the story of the act's passage in Allen D. Hertzke, *Freeing God's Children: The Unlikely Alliance for Global Human Rights* (New York: Rowman and Littlefield, 2004).

10. Ibid., 209–10.

11. Paul Marshall in interview with the author, December 3, 2003.

12. Hertzke, *Freeing God's Children*, 210.

13. Taken from Robert Seiple's keynote address, "The Cry for Help and the Sound of Trumpets," Brandywine Forum, Eastern College, St. Davids, PA, May 19, 2001. Contact the Institute for Global Engagement for copies of the speech. 1300 Eagle Drive, St. Davids, PA 19087.

14. Ibid.

15. Michael Horowitz in interview with the author, December 2, 2003.

16. Interview, December 2003.

17. *Enough*, no. 2 (2003).

18. A version of this material, in response to the torture photos, was carried in the next issue of *Enough*, no. 3 (2003): 14–16.

## Chapter 10  What Works When?

1. *Christianity Today*, March 2003, 48, 50.

2. *Christianity Today*, March 2003, 53.

3. Brother Andrew with Susan DeVore Williams, *And God Changed His Mind* (Old Tappan, NJ: Chosen, 1991), 16–17.

4. Hertzke, *Freeing God's Children*, 30.

5. Ibid., 264–66.

6. "How Can We Support Each Other in the Body of Christ?" *Evangelical Review of Theology* 1, no. 24 (2000): 16–18.

7. See David Aikman, ed., *Love China Today* (Manila: Open Doors Asia, 1977), 204.

8. Interview with Doug Sutphen, July 1999.

9. Ibid., 211.

10. See Barbara G. Baker, "Appeal Denied for Three Uzbek Christians," *Compass Direct*, August 1999; and Felix Corley, "Uzbekistan Pushes through New Church Registrations," *Compass Direct*, September 1999.

11. See, e.g., Marshall, *Their Blood Cries Out*, 162–80; and Herbert Schlossberg, *A Fragrance of Oppression* (Wheaton, IL: Crossway Books, 1991), 191–200.

12. World Evangelical Fellowship's Religious Liberty Email Conference, "Knippers Asks WCC to Defend Persecuted Christians," posted on December 14, 1998.

13. Speech available at http://bradford.anglican.org/newsbyte/04032carey.html.

14. *Are Muslims Hated?* A Mentorn production for Channel 4, UK, broadcast January 9, 2005.

15. Jimmy Carter, *Keeping Faith: Memoirs of a President* (London: Collins, 1982), 207.

16. Vishal Aurora in interview with the author, Dec. 17, 2004.

17. C. B. Samuel in interview with the author, Dec. 17, 2004.

18. According to the United Bible Societies *World Report* #373 of March 2003, the press reached thirty million the same year, although three million of the thirty million were for non-Chinese markets.

19. See Alex Buchan, "U.S. President Bush Appeals for Religious Freedom in China," *Compass Direct*, March 20, 2002.

20. Interview, December 2003.

21. Carol Hamrin, remarks made at the Brandywine Forum, Eastern College, St. Davids, PA, May 2001.

22. Ibid.

23. *China: Why Can't All Christian Bookshops Sell Bibles?* by Hans Peterson, Forum 18 News Service, August 24, 2005. http://www.forum18.org.

## Chapter 11 The Donor's Dilemma

1. Johnstone and Mandryk, *Operation World*, 339.

## Chapter 12 Faith Model

1. See Robert Bellah et al., eds., *Habits of the Heart*, rev. ed. (University of California Press: Berkeley, 1996).

## Chapter 13 Faith Warning

1. Interview in *Compass Direct*, May 1996.

# Acknowledgments

This book is written to discharge a debt. That debt is to the scores of great persecuted believers I have met in twenty-five years of traveling behind the Iron, Bamboo, and now Qur'anic curtains. One Chinese evangelist used to see me off at the train station with these words: "Tell your friends to pray for us, and tell them to remember to suffer." This is my attempt to tell.

Of course, this attempt is not worthy of the lives of many of these great saints, most of whom cannot be named, but my first acknowledgment is to them—those who opened their homes and lives to me, when they had nothing to share but their stories. In their modesty, they didn't realize that their stories were precious treasures. I only wish I had the gift of a Solzhenitsyn to tell the stories well. I don't, but I have learned to offer my work to God and others out of my weaknesses, not my strengths. So here is that offering on their behalf. May God bless it, and may others forgive where I have failed to represent their views as well as I should, or have given unnecessary offense.

It is poignant that the vast majority of the persecuted believers who have been a formative influence on my Christian life cannot be named, as they are still in sensitive ministries among hostile cultures and governments. Some can be mentioned, however—mostly the untouchable elderly and the deceased. I think of individuals like Alexander Solzhenitsyn and Gleb Yakunin in the former USSR, Trian Dors and Paul Negrut in Romania, Wang Mingdao and Moses Xie in China, and mission leaders like Brother Andrew, Peter and Anita Deyneka, Richard Wurmbrand, Paul E. Kauffman, Doug and Meiling Sutphen, and Ross Paterson.

Special thanks, of course, to Open Doors, who not only made it possible to write this book but have also allowed me to interact, report on, and serve the persecuted these past twenty-five years. Thanks especially to Jeff Taylor, who believed in this book almost before I did; to Al Janssen, who used his skills to attract a publisher; and to all the program directors (who cannot be named) who allowed me to make trips into their regions and interview them and their key contacts.

A big thank you goes to my former colleagues at Compass Direct, especially David Miller, Barbara Baker, and Sarah Page, who gave freely of their time and material. Indeed, they have contributed to the text itself by providing some key "faces of the persecuted" profiles in part three. Thanks to Sarah particularly for providing such an excellent critique of the entire manuscript.

In addition to some of those already named, a number of other colleagues ploughed through the manuscript and gave useful feedback: Johan and Anneke Companjen, Jaap Kamphorst, Carl Moeller, and Paul Estabrooks. In addition, Carol Lee Hamrin, Bernhard Reitsma, and Peter Cowell read portions of the book and gave vital input. Thank you also to Gail Wahlquist for her invaluable help with the photos and her "fixing" skills over the years.

Special thanks also to the competent and cheerful Revell publishing team, particularly Jennifer Leep and Jessica Miles for their editorial input.

I owe a big debt to that busy group of people who have dedicated much of their working lives to assisting the persecuted, and who gave me interviews and input over the years: David Aikman, Robert Seiple, John Hanford, Michael Horowitz, Willie Inboden, Carol Lee Hamrin, Brent Fulton, Peter Lee, Paul Marshall, Nina

Shea, Sharon Payt, Bob Fu, Tony Lambert, Felix Corley, Willie Fautre, John Dayal, and the late Jonathan Chao.

While I was traveling, many special people assisted in providing material for particular chapters. Again, I am sorry that some of the most important people who helped cannot be named. Safe to thank publicly are Abraham Mattai, Viju Abraham, Richard Howells, C. B. Samuel, Paul Swarup, Godfrey Yogarajah, Franz Magnis Suseno, Iman Santoso, Yousif Matty, Menes Abdul Noor, and Bishops Thomas, Salieba, and Marshall.

I confess that the manuscript displays an Asian bias. I admit to having far more experience of the persecuted church in places like India, Indonesia, and China than, for example, Africa or Latin America. The fact that the bulk of testimonies comes from Asia is not intended as a slight to the non-Asian persecuted; it just reflects my comparative lack of exposure to those other regions. I mean to put that right in the next few years.

# Further Reading Ideas

If anyone wishes to go to the sources of this book's material and do further research, here is a short guide. For the Internet, the best news resource by far is Compass Direct (www.compassdirect. org), although the websites of the various Open Doors offices (e.g., www.odusa.org and www.opendoorsuk.org) carry a lot more prayer and background information. Outstanding resources for periodic news and analysis are the Center for Religious Freedom (www. freedomhouse.org/religion), where you can find the comments of Nina Shea and Paul Marshall, and the Religious Liberty Commission of the World Evangelical Alliance, whose material is archived at www.ea.org.au/rlc. See also the Forum 18 website for excellent news and analysis on Eastern Europe and Central Asia (though they are now roaming farther too) at www.forum18.org.

Also valuable is www.internationalreligiousfreedomwatch.org, run by former Keston College Director Lawrence Uzzel, and Human Rights Without Frontiers Int. (www.hrwf.net), Willie Fautre's outfit that covers religious liberty issues, particularly in Europe. A tough but important read is the U.S. Department of State's annual report on International Religious Freedom, accessed at www.state. gov/g/drl/irf. (Mercifully, there is an executive summary.) Also see the U.S. Commission on International Religious Freedom website, www.uscirf.gov, which is especially useful for its in-depth coverage on the CPCs (countries of particular concern).

For books, the following is a very subjective list, and more good ones are being published all the time. General books on the topic of persecuted Christians worldwide are rare, however. I really liked Herbert Schlossberg's *A Fragrance of Oppression* (Wheaton: Crossway, 1991), but it is now long out of print. The best factual global roundups were Nina Shea's *In the Lion's Den* (Nashville: Broadman and Holman, 1997) and Paul Marshall's *Their Blood Cries Out* (Dallas: Word Publishing, 1997), but both are nearly ten years old and in urgent need of updating. The global report *Religious Freedom in the World*, issued by the Center for Religious Freedom and edited by Paul Marshall (Nashville: Broadman and Holman, 2000) will soon be available in an updated edition.

Those getting serious with the issues should start with a nodding acquaintance of Samuel P. Huntington's *The Clash of Civilizations and the Remaking of World Order* (New York: Simon and Schuster, 1998), which did much to reclaim religious liberty as an article of foreign policy. Another academic read is Allen D. Hertzke's *Freeing God's Children* (New York: Rowman and Littlefield, 2004), a recent and authoritative write-up of the activism in the United States that brought the issue of religious liberty into the political arena.

Outside of commentaries and dictionaries, it is hard to find books explaining the biblical background of persecution; Glen M. Penner's *In the Shadow of the Cross* (Bartlesville, OK: Living Sacrifice Books, 2004) is the best. I haven't touched much on the history of the church under persecution in *Faith That Endures*, but serious readers—if they have a spare three months—would love W. H. C. Frend's magnum opus, *Martyrdom and Persecution in the Early Church* (Oxford: Basil Blackwell, 1965). A much more accessible and shorter introduction to this period is Herbert B. Workman's *Persecution in the Early Church* (Oxford: Oxford University Press, 1980). A fascinating if not always accurate historical read is Perez Zagorin's *How the Idea of Religious Toleration Came to the West* (Princeton, NJ: Princeton University Press, 2005).

On the human rights front, Robert Drinan's *The Mobilization of Shame* (New Haven: Yale University Press, 2001) is a dry but sane roundup. A livelier read is Mary Ann Glendon's *Rights Talk* (New York: Free Press, 1991), which is not specifically about religious rights but a great primer on how public discourse in the rights arena has gone awry.

As for Islam and Christianity, there are two short texts that are both "musts." One is Sayyid Qutb's *Milestones* (various Islamic publishers), the unofficial bible for most of the world's Islamic extremists, and *Islam at the Crossroads* (Grand Rapids: Baker Books, 2002), by Paul Marshall, Roberta Green, and Lela Gilbert. Going deeper would involve at the very least an interaction with John L. Esposito's *Unholy War: Terror in the Name of Islam* (New York: Oxford University Press, 2002), Bernard Lewis's *The Crisis of Islam* (London: Wiedenfeld and Nicolson, 2003), and Bat Ye'or's *Islam and Dhimmitude: Where Civilizations Collide* (Lancaster, UK: Gazelle Book Services, 2002). These are texts to get one going.

Outstanding books about the persecuted church in specific countries are hard to find, but if you are interested in China, two books really stand out: David Aikman's *Jesus in Beijing* (Washington, D.C.: Regnery, 2003) and Tony Lambert's *China's Christian Millions* (London: Monarch Books, 2006). These China experts are able to peer beneath both propaganda and exaggeration to give the full story of the world's largest Christian revival.

Books of testimonies and devotionals abound. There are two books with 365 daily readings from the testimonies of the persecuted that are of great value. These are *Bound to Be Free*, edited by Jan Pit (Tonbridge, Kent: Sovereign World, 1995), and *Extreme Devotion* by The Voice of the Martyrs (Nashville: W Publishing, 2001). Also from The Voice of the Martyrs comes an excellent little devotional called *Heroic Faith* (Nashville: W Publishing, 2002). Paul Estabrooks's *Secrets of Spiritual Success* (Tonbridge, Kent: Sovereign World, 1996) is a good attempt to apply the lessons of the persecuted to the lives of ordinary western Christians.

There are some lasting classics for me, some difficult to get ahold of now. One is Richard Wurmbrand's *Sermons in Solitary Confinement* (London: Hodder and Stoughton, 1969), and another is *The Sky is Red* (London: Hodder and Stoughton, 1965), Geoffrey Bull's wonderfully rich meditations after his years of jail in Tibet. Then there is the book that started an encounter with the persecuted for so many of us—*God's Smuggler*, by Brother Andrew, first released in 1966 but amazingly still in print today. His latest book, *Light Force*, co-written with Al Janssen (Grand Rapids: Revell, 2004), shares the story of his ministry in the Middle East, and is a great instructor of how Muslims and Christians can coexist yet hold onto the evangelistic distinctives of their respective faiths.

A great novel specifically on the persecuted church has yet to emerge in my view, but I often dip into two Russian Christian writers who have produced great literature. The first is poet Irina Ratushinskaya, whose two books of memoirs are fecund and challenging: *Grey is the Colour of Hope* (London: Hodder and Stoughton, 1988), and *In the Beginning* (London: Hodder and Stoughton, 1990). The second is the great author Alexander Solzhenitsyn. Everything from his considerable corpus is worth reading, but there is a one-volume version of the *The Gulag Archipelago: 1918–1956* (London: The Harvill Press, 1986), available, which contains harrowing stories of Christians in the camps of Siberia. His speeches particularly require close attention as he goes to the spiritual root of things as did few others in the twentieth century. He was fond of quoting this sentence: "Man has forgotten God; that's why all this has happened"—an appropriate ending sentiment for this book.

**Ronald Boyd-MacMillan** has more than twenty years of experience working among persecuted communities. Born in Scotland, raised in Northern Ireland, and a graduate in politics, he became the associate director for research for Open Doors in 1982, traveling to Eastern Europe and the former USSR. After a two-year stint as a pastor in Bristol, he moved to Hong Kong, where he trained as a journalist. In 1987 he cofounded the world's first agency to concentrate on religious persecution, News Network International, and worked as its Asia bureau chief from 1987 to 1991. This took him into many countries, including China and North Korea, and he was a witness to the Tiananmen Massacre in Beijing in 1989.

Ronald then spent five years in Los Angeles gaining a master's degree in divinity from Fuller Theological Seminary, where he also had a ministry leading Bible studies for Hollywood scriptwriters. Returning to Hong Kong in 1996, he became the Asia bureau chief for Compass Direct, a news agency focusing exclusively on the persecuted church. He has traveled extensively among the suffering church communities of Asia, including India, China, and Indonesia, and his articles—under the pen name Alex Buchan—have appeared throughout secular and Christian media. At the end of 2002, he took up a new position as writer-at-large for Open Doors International, which he continues today.

At present Ronald lives in Edinburgh and in his spare time runs a tuition agency for preachers called Points-A-Cross, Inc. He is the author of *Explosive Preaching: Letters on How to Detonate the Gospel in the 21ˢᵗ Century"* (Paternoster Press, June 2006).

For more information on **Open Doors**, or to learn about additional resources and involvement opportunities with the persecuted church, please contact Open Doors at www.od.org.

# One man.
# One incredible story of going undercover for God.

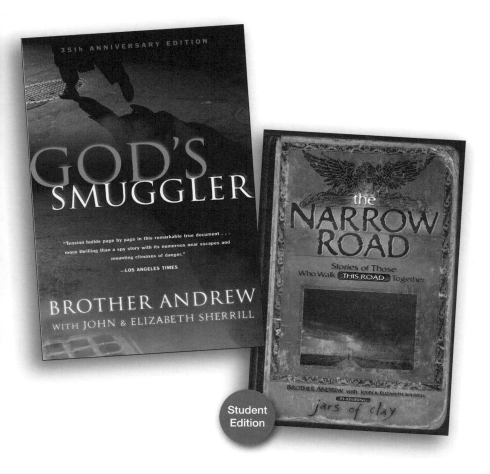

R Revell
www.revellbooks.com

Available at your local bookstore

# You can change the world—
## Brother Andrew shows you how.

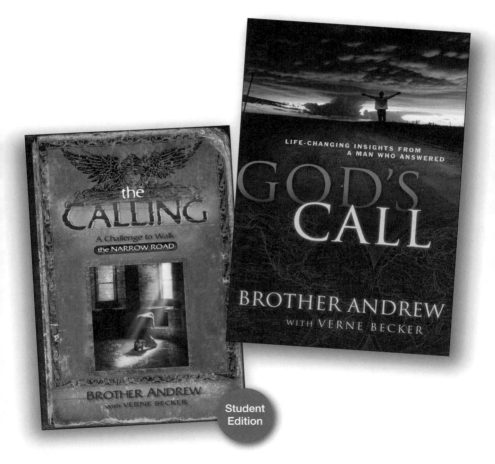

ℛ Revell
www.revellbooks.com

Available at your local bookstore

# Be informed.
# Get involved.

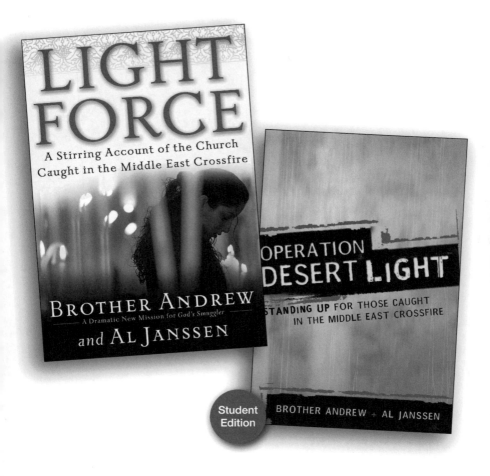

## R Revell
www.revellbooks.com

Available at your local bookstore